CORPORATIONS IN CRISIS

Books by the Editors of FORTUNE

USA—THE PERMANENT REVOLUTION (1951)

IS ANYBODY LISTENING? (1952)

WHY DO PEOPLE BUY? (1953)

A GUIDE TO MODERN MANAGEMENT METHODS (1954)

THE CHANGING AMERICAN MARKET (1954)

THE MIGHTY FORCE OF RESEARCH (1956)

THE FABULOUS FUTURE (1956)

THE EXECUTIVE LIFE (1956)

THE ART OF SUCCESS (1956)

ADVENTURES IN SMALL BUSINESS (1957)

THE AMAZING ADVERTISING BUSINESS (1957)

THE EXPLODING METROPOLIS (1958)

THE NEW WORLD OF MATH (1959)

MARKETS OF THE SIXTIES (1960)

GREAT AMERICAN SCIENTISTS (1961)

THE SPACE INDUSTRY (1962)

THE INSIDERS: A STOCKHOLDER'S GUIDE TO WALL STREET (1962)

FORTUNE'S GUIDE TO PERSONAL INVESTING (1963)

CORPORATIONS IN CRISIS

Richard Austin Smith

DOUBLEDAY & COMPANY, INC.
GARDEN CITY, NEW YORK

UNIVERSITY AND COLLEGE DISTRIBUTION
BY SCOTT, FORESMAN AND COMPANY

To Brownie,
who has had her share
of all these crises

CONTENTS

Preface

A few years ago *Fortune* presented some of the staff with an admirable little book on the elements of style. I've forgotten most of its strictures, for to my way of thinking style should remain a private affair between a man and his typewriter, but I do remember E. B. White's final admonition. "The whole duty of a writer," he declared, "is to please and satisfy himself, and the true writer always plays to an audience of one. Let him start sniffing the air, or glancing at the Trend Machine, and he is as good as dead, although he may make a nice living."

Writing to please one's self, of course, requires a special set of circumstances and a considerable amount of forbearance from all concerned. But it was my good luck to have been hired fifteen years ago by a magazine whose managing editors, Ralph Delahaye Paine Jr., Hedley Donovan, and Duncan Norton-Taylor, raised no more than occasional objections to my writing for that "audience of one" and at the same time for a circulation in the hundreds of thousands. The present book is the result of that happy arrangement.

* * *

It should be noted that the ten chapters, all of which were written as stories for *Fortune* during the Fifties and early Sixties, extend over more than a decade. In consequence they encompass a considerable amount of business history. Yet the point is worth making that what is being presented here is not a series of episodes recounted after the fact, but drama described in the process of enactment. Each of the pieces was put together while the corporation was in the grip of its individual crisis.

It might also be mentioned that at such times truth is hard to come by. Guilt, confusion, and self-justification conspire to conceal the facts, while the wide diversity of viewpoints to be reconciled stretches the writer on the rack of judgment in virtually every paragraph. Further, the assignment and publication of articles about corporations in crisis demands a special brand of perspicacity and fortitude on the part of the managing editor and top management of a business magazine, and entails an extraordinary outlay of time and money. The appearance of such stories in the height of the storm invariably attracts lightning. This has regularly crackled around *Fortune*. But just as regularly the response has been bigger lightning rods, not stories of lower potential.

*   *   *

In conclusion, my special thanks go to Spencer Klaw, whose idea it was that these articles would make a book, and to those members of *Fortune's* research staff who assisted in their preparation: Edith Roper, Mia Fritsch, Claudine Knight, Mary Melville, Elizabeth Swayne, and particularly Shirley Estabrook, my researcher on the Introduction, the electrical conspiracy, and the TFX.

RICHARD AUSTIN SMITH
Port Washington, N.Y.

CORPORATIONS IN CRISIS

Introduction

The typical business story is—and ought to be—a success story. In a highly competitive society such as ours, where enterprises are always under pressure, an account of how somebody made a go of things has an obvious utility, and a stimulating impact. U.S. corporations, moreover, are caught up in the thrust of the world's most successful economic complex and have a far different outlook from those which have to live on the ragged edge of survival. Nevertheless, an exclusive concentration on business success has its dangers. By making business seem easier than it actually is, the success story—if it were to become the universal business story—would blunt its own point. Nothing, they say, succeeds like success; actually, nothing illuminates success like failure.

The significance of this is that management can make the study of failure contribute to success just as surely as pathologists make the study of disease serve the ends of health. But unfortunately for business, there are no great general hospitals where the ailments of corporations can be transmuted into data on how to stay in the pink. When companies get sick, the rule is home treatment by members of the family or management consultants on "house call"; individual communiqués may be issued from time to time but their purpose is to soothe the public rather than contribute to clinical analysis. Even the morgues of business—the bankruptcy files—produce little of value to preventive medicine. Most of the corpses interred there are infants, in size or life span, and whatever can be learned of their fatal malaise has precious little application to those middle-sized corporations on their way to becoming giants, or to the giants themselves, the huge complexes that characterize our industrial machine.

The purpose of this Introduction, and of the book itself, is to try to make up for some of these lacks by bringing together for discussion in one place a number of the ailments common to American businesses. To be sure, *Fortune* often publishes individual "diagnoses" of ailing corporations, and other publications have also probed for the causes of a particular disaster in a particular enterprise. Yet that's been about the end of it. A search of the libraries discloses no book, indeed no article, devoted to a discussion of corporate crises *in general.* Under normal circumstances such a lack would be lamentable enough. But under today's circumstances there is more reason than ever to profit by the mistakes of the past, for the immediate future promises an increase in the tensions, constrictions, and derelictions that cause corporate crises.

In this book the working definition of a corporate crisis comes down simply to Big Trouble, not necessarily fatal, but always making for profound changes. It is an event that oftentimes imperils the entire enterprise or at the very least makes Draconian demands on the energies, ingenuity, and time of top management. Necessarily a book such as this has had to content itself with trying to throw a little light on a big subject. A number of its conclusions are tentative, for some wellsprings of crisis—decentralization comes most readily to mind—are themselves in the process of being explored. But beyond that, several other assumptions and considerations must be made clear if the subject is to be put in proper perspective. The necessary capsuling of case histories tends to make things seem more cut and dried than they actually were, besides raising the inevitable charge that it's always easy to quarterback the game on a Monday morning. Let it be said that in the present book a sustained effort was made to examine the causes of crises *contemporaneously,* as management saw them or could reasonably have been expected to see them. At the same time, the advantages of hindsight were used to the full, for the intent is not to indict but to clarify.

The second essential to perspective is the reiteration of some obvious truths. Business is tough; the making of key decisions is enormously difficult; risk-taking is an essential part of doing business. The greatest disservice a study of the causes of crises could possibly do would be so to envelop the businessman in a fabric of "don'ts" that he'd be afraid to make a move. Some businesses survive only by regularly accepting troubles another business would consider a crisis. Aluminum companies, for instance, are compelled by circumstances to go through regular periods of overcapacity: their pot lines have to be built in blocks which, because they are designed to supply demand five years down the road, must be too big for their current market. Finally, it should be noted that in all but a fraction of the fifty-odd cases on which this book is based—case studies written by the author and others on *Fortune* lie behind many of the generalizations made here—management was innocent of the willful or vicious precipitation of the crisis. By and large they acted according to their own best judgment, fallible and limited though it may subsequently have appeared, and some were neither less experienced nor less intelligent than their opposite numbers in successful enterprises. Nor did they violate a hard-and-fast code of business conduct, a set of rules whose observance would have kept their companies out of trouble under all circumstances. There is none.

Illusions and actualities

The nature of corporate crises is that they seldom occur with the abruptness of a thunderclap; they just seem to. One is startled to hear that "headhunters" like Ward Howell have been commissioned to recruit a whole new sales staff for a certain company, or learns that management consultants have descended on a competitor in battalion strength, or steps off an elevator in Rockefeller Center to find a whole divisional headquarters shrunken down to a couple of rooms full of frightened people. What is being observed here, of course, is not crisis but the sudden materialization of *symptoms*: the crisis itself has been long in the making. It is characteristically the result of years of procrastination, of unwillingness to face up to mistakes or write off failures—indeed, that is the prime reason the cure is so painfully slow.

A second point about the nature of crises is that they seldom if ever arise from a *single* cause, no matter the jungle practice of picking out a scapegoat and blaming everything on him. For every chief executive officer who ran a company into the ditch, a board of directors failed to apply the brakes. For every antitrust action that turned a company upside down, a failure of corporate control, intelligence, and personnel selection contributed to it. For every corporation imperiled by cancellation of a government program, the vulnerability had its roots in failures of timing, alternative product development, or simple foresight. Crises come about from a variety of causes. Typically, one is central, the others contributory.

A matter of men

Since corporations take their tone from the man at the top, it should surprise no one that the central cause of many crises is the Big Boss himself. Sometimes, he just hasn't put in enough time tending the store; one chief executive, for example, held memberships on the boards of directors of thirteen other institutions; this meant, even by the most tolerant arithmetic, that he was spending one week out of every four minding somebody else's business. Absentee management, however, is far less typically the cause of crisis than the failings of an executive all too plainly on the job.

Henry Ford provides the classic example. His enormous energy, will power, and inventiveness were totally harnessed to the Ford Motor Company. He ran it as a one-man show and its early success is in large measure owing to this. The automobile business was new then, the competition was fragmented and weak, and one-man control of a relatively small enterprise had lots to recommend it. But times changed. Henry did not. He still tried to run a billion-dollar company as if it were just bigger but no different than in the Twenties. Thus by 1946 Ford was going through a crisis of the first magnitude. The company's management was demoralized and for good reason. Under old Henry's one-man dictatorship, executives had been periodically demoted so they wouldn't get "uppity," the "ins" ruled over savage little empires, the "outs" were apt to learn of their severance by one day discovering their office furniture piled in the corridor. Its work force was even more demoralized. After years of repression and Harry Bennett's use of thugs as instruments of corporate labor policy, workers employed wildcat strikes and slowdowns to express their collective hatred. Individually they resorted to sabotage. A nut was left off here, a weld there, or live rats and pop bottles were walled up in Lincoln door panels. The company had no research department, though it then sold one out of every five U.S. cars; and though its sales amounted to nearly $1 billion, it had no more cost-control system than a country store. Consequently, as Ford struggled with reconverting to domestic production after World War II, it was losing money at the rate of $10 million a month, going sixty-two dollars in the red on every vehicle turned out. Yet nobody could tell what was responsible for the losses because there were no cost breakdowns; there was just the cash account, a simple totting up of the dozens of bank accounts Ford had scattered across the nation. It was only when *young* Henry took matters in his own hands and got Ernest Breech in to help him that Ford became an up-to-date corporation, its organizational deficiencies remedied, its cost-control problems resolved, its management vacuum filled, and its labor troubles mitigated.

On the other hand, Montgomery Ward's trouble-at-the-top had its origin in the preservation of an anachronistic policy rather than an outmoded philosophy of management. That policy was to run Montgomery Ward in conformance with Chairman Sewell Avery's dogma that the postwar inflation was certain to end in a crash as devastating as 1929. Certainly the policy was one a lot of other corporations pursued in the last of the Forties. A feeling of bearishness pervaded the whole business community; outlays for capital investment stood at apprehensive levels; unemployment was expected to top four million, a level associated with full-blown depressions. Chrysler even went so far as to experiment with a depression edition of the Dodge, a stripped-down, dechromed, rudimentary vehicle priced for thin purses. But the difference was that Chrysler and the other corporations altered their strategy in keeping with conditions. Montgomery Ward did not. Sewell Avery's fixation was pursued to the point where it stunted the company's growth. Year after year Ward continued to hoard cash against the holocaust that was never to come. It opened no new stores and its sales remained frozen around the billion-dollar mark while arch rival Sears, Roebuck, making the most of its own opportunities, pushed sales from $1 billion in 1946 to $4.3 billion in 1961. Avery's aberrant performance at a stockholders' meeting in 1955 finally proved too much for even the most sentimental of his supporters and he was forced out as chief executive officer. But unhappily for Ward, the consequences of his *idée fixe* still have to be reckoned with. Since the prime store sites were already bought up by Sears, Montgomery Ward had to take second best in many instances (and pay through the nose for that). The net profit in 1960, $15 million, was the lowest since 1936.

The object lesson offered by Montgomery Ward, however, contains more than a warning that trouble can be expected whenever a chief executive pursues some policy beyond the bounds of reason. It should also underscore the point that the license he had to indulge the bee in his bonnet constituted a failure of control at the board level. Montgomery Ward was no family-owned corporation like Ford, where criticism could be silenced by chopping off heads or just arguing that if the enterprise was going to the dogs, the biggest loser would be the boss himself. Avery was not even a majority stockholder. Since the board of directors had the power to check him and didn't do so, their dereliction must be set down as a cause of the crisis. Indeed, with the decline of the family-owned corporation, the eccentric executive typically does his damage with the acquiescence of the board. Such, in fact, was the combination that led to the demise of RKO, the nation's fifth biggest motion-picture studio.

The sad story there was Howard Hughes (see Chapter II, "RKO: A Crisis of Responsibility"). He took over a strong company from Floyd Odlum, but then neither ran the studio himself nor delegated authority to anyone else to run it. In fact, he never visited the place, despite its piling up $20 million in losses; the nearest thing to a visitation was a flight *over* the studio one morning on his way to Tucson. He thought it looked shabby, phoned back to have it painted.

Why didn't somebody step in and stop the demolition of RKO? With its stock widely scattered among fifteen thousand stockholders, few had the economic incentive, the resources, or the information either to wage a successful proxy fight or to bring a suit. Moreover, nobody wanted to tangle with Howard Hughes. His substantial investments, reaching into aircraft, electronics, the oil industry, transportation, beverages, tools, and movies, were diversified enough to suggest plenty of room for reprisals. But desperation finally impelled some stockholders to file suit and the litigation induced Hughes to buy up all the assets of RKO. These he used no better than before and in 1954 film production stopped altogether. Next year Hughes sold out, starting the company on the way to dismemberment, its studios for sale here, its film library there, until the only thing left was the name. Even that has nothing to do with movie-making, for as a division of General Tire & Rubber, its concern is now with radio and television stations.

The perils of change

As might be expected in a fast-moving society such as ours, there's an important correlation between change and corporate crises. Most big companies have a built-in immobility. Their plants cannot be easily shifted about, their product lines are not susceptible to sudden alteration, their equipment is not all-purpose but must be designed for particular kinds of production. Consequently, some changes in their markets or competition demand a degree of flexibility they simply aren't capable of, and could not reasonably be expected to possess. In the transportation field, for example, the airlines got into deep trouble because of the unavoidable shift from propeller-driven aircraft to jet transports; the combination of the jet's high acquisition cost and a passenger volume far below the jet's tremendous carrying capacity was the main reason five of the major airlines operated in the red in 1961. Similarly, an overwhelming change in basic economic circumstances has caused the virtual disappearance of U.S. coastwise shipping. Ever since the Interstate Commerce Commission got jurisdiction over the domestic *maritime* rate structure in 1940, the railroads have been allowed to bid for ocean freight with sharply reduced rates, making up for the losses in higher rates elsewhere.

What happened to Luckenbach Lines under this sort of competition was typical of coastwise shipping in general. Luckenbach vessels had profitably carried cargo between Seattle and Portland, Maine, for more than a hundred and ten years, but they went $2 million in the red for 1960. Then in 1961 the company was confronted both by the ICC's approval of a twenty-cent-per-hundredweight reduction in *rail* carrier charges on canned goods, long a mainstay of Luckenbach's eastbound vessels, and by the Maritime Board's refusal to insure a $57-million loan the corporation needed for the conversion of five fast freighters into "container" ships. Facing further traffic losses to the railroads on the one hand, and unable to cut costs via container ships on the other, Luckenbach decided the changed circumstances were more than it could cope with. The line withdrew completely from domestic trade and leased its ships abroad.

Unhappily, corporate difficulties are more often the result of inaction in the face of a dangerous change than of being the hapless victim of circumstances. It's the exceptional executive who can bring himself to admit that a crisis is in the making; the unexpected report of trouble, like Banquo's ghost, just doesn't fit into the scheme of things. Even fewer are the executives with the courage to take drastic action *in time*. On the contrary, case histories reveal too many instances where top management procrastinated about an emergent crisis. General Dynamics (see Chapter III, "General Dynamics: A Crisis of Control") might have got out of its plainly ill-starred jet-transport venture at a cost of $50 million, in 1957. But by failing to face some embarrassing facts and remaining ignorant of others, the company wound up $425 million in the hole, the biggest product loss ever sustained by any enterprise.

There are, of course, extenuating circumstances in almost every instance of managerial procrastination, but the following examples make clear a number of the consequences. United Fruit clung to its belief that the banana would remain the autocrat of the breakfast table, despite the growing popularity of frozen juices, virtually until the day in 1959 when dwindling profits forced it to pass a regular dividend, for the first time in sixty years. Baldwin-Lima-Hamilton continued to hope against hope that the Iron Horse would somehow survive the rising competition of the diesel locomotive. G.M., however, had got an immense headstart during the war and it continued to win over Baldwin's customers until finally diesels ran steam engines right off the latter's production lines. Knox Glass and Hazel-Atlas also couldn't bring themselves to face the facts. They stub-

bornly refused to recognize that the universal availability of natural gas
had changed their once important economic advantage, location, and
that they would have to install the most modern glassmaking equipment if
they were to remain competitive. The result for Knox was a loss of $288,-
000 on 1961's sales of $45 million. Ailing Hazel-Atlas actually disappeared
as an independent company. It was acquired in 1956 by Continental Can,
which immediately began installation of the modern machinery. And Curtis Publishing got into difficulties by violating a precept of its most famous
editor, George Horace Lorimer, that the time to change was not after
things started going bad but when they were still going fine. It put off too
long doing something about revamping its magazines and management to
cope with ominous changes in circulation, costs, and the nature of the
competition. In 1961 the company reported a loss for the first time since
its infancy.

But perhaps the most notable example of a company whose inability
or unwillingness to adjust to change involved it in a corporate crisis is
Curtiss-Wright. One of the nation's most famous aircraft companies,
founded by the Wright brothers themselves, Curtiss-Wright produced more
pounds of airframe than any other manufacturer in World War II and
was also an important engine manufacturer. However the trouble was it
hadn't been able to develop important new engines to hold its own against
Pratt & Whitney. Such new products as did see the light of day were of the
razzle-dazzle variety—like an air car, touted with full-page ads in the *Wall
Street Journal*. These produced a momentary flurry in C.-W.'s stock, but
their very flamboyance underscored the inability of Curtiss-Wright to come
up with something solid. Aerospace, the real postwar opportunity capitalized upon by virtually every other major airframe manufacturer, was allowed to slip by.

This inability to change with the times eventually became a sort
of creeping paralysis that spread to the company's traditional product lines.
It dropped entirely out of airframe production and then all but stopped
aircraft-engine production save for spare parts. Even in parts, C.-W.'s iner-
tia earned it the enmity of the airlines for poor quality control and for
sometimes taking as much as two years on delivery. Sales dropped from
the $571 million of 1956 to $203 million in 1961, profits from $43 million
to $6 million; 1962 showed only slight improvement, leaving a grave ques-
tion about what will happen to the company in the future when its spare-
parts business, the primary reason it has survived at all, comes to a final
sputtering end.

Why wasn't Curtiss-Wright able to keep pace? Fundamentally because
ex-President Roy T. Hurley was obsessed with short-range profits. He re-

fused to spend the money necessary for long-range development, the life-blood of aircraft companies. In an industry where it then took five years and $50 million to $75 million even to develop a new engine, he missed the main chances by insisting that if C.-W. couldn't break even on any project in two to three years, it wasn't worth doing.

When fate steps in

Not uncommonly a crisis will come about from bizarre or quixotic causes, as if destiny had mischievously taken a hand in corporate affairs. Some "Dangerous Corner" will be turned, as in J. B. Priestley's chilling play of that name, and from then on things will be beyond help. General Motors' dangerous corner was turned back in 1953 at its new $35-million Hydra-Matic plant in Livonia, Michigan. It began when a welder went to work on an overhead duct at this "factory that couldn't burn." A tiny spark from his torch ignited the oil in a conveyer-belt drip pan. This spread to the creosoted wood-block floor and soon touched off a dip tank of the same oil. When the whole plant went up in flames—it was the biggest industrial fire in history—every automotive division at G.M. was affected, Pontiac being virtually out of the running for the five frantic months it took to get a substitute facility (Kaiser's old Willow Run plant) in full operation.

In the case of the ailing Crane Company, destiny took a hand in corporate affairs through an inexplicable plane crash (1956). Crane's director of branch sales, two of its three vice-presidents in charge of sales divisions, and three of their top assistants were wiped out in that single tragedy. Another company might have been able to handle such a loss, but Crane was peculiarly vulnerable. Its management was already stretched perilously thin and an enormous gap existed between the aging group at the top and the youngsters at the third level. This made it virtually certain that some raider would be attracted to Crane, as Thomas Mellon Evans was the next year. By 1960 Evans had seized control of the company and virtually turned it upside down. He ousted four of its vice-presidents, hastened the departure of six directors, closed up or sold off forty-three of its 130 supply outlets in a take-over described by men who worked at it with him as "crude and brutal."

The most quixotic of crises, however, was undoubtedly that of the Glenn L. Martin Company (predecessor of Martin Marietta) in the late Forties: the old-line Navy plane maker almost went to the wall because Glenn Martin had taken a hand in the celebrated "Admirals' revolt."

To be sure, the company had been in difficulties before then, for founder Martin ran a one-man show where people of spirit and ability seldom lasted long. Moreover, it had suffered along with the rest of the airframe industry in the general cutback of government orders for aircraft. But the purposes of the "Admirals' revolt" were two, both anathema to the Air Force: (1) to clip the wings of the Air Force, (2) to increase the power of the Navy. Thus the Martin Company in general and Glenn Martin in particular became the personal targets of the Air Force, whose secretary was Stuart Symington. Not only was the company cut off from future Air Force orders, but when Martin hurried into the RFC for a loan to save his foundering company, he found himself blocked there too. Symington was the new head of the agency. It was only when a White House conference brushed aside Symington's contentions (Glenn Martin was senile, the company was badly run, and there were too many airframe manufacturers anyway) that Martin was saved with a government loan.

Companies on a tightrope

An increasing number of corporate crises are conceptual in origin in the sense that they arise from the faulty application of a structural, organizational, or managerial concept. Decentralization, for one, is too often embraced by companies that have an incomplete understanding of how it suits their requirements or the special controls necessary to hold a decentralized enterprise together. They tend to look at General Motors—not a single major error of commission since it was decentralized in 1920—and think along the lines of what's been good for G.M. should be good for us. Yet decentralization on too grand a scale was the prime cause of Blaw-Knox's 1955 profits diving to the lowest level since 1944. It was only when management de-decentralized, centralizing cost controls, budgets, forecasts, and marketing surveys, that this venerable manufacturer of construction equipment began to roll again. At Consolidated Freightways, largest motor common carrier in the United States, all-out decentralization was again at the root of the difficulties. With the carrier split into thirty virtually autonomous divisions, tight control over costs was impossible. Management could only guess whether the company as a whole was profitable—and sometimes it wasn't, until part of the divisional autonomy was withdrawn and the powers transferred to headquarters.

The common source of the trouble would seem to be an inability to preserve proper balance. Under decentralization, the divisional vice-presidents must be granted considerable latitude to run their own affairs, for characteristically the decentralized enterprise is too big or too diverse to be run from any headquarters. At the same time headquarters must know precisely what the division chiefs are doing, and this calls for some centralized controls.

Two recent examples should make the point. A crisis materialized in the heavy electrical apparatus divisions of General Electric (see Chapter V, "General Electric: A Crisis of Antitrust") because the front office hadn't established such controls. G.E. made the fatal error of putting the managers of the apparatus group under heavy pressure to produce profits, without keeping itself fully informed about just how they were producing those profits. At General Dynamics, the castastrophe was exacerbated by the fact that corporate management in New York not only didn't know what was going on at the Convair Division in San Diego, but had persuaded itself it *couldn't* know.

Going overboard about diversification has had some equally unpleasant consequences. Most companies would agree with the proposition voiced by Paul Davies, chairman of FMC Corporation (agricultural equipment), that "The manufacturer of a very durable mousetrap would readily see the advantage of owning a stabilizing cheese business." Diversification does help stabilize earnings, particularly in enterprises subject to seasonal peaks and valleys. But headlong diversification is something else again. In 1958 giant Olin Mathieson's profits dropped 69 percent below 1957's (see Chapter I, "Olin Mathieson: A Crisis of Growth"), borne down mainly by the attempt to manufacture what must have been the widest assortment of products made by any corporation in the United States. This hyperdiversification came about through a policy of growth-by-acquisition on the one hand and, on the other, the inability of top management to clean house. With management defaulting on a definition of goals, product lines grew more exotic as one hand toyed with the atom, the other tried to get down to earth in the fertilizer business.

Easy does it

Such crises, to repeat, underscore the obvious fact that some corporations get into difficulties not from an inherent flaw in the concepts of decentralization, centralization, or diversification, but rather from going overboard about those concepts. Anything done to excess is as certain to bring on big trouble in business as in daily living. But if excess is a general cause of crisis, so are shortcomings. Ford lost $200 million on the Edsel, in the main because of inadequate market research. It had no inkling until too late that reports on the medium-price car market were overblown. When the Edsel began rolling off the assembly lines in 1957, the customers were looking the other way—for the compacts. Kaiser's shortcoming was a lack of experience. The company jumped into the highly competitive automobile business in 1948 as if its successes in steel, cement, and shipbuilding would somehow stand it in good stead. But Kaiser didn't know how to build up an efficient dealer organization from scratch, or how to produce a competitively priced car. The going got so rough by 1955 that Kaiser not only got out of town, it got out of the country, taking the Willow Run machinery down to the greener grass in Argentina. The big trouble at J. I. Case stemmed from inadequacies of engineering coupled with an inability to sell at all levels. President Marc B. Rojtman, replaced in 1960, loaded up the dealers through his flamboyant sales methods, but then did little to get the farmers to buy Case tractors in an equal volume. Huge dealer inventories piled up, fed by the recession of 1958, by mechanical problems with the tractors that the engineers failed to correct, and by more production. By 1959 the $200 million in sales reported by the company represented nothing save sales to the dealers. In 1960 the roof fell in. Case reported a loss of $39,800,000, almost a dollar in the red for every three of sales. And finally, to round out the list of dangerous excess, there's the causal relationship of crisis to size, companies being either too small or too big.

The problems of proportion

Small companies find it easy to get started in a new industry—helicopters, aerospace, and electronics are three contemporary examples—and for a long time can make ideas compensate for lack of capital, management skill, and organizational framework. Electronics companies in particular have been built around a couple of brilliant scientists and a half-dozen associates; as a matter of fact, initial success often leads them to disdain conventional management. But the day inevitably dawns when the industry grows up: no longer is everyone "equal," the one-product firm finds itself competing with multiproduct companies, and management is faced with the decision of growing or withering on the vine. Thus, Stavid Engineering, which had worked up to annual sales of $10 million, discovered the only way it could get the plant, capital, and customer confidence for $20-*million* jobs was to become part of a bigger company, Lockheed. And thus Piasecki, though saved once from having its sales drop to zero by the heroic investment of 25 percent of its net worth in one product, the successful V-107 helicopter, finally decided the only way it could survive competition with Sikorsky (a division of big United Aircraft) was by getting big itself through acquisition by Boeing.

As for the giants, their troubles seldom fall neatly into the Brandeisian generalization that the efficiency of big business is limited by size. Many modern corporations, as Adolf Berle has pointed out, have grown to a size twenty times that which Justice Brandeis thought capable of efficient organization, and are doing very well indeed. Where crises occur, they do so far less from any orginal sin of size than from one or more wholly correctible transgressions, such as the previously cited failure to see that the control system keeps pace with the size of the company, particularly in providing adequate G-2 (intelligence).

Though it may come as a surprise, in light of all the foregoing travail, there are instances where corporate crises have had salutary side effects. G.E., for one, was alerted to the need of a tighter control system as the result of having put the careers of a score of its executives (those involved in the electrical conspiracy) under uncommon scrutiny. It is now far less likely that a department manager will get away with "mining the company," as one did before in making his profit record look good, crowding equipment together to escape being charged for the floor space, even deferring maintenance to a point where his successor—not he—had to be charged for the repair of a leaking roof. American Motors, to cite another example, owes a good bit of its regeneration to the threat of a raider, Louis Wolfson, who became the company's largest stockholder in 1958: when President George Romney made it clear to top management that only success would save them from being gobbled up by the wolf at the door, the adrenalin of crisis came powerfully into play.

Prevention's pound of cure

For most companies, however, a corporate crisis is regarded even in retrospect as unmitigated trouble. Few of them, to be sure, become actual fatalities. Big enterprises are hard to kill. Many people have a stake in their survival and their wellsprings of vitality can run deep. Yet the experience is a bitter one for all that; years of lean purses and long hours commonly go by before the company can be "turned around" again. What then is needed to prevent these corporate upheavals? As noted before there is no hard and fast code of conduct whose observance would keep a company out of trouble under all circumstances. Yet the more crises one examines, the clearer it is that many of them might have been avoided if management had just done the things that could reasonably have been expected of it: keeping fit through keeping competitive, always reaching out but not so far as to go overboard about anybody or anything, making sure the chief executive officer rides herd on the enterprise and the board of directors rides herd on him—most important, developing the skill to distinguish real trouble from normal operating difficulty and mustering the courage to face up to it in time.

CHAPTER I

Olin Mathieson: A Crisis of Growth

Prologue

Almost everyone is familiar with the manifestations of the acquisitive instinct, one of the strongest of human drives. In the home, it has a way of turning decorative harmony into a mere clutter of possessions, unless a firm hand is taken to weed out things that just don't fit in. In great corporations, particularly those whose size is more the result of acquiring other companies than of self-development, failure to take a firm hand inevitably brings on crisis. The trouble with this great chemical company in September of 1958 was rooted in the fact that for years Olin Mathieson had piled one inharmonious acquisition upon another, building up debt, eroding profits, scattering its strength, paralyzing management.

*   *   *

"Goat-feathers," wrote Ellis Parker Butler, who died long before the Olin Mathieson Chemical Corporation came into being, "are the feathers a man picks and sticks all over his hide to make himself look like the village goat. . . . [They] are the distractions, sidelines, and deflections that take a man's attention from his own business and keep him from getting ahead. . . . Even a cow does better if she sticks close to the business of eating grass and chewing the cud. When a cow strays from plain milk-producing methods and begins climbing trees and turning somersaults, she may be more picturesque, but she is gathering nothing but goat-feathers."

Doubtless it would surprise Mr. Butler to learn that his rustic little essay on singleness of purpose had its broadest readership during the late 1950s in the big-city offices of a very big corporation. In Olin Mathieson's Manhattan headquarters, harried executives even pressed Mr. Butler's tract upon an outsider, with no comment other than a wry smile. For the criticisms Butler had directed against himself were manifestly applicable to the nation's fifth-ranking chemical company. Olin Mathieson, in Butler's phrase, had certainly *not* been "getting ahead."

Four years after the corporation was created (out of the merger of prosperous Olin Industries with dynamic Mathieson Chemical), long-term debt had more than tripled, to nearly 60 percent of the combined capitalization, an unusually burdensome ratio for any industrial enterprise. With net earnings for the first half of 1958 down 50 percent from the same period in 1957, the corporation fell some 26 percent short of the $13 million needed to pay the usual fifty-cent dividend in the first and second quarters of 1958. Early in August of that year its embattled management—just beginning to progress on a new program instituted by a new president, Stanley de Jongh Osborne—had to take time out to chew over the question of dividend payments for the third and fourth quarters; they decided to cut them to twenty-five cents.

And what kept Olin Mathieson from fulfilling the promise implicit in its creation? "Distractions, sidelines, and deflections"; in short, goatfeathers.

Rather than bringing its multiform affairs to a burning focus, Olin Mathieson scattered them, much as if it believed the essence of business was simple busy-ness. It had been manufacturing what was probably the widest assortment of products of any corporation in the United States, among them industrial chemicals and agricultural chemicals, brass and aluminum, cigarette paper, cellophane, flashlight batteries, Winchester guns and Winchester-Western ammunition, hardwood flooring and lumber, antifreezes and brake fluids, explosives and powder-actuated tools, nuclear fuel elements and high-energy fuels, Squibb drugs and pharmaceuticals. To be sure, a policy of diversification has served many companies well. But the trouble at Olin Mathieson was that its fifty-odd plants and enterprises were never effectively coordinated. In consequence the economic power of the corporation could be no greater than the simple sum of its parts, and indeed was becoming somewhat less. The stature it might have achieved as a coherent enterprise with $593 million in sales (1957) was drastically circumscribed by the lack of orientation and central purpose. Top management was at sixes and sevens as to just what kind of enterprise it was supposed to run: should this be an out-and-out holding company (which would make it easier to accommodate Olin Mathieson rockets and Olin Mathieson roller skates within the same structure) or should the deadwood be eliminated, along with the sentimental sanctuaries and potluck acquisitions, and the more compatible remainder put under strong centralized control? With management defaulting on this essential decision for over three years, corporate affairs quite naturally followed the line of least resistance. The company degenerated into a loose confederation of tribal chieftains. Executive vice-presidents proliferated (there were ten in 1957). Division chiefs assumed the power and perquisites of corporation presidents. Product lines grew more exotic as one hand toyed with the atom, the other grubbed in the fertilizer business.

Specific examples of Olin Mathieson's affinity for goat-feathers abound. It dashed into the production of boron high-energy fuel, where a less headlong approach would undoubtedly have resulted in the government, rather than money-short Olin Mathieson, shelling out $9 million for new plant, start-up, and other expenses. In research, lack of a centrally coordinated program caused the frittering away of time and talent. It wasn't until spring 1958, when a hard-driving new research vice-president (William E. "Butch" Hanford) herded his people together to initiate just such a company-wide program, that all of O.M.'s thirty-six research chiefs met each other for the first time; two of them—one in industrial chemicals, the other in organic chemicals—then made the embarrassing discovery that both were engaged in identical projects to produce an oil additive. And on occasion, as in its chronically short-circuiting electric-battery venture and its Morgantown, West Virginia, chemical plant, the company allowed itself to be bogged down by the worst of its enterprises rather than making the most of the best. Morgantown was once a good proposition—in the early Fifties, when Mathieson Chemical rented it from the government and thereby got a large amount of ammonia capacity at a time when there was a national shortage of this chemical. But it was a high-cost installation to begin with, and soon disadvantaged by events. New low-cost plants were built closer to the prime marketing areas, while a shift in basing points burdened some of Morgantown's own shipments with a $12-to-$15-a-ton freight differential. Olin Mathieson, however, kept sending good money after bad, presumably in the expectation that the government would cough up the $10 million required for a complete plant modernization. Commented a senior vice-president, when the creaking facility was finally closed down in 1958: "If the time and effort we spent trying to straighten out Morgantown had been put to other things, we'd be millions of dollars ahead."

When Olin Industries joined with Mathieson Chemical to form the new company, in September 1954, it looked as though both boards had had a good idea. Mathieson's caustic soda, sulfuric acid, ammonia, and chlorine, for example, would be going into Olin's explosives, cellophane, and paper, while Mathieson's antifreeze and fertilizer would find a way into almost every hardware store in the country through doors held open by Winchester. Olin Mathieson's sidelines, deflections, and distractions, however, quickly exacted their toll. Poorly conceived projects mortgaged the future of really worthwhile ones. To make up for ill-spent funds, very costly financing had to be undertaken. The company's judgment and sense of timing underwent a subtle corrosion. Corporate luck began to run out, for it was circumscribed by too many adverse circumstances. The company's excursion into aluminum brings all these factors into focus. As an example of somnolence, slipshod planning, and getting out on a limb, it has few equals.

Misadventures in aluminum

The heart of Olin Mathieson's aluminum operation is Ormet, a 180,000-ton smelter at Clarington, Ohio, owned jointly with Revere Copper & Brass. Its cost was roughly $250 million (including $17,500,000 of initial working capital) and Olin Mathieson, in an exuberant mood, committed itself to guaranteeing two-thirds of Ormet's annual obligations. These obligations are little short of backbreaking. The smelter, getting into operation in a glutted market, was financed with only the thinnest of equity money, $31 million. Thus its ratio of debt to aluminum-smelting capacity, $1111 per ton of metal, is roughly double that of Reynolds and Kaiser Aluminum. Debt installments are consequently formidable: repayment to banks of the first $100 million (in promissory notes) must begin on March 31 of next year and continue in equal installments through September of 1963. In return for its annual 120,000-ton share of Ormet's aluminum, Olin Mathieson will have to pony up $14 million a year to meet the debt schedule; it is committed to paying two-thirds of the operating costs.

The present softness of the aluminum market, quite apart from the difficulties of a newcomer trying to break into the business, suggests that Ormet deficits could be sobering indeed. Ormet has a considerably higher breakeven point than any of the established producers. To stay out of the red it will have to keep four of its five pot lines (80 percent of capacity) in operation. The problem will be to find a buyer for these 144,000 tons of *new* metal in the next year or so. Metals Division Vice-President Jess

Williams doesn't think that the company will be able to sell even 60,-000 tons of metal in 1959. "We expect the pull-out to come in 1960," he commented recently, "certainly not before then." The outlook, as of now at least, hardly warrants his being any more optimistic. The industry had reduced production by roughly 30 percent by midsummer. Kaiser's new 145,000-ton Ravenswood, West Virginia, smelter was operating at only 50 percent of capacity. Meanwhile foreign aluminum companies are shipping in shapes and fabrications at 10 percent under American posted prices, duty paid. Next year, just at the time when the government will stop taking 250,000 tons a year maximum off the market, the total aluminum supply will have expanded to some 3,300,000 tons. If consumption is no better than the two million tons of 1957, new markets will have to be found for over a million tons of metal to keep these new facilities going. In the first few months of 1958, Olin Mathieson shelled out $6 million for its aluminum program, holds it responsible for almost half the 50 percent drop in its net profits for the first and second quarters, 1958 vs. 1957. Chances are that aluminum will gobble up an additional $9 million or $10 million by year's end.

Olin Mathieson argues that no one could have predicted in 1956, the year its aluminum program was started, that the completed facility would have the bad luck to run head on into both a metals depression and a general recession. Perhaps not, though enough storm signals were flying to warrant extreme caution, particularly in a venture that would, if it failed, undermine the whole structure. For example, it was quite clear in 1955, when the government stopped stockpile buying, that the aluminum industry was in for trouble. The next year the domestic aluminum producers began importuning the General Services Administration to help them out of an increasingly distressing inventory problem. That was the year Olin Mathieson launched Ormet and, in a sense, made its own bad luck. The company's subsequent moves were of a piece with the original inexpert decision. Some of them:

Product mix—Though Olin Mathieson's production is only 7.9 percent of the total market, the company complicated matters for itself by skimping on facilities at Omal in Ohio, the new $65-million rolling mill it built nearby to take Ormet's ingot. Nearly 80 percent of Omal's narrow product mix is concentrated in sheet and plate. But sheet and plate last year comprised almost 50 percent of the total tonnage of the whole aluminum industry. If Omal is to attain 7.9 percent of the total market, it figures it will have to displace more than 14 percent of the present market for sheet and plate. The prospects of Omal's bringing off that achievement are not bright, particularly after a slow start in getting the aluminum sales organization established. The Personnel Department failed to turn up an industry-trained candidate for the aluminum sales vice-presidency, though a half-year was spent searching for one. The executive who was finally hired for this critical post was fired last December after six months on the job. His successor, Derek Richardson, though able, is inexperienced in aluminum.

Raw material—Olin Mathieson launched into the biggest and riskiest investment in its corporate history without a captive source of bauxite, the basic raw material of aluminum, or even a long-term contract for the ore—and did so in the face of the bitter experience that companies like Reynolds had in going into aluminum production without first assuring themselves of a substantial long-term supply of bauxite. O.M.'s agreement with Billiton for delivery of Surinam bauxite extended only through 1966. The bargaining disadvantages the corporation would encounter at renewal time, with prime sources of bauxite in habitually short supply, were obvious.

Product development—As of today, there are no new products or developments of its own with which Olin Mathieson can ease its entry into the aluminum market. Completion of the company's $5-million Metals Research Center at New Haven next year is just a starter in this direction; consequential product development is at least two years distant. In the interim, O.M. will have to content itself with a large amount of sales in the most rudimentary (and unprofitable) form, ingot. The trademarked product "Roll-Bond," made by a novel hydraulic inflation process, which in the case of heat exchangers eliminated the costly drawing and brazing of tubes, was once Olin Mathieson's white hope. Indeed, the corporation sank $6 million in a new plant just to produce this "patented" product. But General Motors (Frigidaire), exploiting almost unbelievable carelessness and procrastination by Olin Mathieson, maneuvered itself into a position where it now holds the patent in some foreign countries and a cross-licensing agreement in the United States. Ironically enough, Olin Mathieson's ebullience about the future prospects of Roll-Bond was in part responsible for its making a commitment to buy a supplementary supply of aluminum—100,000 tons of the metal—from Alcoa, Kaiser, Alcan, and Anaconda in 1958 and 1959. This $50-million obligation, a superfluity in today's market, has simply compounded the difficulties of the whole aluminum program.

A bull in the street

Unhappily for Olin Mathieson, supercharged forecasting was not confined to aluminum. In 1956 it was present to an alarming degree in almost every division, when John W. Hanes, the experienced chairman of
the finance committee, was himself carried away by the grandeur of the
growth projections submitted by O.M.'s division chiefs. In a major speech
to the Philadelphia Security Analysts that year, he put his own prestige,
and the company's reputation, behind a forecast that total sales would
hit close to a billion and a quarter by 1960. Net profits after taxes were
expected to reach $111,400,000 the same year; the total five-year profits
projection: $391 million. In the cold light of 1958 the chances of either
the profit or sales projection's coming true are practically zero. Net income for 1956 and 1957 totaled $81,200,000, 1958 earnings are now run-
ning at an annual rate of less than $20 million [they actually ended the
year at $12.1 million vs. 1957's $39.6 million]; which would leave the
mountainous amount of $291 million still to be earned in 1958 and 1959.
Sales would have to jump more than half a billion in the next two years.
But even in the heady atmosphere of 1956 there was a murmur of disbelief from Wall Street. Indeed, some clearheaded financial men, far from
sharing these extravagantly optimistic views, were so convinced that Olin
Mathieson was hurting for money that they made a series of offers to buy
the Squibb Division. The longer one looked at Olin Mathieson the more
messed up its affairs appeared to be. For underlying the symptomatic
deviations and other weaknesses were two basic ailments.

Patriarchy and dilution

First, neither Olin Industries ($228 million in sales) nor Mathieson
Chemical ($244 million) had shaken down individually at the time of
the 1954 merger. Olin Industries had just emerged from a patriarchy and
was in the process of revamping its entire approach to business. Mathieson
Chemical, which had shot up from an enterprise with $66 million in as-
sets in 1947 to a $339-million corporation in 1954, mainly by acquisition,
had undergone continuous disruption and dilution; indeed, in 1952,
when Mathieson acquired Squibb for 40 percent of the total Mathieson
equity, there was considerable wonder within the company about who had

taken over whom. Compounded of two still-to-be consolidated corporations, Olin Mathieson itself needed a great deal more shaking down than
the usual merger-created company.

Second, after the merger, there was a lack of the kind of leadership that
could bring about the necessary consolidation. Mathieson's Thomas S.
Nichols, who became president of Olin Mathieson, was brilliant as a pro-
moter; it was he who had singlehandedly put together the Mathieson
complex. But as an administrator he was constantly leading from weakness.
Communication from him *up* was no doubt excellent, but from him down
it was sporadic, mercurial, or nonexistent. When the first attempts were
being made to buy Squibb from Olin Mathieson, the entire division was
kept in a state of extreme uneasiness for lack of any word from Nichols
as to what was going on. The trade press, meanwhile, was getting plenty
of linage out of the rumors, and the local grapevine was buzzing with
apprehension, for the prospective buyers had stopped off first at the Squibb
Division before making their bid to Olin Mathieson's president. It was
not until the divisional vice-president took matters in his own hands,
and told his senior staff that their jobs would be guaranteed by any potential buyers, that things simmered down.

John Olin, who became chairman of Olin Mathieson, might once
have undertaken something as complicated and bloody as consolidating
this vast new corporation. But that would have been twenty years ago.
Moreover, the shakedown job was really Nichols' and not his.

John Hanes commented to Nichols at the time of the merger negotiations, "You want to be Mr. Big and John Olin wants to be Mr.
Big, and I want out." But Olin Mathieson's management problem was
that neither the president nor the chairman was big enough to be Mr.
Big.

This unhappy state of affairs continued until last year. By then both
Olin and Hanes had made up their minds that something drastic had to
be done. Nichols relinquished the presidency for the chairmanship of the
board. John Olin, now sixty-five (at sixty-four he used to say that
ninety was the right age for retirement), accepted the post of chairman
of the executive committee. Hanes, who had wanted out, got out of the
finance-committee chairmanship (though he is still a director). Stanley
Osborne, then fifty-two, went in as president on May 17, 1957. A new
entity, the Financial and Operating Policy Committee, was set up as a
sort of board of review, where Osborne's recommendations would become
corporate policy—if they met with unanimous approval. The committee's members were Osborne himself, Nichols, Hanes, and Olin (chair-

man). But who was really calling the turn, in view of the membership of the F.O.P. Committee and the heavy stockholdings of Olin, Nichols, and Hanes? The complete answer was supplied by the character and actions of the new president himself.

One pats, the other slices

Financial vice-president of Mathieson Chemical, Osborne had gone on to two important posts in the merged corporation: executive vice-president in charge of the International Division (1954), and executive vice-president for finance (1956). One job gave him a considerable insight into the strength of the Olin Mathieson divisions in worldwide markets (he managed to expand foreign sales from $55 million to $84 million in three years), while the other put him in the know about the corporation as an entity.

Osborne was not willing to be bounced around to just any job so long as it could be construed as a promotion; he had had his eye fixed on the main chance, the presidency of some corporation, ever since 1950, and had trained himself accordingly. As an administrator, he expected complete preparation from anybody requiring a decision from him ("I usually bring a briefcase full of data," says one vice-president). But people could get right to the heart of any corporate matter with him. Henry Arnold, head of Squibb in Argentina, had been about to quit for lack of effective communication with the home office, when someone suggested he make his beef to Osborne, just established as head of the International Division. Within an hour and a half Arnold had got decisions on twenty-five major problems, some of which had been hanging fire for years.

The new president's view of his job was realistic: he had to pat backs with one hand and slice heads off with the other; he had to reform and regroup the entire corporation, but not paralyze it in the process or dissipate any of its manageable strength; and he had to be prepared to be the lonely man in the crowded room.

"You gotta"

His character makes it easy for him to establish rapport with widely varying personalities. "Stan Osborne," says Hanes, himself a sophisticated man-about-finance, "is a diligent, intelligent, and civilized fellow who is not dogmatic and so is able to gather a lot of good men around him. He has finesse, prestige, and finality." "Stan Osborne," observes the veteran Ed Block, a dynamic, hard-shelled industrialist who sold his successful chemical company, Blockson, to Olin Mathieson in 1955, "is a fighting little banty rooster. He'll tell anybody off. He'll come to grips with anything. He's trained for organization and is the best damned organizer I ever saw. When he called me in about taking over the Chemical Division, it wasn't 'Will you?' but 'You gotta.'"

Osborne brought to his job not only business ability but the perspectives of the historian and the illumination of the teacher. One day he hopes to publish a history of Spain that he works on at home "for recreation," and one day, on retirement, he hopes to get back to the teaching he enjoyed so much, if so briefly, as a young Harvard instructor. Meanwhile, here is a man who really relishes being president of Olin Mathieson, no matter how ominous many of the problems confronting him.

Osborne's first move was to spend a little time in Nassau mulling over what he was going to do. At the end of two weeks he hurried into the company's Park Avenue offices with a fistful of yellow sheets on which he had made his notes for the renovation of Olin Mathieson.

Rudimentary remedies

Necessarily, some of the remedies Osborne had to prescribe were the sort of thing most well-run companies consider rudimentary. For the first time every product in the company is being individually examined to see what it really costs, how well it fits into the line. And for the first time the division heads are having their operations reviewed on the basis of precise and detailed figures, examination of the figures themselves often being sufficient to put the division on the right track. Elementary or not, Osborne's approach has brought substantial progress in the past sixteen months. Some of the highlights:

Rag, tag, and bobtails—The Morgantown chemical plant was closed down July 15 and a deal consummated with Sun Oil for the use of Sun cash and O.M. technical skill in construction and operation of an efficient urea plant in the Philadelphia area. An appraisal of the electric-battery operation at New Haven is now in process. Roller skates were dropped.

Bauxite—O.M.'s need for a captive source of bauxite for its aluminum operation was filled by Osborne through participation in the Fria Project.

A joint $135-million venture with British Aluminum, Pechiney and Ugine of France, and Aluminium Industrie/A.G. of Switzerland, Fria will have a 480,000-ton alumina plant in limited operation in French Guinea by 1961. O.M. will own 53.5 percent of the stock, have 36 percent of the voting power, and is entitled to 53.5 percent of the alumina. Fria's own bauxite reserves plus its rights to adjacent mineral deposits are estimated as sufficient to keep the alumina plant operating for seven hundred and fifty years.

A commitment to take half of Fria's alumina beginning in 1961 has been postponed to the more manageable date of 1965. Financial obligations, other than the $6 million already paid, have been altered so that Olin Mathieson can defer payments on the principal. Osborne has worked out an arrangement whereby most of the $50 million worth of aluminum O.M. had contracted to buy from other producers this year and next will be spread over a six-year period.

Capital expenditures—A $4,500,000 commitment involving effluent control at a calcium chloride plant in Virginia was altered to provide an equally efficient remedy at a fraction of the cost. A capital expenditure for the Chemicals Division, which became imperative after a power dam in upstate New York collapsed, was distributed over three years instead of one.

Cost-cutting—Beginning with a $30,000 reduction in his own $145,000 salary, and equal cuts in those of Olin and Nichols, Osborne served notice on the senior executives that he'd expect them to volunteer reductions in their salaries, too. (Their cuts ranged from 10 to 15 percent.) Executives making $15,000 and up were put under his personal review. Requests for capital-asset improvement were subject to the most searching scrutiny; budgets for this are 22 percent lower in 1958 than in 1957. Particular attention was also directed at reducing expenditures for services, inventories, and receivables. One million dollars was saved by cost-cutting in the Chemicals Division. Research was put under equally strict surveillance.

Financing—Under heavy pressure from its aluminum venture, Olin Mathieson had to replenish its capital. The costs of building Ormet were not only formidable, they were 5 to 10 percent ($10 to $20 million) above estimates. Unhappily, equity financing was out of the question— the company had already experienced a substantial dilution of equity— so it was decided to use debentures. These bore an interest rate of 5.5 percent and could be converted into Olin Mathieson common stock at fifty dollars a share until 1962. Osborne would have preferred going into the market for the necessary $100 million ($40 million of which was to retire some senior obligations) at one crack. But the legal complications over the financing of the Fria project argued for a more circumspect approach, so he split the debenture issue. The biggest chunk, $60 million, went on the market in November 1957, $40 million in March of 1958. To his dismay, however, the timing of the first issue was marred by the Federal Reserve's abrupt lowering of the rediscount rate. This meant, of course, that all interest rates would subsequently decline and Osborne might have been able to offer his debentures more advantageously later on, at rates less than 5.5 percent. But Osborne just couldn't afford to wait. By the time the second offering came on in March, interest rates had been steadily declining, but now O.M. couldn't afford to risk anything less "sweet" than the 5.5 percent of November. Osborne found consolation in the fact that when the debentures are converted, stockholders' equity will rise to 66 percent of the total capitalization.

He was also making progress on another of his major financial objectives. "What I hope to do," he explained a few weeks ago, "is to write off all of the start-up expenses this year, so that next year none of the start-up costs of aluminum, high-energy fuel, nuclear fuel, explosives, or paper will be a drag on earnings. The balance sheets will be clean. That will be costly, demanding probably $15 million before taxes."

Organization—Osborne's organizational program for O.M. clarified the attitude of the company toward both staff and line functions, clearly established the areas in which the staff could act for him, set up company-wide grants of operational authority and limitations on that same authority. He had the heads of the fourteen operating divisions reporting directly to him for a full year. By June of this year the organizational plan was complete. The number of divisions, through consolidation and elimination, was compressed from fourteen sprawling entities to seven compact ones.

Profits and potentialities

O.M.'s seven new divisions present a mixed picture today, in part because of the recession and in part because they are still in the process of reorganization.

Industrial chemicals are down 15.1 percent in sales for the first half of 1958 vs. 1957, 24.8 percent in net profits. The key to the future, says Ed Block, is more research.

Arms, ammunition, and explosives are down 29 percent in sales, almost

60 percent in net, the latter figure including the cost of facilities and development of O.M.'s new solid propellants. There is not much hope for substantial growth in arms and ammunition, under present policies. Moreover, with any construction man able to make his own explosives by compounding bunker oil and fertilizer-grade ammonium nitrate in a cement mixer, the dynamite business is on the rocks. The efficiency of Olin Mathieson's own explosive organization is currently low.

Drugs and pharmaceuticals (Squibb), a taut show run by John C. Leppart, whose talent for administration has been proved in twenty years of top-level posts, came up with an 8.7 percent increase in sales and a 2.6 percent rise in net last year, the biggest in Squibb's history. During Leppart's five-year tenure Squibb sales have been pushed up 50 percent while profits jumped 360 percent. After industrial chemicals it has been Olin Mathieson's biggest money-maker. Over half of last year's sales came from products introduced since 1952, pointing up the fact that in a pharmaceutical company, research has to be operated almost like a production unit.

Metal sales are down 6.3 percent, while profits, burdened by the aluminum start-up expenses, have dropped 210 percent. Brass has been caught in the metals depression that was accentuated by the slump in automobile sales. Imported standard brass products are now being marketed in the U.S. at 10 to 15 percent under American prices, a situation that is likely to persist for some time.

High-energy and nuclear fuels are full of glamour but devoid of profits. Sales, all to the government, are up 29.7 percent, but the net, again with a heavy burden of start-up expenses, is down 208.2 percent. Olin Mathieson's breakthrough in boron fuels gave it plenty of publicity, but nothing in the way of a commercial market. Boron, which enables O.M. to get into both solid and liquid propellants, has the potential of a big money earner for the corporation but at this juncture its profit outlook is minuscule and its potentiality obscure.

International, up 1.1 percent in sales and down 11.4 percent in profits, should just about equal 1957 by the close of this year.

Finally, film, paper, and forest products may be in for something more than a 1.2 percent increase in net and .8 percent decrease in sales. Cellophane capacity has been doubled (80,000 pounds) and the new plant is now confronted both by an oversupplied market and by heavier competition from polyethylene film. On the other hand, this division is run by R. H. Evans, one of the smartest executives in the company. O.M. has recognized the advantages of offering a customer a complete packaging service: paper bags, cardboard cartons, cellophane and polyethylene wrappings, a line that might get 30 percent of the customer's business where only 20 percent could be had by offering single or unrelated items.

Short rations

The reformation of Olin Mathieson has not solved all its problems. The corporation will be needing money and embarrassingly soon, for chemical companies don't do well for long on short rations; the nature of the business is such that you either go ahead or you go back. In a very real sense, the fate of the company is tied up with its aluminum venture and the future of that is dependent upon the aluminum market. Ormet should eventually be quite profitable. Its initial power ratio of 7.3 kilowatt-hours per pound of metal suggests low-cost production when all pot lines are operating.

For the next couple of years the general forecast for Olin Mathieson is "hard going." It would seem to make sense for the company to keep on disposing of sidelines. Marquardt Aviation (25 percent stock ownership) is one that could go, and McGraw Engineering (44 percent) is another. At Winchester-Western Division the hundred-odd modifications of twenty-three models, some of which don't bring in more than a dozen sales a year, could be drastically cut. Reducing the cost of shotgun shells, a prime deterrent to increased recreational shooting, might well be a major target of Western Cartridge.

Over-all, the matter of further consolidation should not be regarded as settled on the basis of the present studies. Olin Mathieson's management is still spread pretty thin and the corporation as a whole, because of the multiplicity of its interests and because of its economic circumstances, will be hard put to do justice to the most promising lines.

On the main line

Happily, one of the most important ingredients in any change for the better is the feeling that change is on the way. If Osborne can hold things together for the next two or three years, aluminum should be coming to his aid with a substantial plus. Meanwhile, morale around Olin Mathieson is high, nerves are surprisingly steady, candor has replaced secretiveness. "The time we waste in excursions off the main line of our road to our goal is the difference between success and half-success," wrote Ellis Parker Butler at the conclusion of his essay on goat-feathers; "often it is the difference between success and failure." Osborne would agree, and he's just started to get on the main line of Olin Mathieson's road.

Epilogue

Olin Mathieson had a very rough go of things over the next several years, for much had to be done, and done under combat conditions. Sales never came close to $1.2 billion for 1960, the figure so ebulliently presented to the Philadelphia Security Analysts in 1956, nor did profits hit the $111 million forecast; they stood at $690 million and $35 million respectively. The next year showed little improvement, revenues climbing slightly to $700 million, but profits falling to $32 million. This gave Olin Mathieson a ratio of only 4.6 percent per dollar of sales, far below the top, Du Pont's 18.8 percent, indeed well under that of Allied (6.3 percent), the lowest of the other major chemical companies. Moreover, the long-term debt, which had reached the equivalent of nearly 60 percent of the combined capitalization in 1958, climbed to 82 percent of the capitalization in 1962. But for all of that, President Stanley Osborne has done a monumental job of setting Olin Mathieson to rights. He not only recognized the company's problems for what they were, but let neither hell nor high water stand in the way of his attack on them.

The prime reasons for Olin Mathieson's crisis, it will be remembered, were (1) the corporation had never shaken down, (2) its strength was steadily sapped by "distractions, sidelines, and deflections," and (3) it had never had the kind of leadership that could bring about consolidation of its manifold elements. Osborne first proceeded to give Olin Mathieson the necessary unity. He moved in vigorously to eliminate the old interdivisional rivalries and jealousies that had hamstrung the enterprise, and he somehow got executives to understand they were not "Olin men" or "Mathieson men," but colleagues in a common endeavor. Engineering was reorganized, personnel and finance were centralized, two of many moves to curtail the excessive autonomy of the divisions. New blood was brought in—seven divisional heads and general managers all told, both to replace the refractory and to shore up weaknesses. All this helped make Olin Mathieson a federated corporation instead of the "loose confederation of tribal chieftains."

Next Osborne took to plucking goat-feathers with a zeal that would have

won an accolade from Ellis Parker Butler himself. He got Olin Mathieson
out of F. H. McGraw Company (engineering), the irrigation business,
the retail fertilizer business, Marquardt Aircraft, a small insurance company, the perfume business, the rocket company, collapsible metal tubes,
flashlights and batteries, and he spun off Hunter Engineering Corporation.
In the process of achieving all this, he resolved Olin's third problem: leadership at the top. Previous management, led by John Olin and Tom Nichols,
had consented to let him take over, displacing them in the hierarchy, only
if the special Financial and Operating Policy Committee were established
with both of them members and Olin the chairman. This committee of
Olin, Nichols, Hanes, and Osborne had the power to disapprove the last-
named's recommendations if so minded. But the sort of leadership Osborne demonstrated was its own argument for his being given a free
hand; one day the committee simply shut up shop and Osborne became
chief executive officer in fact as well as in title.

There is, perhaps, no such thing as complete victory over a corporate
crisis. They take time to resolve and all the while time works changes of its
own. But Olin Mathieson would seem to have successfully surmounted the
crisis of 1958. This is not to say that the cost-price squeeze or changing
markets or heightened competition won't give it trouble tomorrow, but the
effort that had to be spent shoring up bulkheads, plugging leaks, and man-
ning the pumps can now be devoted to the normal labor of running the
ship. It is a reoriented, rejuvenated company, and because Osborne was
able both to transform the corporation and to hold it together in the years
required to liquidate most of the heavy aluminum obligation, once-dan-
gerous Ormet can now become a plus on the profit-and-loss sheet. In
September of 1963 the last $20 million of Ormet's $100-million short-term
indebtedness for that aluminum facility will have been paid off. This promises the release of funds equivalent to thirty-seven cents a share in 1964
($5.5 million), a well-earned reward for a well-fought battle.

CHAPTER II

RKO: A Crisis of Responsibility

Prologue

There are two ways to run any company: either you run it yourself or you delegate real authority to someone else to do the job. What created a crisis at RKO was that Howard Hughes did neither. He took over a strong enterprise from Floyd Odlum in 1948 but over the next five years hamstrung the efforts of management to keep the studio going; at the same time, he never even set foot on the lot himself. As talented producers like Dore Schary threw up their hands in despair and the departure of top executives became an exodus, losses climbed past the $20-million mark. By 1953, as this chapter discloses, the light had gone out at the nation's fifth-biggest studio and what value remained was as so many parcels of real estate, so many cans of old film.

*   *   *

In October 1952 when Hollywood got its first good whiff of the newcomers who had bought working control of RKO Pictures, the fifth-largest studio, there was an immediate yelp of dismay. The aroma that surrounded three members of the five-man syndicate was vastly disturbing to an industry already overloaded with trouble. The one thing nobody wanted was a public scandal involving the directors of a major film company. What the proportions of the "scandal" actually were may never be known, but regardless of that, "the mass of unfavorable publicity" and Hollywood's way of *behaving* as if quick-money men were out to loot RKO knocked the syndicate's plans in the head. After fifteen harried weeks its members forfeited $1,350,000 in cash, handed back the majority stockholdings to their former owner, Howard Robard Hughes, and blew. The movie industry shook hands all around, then settled down again to worrying about

TV and three-dimensional film; the *Wall Street Journal*, whose muscular reporting first uncovered the mess, returned to more conventional journalism. Another episode in the mottled career of RKO was over.

The ironic aspect of this whole affair is that the syndicate, by its very eagerness to make a fast buck, might have been a distinct improvement over the sort of management RKO had had in the previous five years. To be sure, there was a world of difference between, say, Ned Depinet and his successor as president of the company, syndicate man Ralph Stolkin; or between Howard Hughes and the syndicate member (Abraham Koolish) who took his place on RKO's board of directors. A good bit of the business history of Messrs. Stolkin and Koolish has been memorialized only in the files of the Better Business Bureau, the Federal Trade Commission, and the Post Office Department, which organizations, at various times, took them to task for operations in direct-mail merchandising, insurance, and punchboards. Ned Depinet, on the other hand, has had a lifelong and apparently blameless career as a movie executive. As for Howard Hughes, the real power at RKO, he has been making some sort of history during most of his forty-seven years; in 1928, he won the Motion Picture Academy Award for *Two Arabian Knights*, the best comedy of the season; in 1930, he released his epochal *Hell's Angels*; in 1941, he won a special Congressional Medal of Honor for a record flight around the world; in 1943, he put the bust in the box office with Jane Russell's *The Outlaw*, and in the same year saw his conception, the Constellation, take to the air. Nobody, in short, could legitimately discuss RKO's previous management in the same terms they might apply to Messrs. Stolkin and Koolish. Indeed, legitimately or not, nobody has, for there is a bone-deep feeling in Hollywood that Howard Hughes is a $200-million bundle of eccentricities with powerful influence. But for all of that, the 1948–52 record of the Hughes regime at RKO was about as dismal as it could possibly be.

In his five years the studio piled up losses of over $20 million, a whopping deficit in every year except one (stated profit for 1951: $300,000).

Production went to pieces, from either crotchety perfectionism or laggard decisions. RKO produced twenty-eight pictures the year before Hughes, ten the year he left.

Studio talent, more of an asset to a picture company than real property, was squandered. Studio payroll fell off from two thousand in 1948 to fewer than five hundred in 1952.

RKO got to such a state by 1953 that banks would not grant it working capital unless Howard Hughes personally guaranteed the loan.

Old-timers, of course, will remember RKO as the studio that had been in and out of hot water during most of the twenty-four years it had been making pictures. It seems as if somebody had always been holding it together by the power of his personal signature. These recollections, however, are perhaps more colored by what happened under the Hughes regime than by the actual performance of previous managements. There was a period, believe it or not, when RKO made a lot of movies and a lot of money. That was in the reign of Floyd B. Odlum.

From mermaid to movies

Back in 1935, when Floyd Odlum first got interested in RKO, the company had little to distinguish it save the size of its deficit and the fact that its origin traced back more than fifty years, from the Keith-Albee-Orpheum vaudeville circuit to Benjamin Franklin Keith's Gaiety Museum and the great showman's original attractions, a midget and a stuffed mermaid. But Odlum knew value when he saw it; indeed, his shrewd appraisals had accounted for the growth of his own Atlas Corporation (investments) from a $40,000 company to one worth $75 million. Even though RKO was then in receivership, he bought a large block of stock and hung on to it. When the receivership was ended five years later, the new company (Floyd Odlum, chairman) started off with a sound reorganization plan (Odlum's), no outstanding debt, and enough hard cash ($8 million) to handle double its current liabilities.

Odlum's approach to RKO was simplicity itself. He was not a boyish personality bent on amusing himself with a motion-picture studio (from an adolescent's point of view probably the most irresistible toy that man has ever devised). He had no neurotic appetite for power over people. Nor was he an egocentric, determined that every foot of film should bear his personal imprimatur. He simply wanted to make RKO into a vigorous, profitable company, then sell out his stock at a price reflecting that improvement. But even with these intentions, the first several years were troublesome for the reconstituted company.

George Schaefer, the president who had been pressed upon Odlum by the Radio Corporation of America (alias David Sarnoff) and Rockefeller Center, Inc. (alias Nelson Rockefeller), majority stockholders, had some movie-making ideas of his own. He decided to sweep out the independent producers who had been making contract movies for RKO and replace their production with more film made at the studio, for the studio. Unfortunately, while the independents knew how to produce, RKO did not. At a time when the rest of the industry was rolling in box-office receipts, RKO Radio Pictures, Inc., the picture-making subsidiary, turned in a half-million loss in 1941, was running at a rate that put it $2,300,000 in the red by the end of 1942. Out went Schaefer. Out too went R.C.A. and Rockefeller Center via the sale of their holdings.

To get distribution and production rolling again, Odlum put the company's crack distribution man, Ned Depinet, at the head of RKO Radio Pictures, Inc., and set up Charles Koerner, who had made a name for himself in RKO Theatres, Inc., as vice-president in charge of production. The Koerner schedule called for twenty-three pictures in eleven months, and, miraculously, it was met. Two quickies, *Hitler's Children* (cost: $175,000) and *Behind the Rising Sun* ($210,000), produced for RKO by Edward Golden, a onetime dentist turned film distributor, materialized as the biggest low-budget money-makers in screen history. Gross revenues: $2 million to $3,500,000 apiece. This single harvest (really sown by ex-president Schaefer) was enough to assure Charlie Koerner of a movie-making profit, but wartime audiences, worried and uncritical, were ready to do even more for him or any other studio head who would just produce pictures. With Charlie just producing, RKO wound up 1943 with the greatest picture-making profit ever: $7,596,000. Total net profits for the corporation (picture company plus theater company and subsidiaries) after taxes amounted to almost $7 million, nearly ten times greater than those of the previous year.

The following year's performance, though brilliant by previous standards, was somewhat down from 1943. Picture-making profits slipped from $7,600,000 to $5,100,000, the consolidated net from $6,900,000 to $5,200,-000. In 1945 studio profits fell off even more (to $4,995,000). Charlie Koerner had not stumbled across any "sleepers" like *Hitler's Children*; nor had he proved himself notably sharp at the incessant horse-trading in talent that, almost as much as production, governs success in the movie business. Nevertheless, when he died quite suddenly of leukemia in early 1946, RKO could look back at his administration of the studio as the only "Golden Age" in its history.

End of an age

Some of Koerner's momentum, fortunately for the company, carried over into the latter months of 1946. Picture-making profits rose to $6,-300,000, but actually RKO was in trouble again. Production was virtually at a standstill. The studio had been unable either to develop or to hang onto stars and producers. Moreover, most of the movies that bore its label were made by others. Its studio had degenerated into a kind of rental lot and the whole picture operation was fast becoming a mere appendage of the theater chain. Earnings under such circumstances could hardly go anywhere but down.

The studio chief brought in to pull RKO out of its difficulties was Dore Schary. Though not then the first-rank film executive he eventually became, Schary soon generated a sense of enthusiasm and accomplishment within the company. He himself had come up through the ranks, beginning as a writer, winding up as a producer. Under his one-man studio control ("committees are death on creative people"), RKO brought in talent and made maximum use of the capabilities on hand. Schary believed advance planning could cut production costs to the bone. His method, something of an innovation in a Hollywood given to overblown scripts rectified by expensive retakes and cutting, was to get the script right before shooting began. That way, he might even find that "the material itself becomes a star" and the film could be made with virtual unknowns. With him RKO achieved a *succès d'estime*, but did not avert a financial deficit at the studio (1947: $1,800,000) nor, consequently, deflect the piercing glance of Floyd Odlum.

Sometime in 1947 Odlum had decided to sell his RKO holdings. He was disturbed by Congressman J. Parnell Thomas' Communist hunt of that year, but the decisive reason was economic. Foreign receipts were frozen as a consequence of the dollar shortage. Odlum thought less prosperous days were ahead for Hollywood, his own studio experiencing the first loss in five years, and it might be six months before Schary's program started making money. The time had arrived to unload and invest the proceeds elsewhere.

Certainly Odlum had something to sell. RKO (studio *plus* theaters) had $69 million in assets when he took uncontested control in early 1943; it had a surplus of only $562,000 and a microscopic net profit—$736,000. At the end of his fourth year the company was worth $114 million, had an earned surplus of $23,500,000 and a net profit of $5 million. Net profits had stayed between $5 million and $7 million every year except 1946, when the greatest movie-going boom in U.S. history (one and a half billion admissions) pushed the corporate net to over $12 million. Dividend payments averaged $3,500,000 a year over the period. But individual buyers with enough cash to pay his price—roughly $9 million for 929,000 shares—were not to be found mooning around the studio gates. Finally Odlum got his first serious bite: in mid-January 1948, Howard Hughes flew down to San Diego to talk things over. After an hour's discussion he flew back to Beverly Hills to make up his mind. Impatiently, Floyd Odlum complained to the press: "Under today's almost panicky conditions in Hollywood, [no one] has the combined money and nerve to meet the faith of Atlas Corporation in the industry."

This statement, a rather transparent one from somebody bent on unloading his own holdings, quite naturally failed to challenge Hughes. He had just begun to back and fill, and would be months at it. News of the negotiations, however, did start some unpleasant conjecture on the RKO lot. Studio people began piecing together what they knew or had heard about their prospective boss. It was far from reassuring.

The Texan seemed incapable of keeping hands off any enterprise he was interested in. In 1944 he and the brilliant writer-director-producer, Preston Sturges, formed Sturges-Hughes, Inc. to make some twenty films. Said Hughes: "I want to make one thing clear, I can't devote any time whatsoever to the motion-picture business until the war is over. . . . He [Sturges] is one man in whom I have complete confidence. I am happy to turn over to him the full control and direction of all my motion-picture activities." In 1946 a completely frustrated Sturges dissolved the partnership because of "disagreements over budget, production procedures, and minor casting." No films had been released.

A plunger who played his hunches to the limit, Hughes sometimes achieved fabulous success. His first major movie, *Hell's Angels*, in 1929 the most expensive production ever filmed, was completed as a silent picture at a cost of $3 million. Then Hughes saw his first talkie. He gambled another million that *Hell's Angels* would make more money in sound, replacing Greta Nissen and her Swedish accent with an untried girl, Jean Harlow, and reshooting much of the picture. The payoff: gross receipts of $8 million.

Like many rich men, he haggled over pennies but spent dollars to get ten cents' worth of something he wanted. A fancied six-dollar room overcharge at a hotel would cause him to assign an expensive henchman to a fortnight of wrangling with a management only too willing to make him a present of the room, while on the other hand he would let actor Jack Buetel sit around for seven years, at $1050 a week, while he made up his mind about casting him in a picture.

His early movie-making (*Hell's Angels, Scarface, The Front Page*)

had often been distinguished by technical innovation and a preoccupa-
tion with violence, high speed, and sex. Lately this had coalesced into a
commercial pertinacity about Jane Russell's bosom. During a flogging
sequence in one of her films, Hughes decided her chest did not gyrate to
the best effect. He designed, on the spot, a brassière that produced realism
at the pull of a string.

Subordinates usually found it impossible to reach him, no matter how
important the occasion. He called them at his convenience, days after
notification, often in the middle of the night, and then as likely as not
turned things upside down. A $30,000-a-year adman, with a $10,000 to
$15,000 layout book of ads for *The Outlaw*, had been summoned by
Hughes for an O.K. He left New York by plane, then spent three weeks
at a hotel before Hughes contacted him. He was told to meet a certain
man at a certain gas station at night. Eventually he got to Hughes, at
another hotel; Hughes ripped up the display book, and in ten minutes,
on hotel stationery, sketched the ads that were finally used.

As an antagonist, he fought in the rough-and-tumble tradition of
the frontier, calling on the memory of an elephant, the resources of Croe-
sus, and the license of a Bushman to speed his arm. His free-swinging suits
and court fights routed the Hays office in its efforts to ban *The Outlaw*;
his vituperation and mastery of the insinuating question defeated Senator Brewster in a celebrated congressional rhubarb over his plane building for the government.

In May 1948, four months after the meeting with Odlum, Howard
Hughes was head man at RKO. He had finally bought Odlum's stock,
following some of the most bizarre negotiations in film history, for $8,-
825,690 ($9.50 per share), slightly above the market price. His motivation
must remain conjectural; at the time it did not suit his purposes to switch
from a habitual reticence to an equally serviceable loquacity. Best guesses
are that Hughes was moved by two of his abiding interests, prestige and
money. His aviation ventures were somewhat beclouded: he had almost
killed himself in the 1946 test flight of one photo-reconnaissance plane
he was building for the Air Force, no orders had been placed for its
successor, and about all that could be said for the giant Hughes flying
boat ($18 million of government money, $7 million of his own) was that
it had got seventy feet off the water before going into seclusion again.
Control of RKO, which could be had for nearly the same amount of money
he had sunk in the five-year-old plywood flying boat, provided prestige,
production facilities, and a chain of 124 theaters. The last could be use-
ful in bailing out Hughes's investment in two of his own films, *Mad*

Wednesday ($2,400,000) and *Vendetta* (unfinished, $3 million). There should have been nothing conjectural, however, about what Hughes was going to do once he had bought control of RKO. It was an old story.

The exodus begins

The circumstances of Hughes's accession were later explained by ex-President Peter Rathvon, Odlum's smart and amiable finance man, from the perspective of his Paris offices on the Carré de Pétrarque. Both Odlum and he believed that Hughes was a responsible buyer "although we knew he was not an experienced executive. But prior to the sale, Mr. Hughes had declared his intention to devote himself almost exclusively to his aviation interests. Furthermore, at Mr. Hughes's request, I agreed to remain as president on the understanding that I would function without interference from Mr. Hughes and would continue to be responsible only to the board of directors. Mr. Hughes told me that I could expect to have a freer hand in management than ever before, that he would not himself become a director. . . . Mr. Dore Schary, head of production, was assured that he would continue under my supervision. . . ." Dore Schary was the first casualty.

Hughes and Schary never met until a week after the stock purchase. It was an edgy occasion. Politically and temperamentally the men were poles apart. Schary had been pretty glum about Hughes's coming since he first heard of the bid in January. He had taken no more comfort from Odlum's assurance that "it would be good for the stockholders" than were the stockholders ultimately to take themselves. Said Hughes, after the introduction: "I hear you don't like me." Said Schary: "Well, I hear you don't like me either. We can either talk in terms of gossip or talk business." Said Hughes: "You can run the studio—I haven't got any time."

Two weeks later, while Rathvon was on a business trip to Mexico, Hughes politely asked Schary what his reasons were for making *Battleground,* a movie of the Battle of the Bulge. Schary's reason: he thought war films were sure to have a vogue soon and he wanted to lead not follow the parade. Hughes thought war pictures were not a good idea at that time; the polls had reported against them. Next question: Why film *Bed of Roses* and why star Barbara Bel Geddes in it? (The movie was scheduled for shooting a few days hence, sets were built, all preparations made.) Schary explained both he and director Anatole Litvak thought Geddes an unusually talented actress and, since RKO was going to have to start building its own stars, she was one the studio had more or less decided on. Upshot of the conversation was that Hughes, though customarily positive about the women he wants in a film, did not overrule Schary on either *Bed* or *Battleground*. Two days later, around midnight, Hughes called, and in the course of conversation told Schary he wanted production on the films stopped. The studio chief promptly resigned. Said Hughes, for publication: "It saved me paying him two weeks' salary."

It was the kind of crack that always comes home to roost. Schary went to M.G.M., the industry's biggest and most glamorous studio, as head of production, and in the following year made sixty-four of the sixty-seven pictures he announced he'd make, more than three times the studio's 1948 output. Moreover, he bought the *Battleground* script from Hughes, filmed it for $1,780,000, turned it into the No. 2 box-office success of the year with an indicated eventual gross of $4,550,000, and started a fashion in war films.

The man who wasn't there

Next to go was Peter Rathvon. RKO's president was soon convinced that Hughes did not intend to pursue the promised hands-off policy. He submitted his resignation to Odlum, still chairman of the board by virtue of the 300,000 stock warrants he had retained. Odlum, acting as peacemaker, prepared the form of a letter to be sent Hughes by Rathvon, defining an acceptable division of authority. Although he believed it gave Hughes wider latitude than their original understanding, Rathvon agreed to send it if Hughes would just accept it in writing. Hughes refused. Rathvon resigned.

Certainly nobody could say that Hughes had violated the assurance he'd given that there would be a sixty-day moratorium on hiring and firing. Schary and Rathvon had resigned, in a way. But with the moratorium over, the ax bit deep. Seven hundred employees (150 of them temporaries) were fired during the summer of 1948, the cuts in most departments running between 50 and 75 percent. Odlum resigned as chairman to be replaced by Hughes's alter ego, Noah Dietrich, the suave, agile president of the $81-million Hughes Tool Company (owner: Howard Hughes). Ned Depinet was elected president. An executive committee, composed of the experienced producer Sid Rogell and two nonproduction men, began work administering studio output. Hughes himself kept away from RKO. He preferred to retain his offices in the Goldwyn studios a mile distant, making his wishes known by messenger or telephone, and indeed never set foot on the RKO lot at all. The nearest thing to a visitation, according to a ranking member of his entourage, was a flight *over* the studio one morning on his way to Tucson; he thought it looked shabby, phoned back to have it painted. The extent to which this separatism complicated studio routine can be measured by the story that on one occasion an entire movie set had to be dismantled and shipped over to the Goldwyn lot to get his approval.

But despite the fact that he insisted on absentee management, Hughes was active in RKO affairs, up to the armpit. Three of the films he personally owned—*The Outlaw, Mad Wednesday,* and *Vendetta*—were acquired by RKO from himself and United Artists, holder of the release rights.[1] He signed up Polan Banks Production, Inc., to make three movies for RKO starring Ann Sheridan, the first to be *Carriage Entrance.* Next he got the rights and partially completed screen play of *Jet Pilot* from independent producer Paul Short for "a substantial sum" in the expectation of making it a modern *Hell's Angels.* By December, however, the studio announced that it would suspend production over the holidays (as two other studios had). The final picture worked on that year was the Groucho Marx-Jane Russell-Frank Sinatra comedy *It's Only Money.* RKO's only money connected with picture-making was a cool loss of $5,600,000 for 1948.

One man's meat . . .

The year 1949, of course, would be better, much better. RKO announced its plans to release forty-nine major films in 1949–50 and make thirty-one of them itself. The trouble was Howard Hughes. Nobody in Hollywood quarreled with one-man studio control, so long as it was consistent and permitted the usual departmentalization. But Hughes was both running things and not running things. Decisions had to be made by him, yet often he couldn't be reached quickly enough for the company to pluck any plums in what is one of the nation's most competitive businesses. "If you were lucky enough to get wind of a good story property," said an ex-

[1] The acquisition of these and other Hughes films by RKO was one of several grounds for a minority stockholders' lawsuit against Hughes filed in the fall of 1952. "Hughes," said the complaint, "was sitting on both sides of the negotiating table."

RKO executive, "you couldn't even buy an option on it. If you were still luckier and succeeded in interesting a star in that story, you had to move on *both* deals within a few hours. The chances were that even by next day both possibilities would be snapped up by somebody else. Chances also were that it would be three weeks later that Hughes let you know the option might be okay. . . ." On the other hand, there were times when producers "saw" all too much of him. "Working for Hughes," said one veteran, "was like taking the ball in a football game and running four feet only to find that the coach was tackling you from behind."

. . . is another man's poison

Some members of the board of directors were also getting a bit uneasy about the Hughes technique. They didn't object to autarchy so long as the autocrat was making money, but when the film company was deep in the red, and the onus was shared by them, they wanted influence proportionate to their responsibility. They didn't get it. Moreover, there was the question of RKO (as Howard Hughes) buying Howard Hughes's personally owned films, for distribution through the corporation. Some of the directors wanted to pass on each acquisition, not simply be informed after the fact, as in the 1949 purchase of *Montana Belle* (Jane Russell). And there was a question raised as to the suitability of re-releasing *The Outlaw* during the school holidays around Christmas, both the most profitable time of the year and the most sensitive from the standpoint of taste. It had already been released three years before and its mood was about as far as anyone could get from Peace on Earth, Good Will to Men. Indeed, as a Baltimore judge had said in upholding the state's 1947 ban on the film, Jane Russell's breasts "hung over the picture like a summer thunderstorm spread out over a landscape. They were everywhere. They were there when she first came into the picture. They were there when she went out."

Hughes's response to criticism, however, was more Hughes. He got himself elected Managing Director—Production. His personality aside, RKO could use both managing and direction.

It's Only Money (which became *Double Dynamite*) was not finished in 1948. In fact it wasn't released until 1951. Hughes disliked the gowns Jane Russell wore, ordered complete reshooting on her scenes.

Carriage Entrance did not get started. In the following spring, Polan Banks sued RKO for $670,000 damages, charging breach of contract after the studio had disapproved the scenario. RKO came to terms by buying the scenario, then turned around and got into a contract squabble with Ann Sheridan over the choice of her leading man.

Jet Pilot ground-looped. It had not been released even by 1953. Planes and uniforms were by then obsolete. The $4-million estimated cost still awaited justification by Hughes's movie-making yardstick: "Movies are a cinch. The more you spend, the more you make."

The final box score for the year 1949 was quite different from the announced plan: thirty-one major films to be made by RKO, eighteen by independent producers releasing through the studio. RKO put twelve majors into production, the independents none. Naturally the proceeds from each film had to bear a larger share of studio overhead (then about 40 percent) than they would if it had been possible to spread the charge over more movies. Potential profits were never realized. RKO Radio Pictures turned in another loss, $4,200,000.

Word trouble

In the first part of 1950 two directors, sensing a trend, handed in their resignations. Their departure, since it left only Hughes's men on the board, simply made matters worse. The executive committee—the chairman, president, executive vice-president, and two directors—was scrapped. Production man Sid Rogell also decided he had had enough. Hughes was surprised, and hurt. Expert mechanically, he never seemed to understand the workings of the human mind. While Rogell was waiting around for Hughes to get over his surprise and dig up another executive producer, a situation occurred that underlined the state of affairs at RKO.

After months of negotiation Rogell had got everything ready to close a deal with independent producer Jack Skirball of Gold Seal Productions, Inc. Skirball was to make *Appointment in Samarra*, tentatively starring Gregory Peck, for RKO release. Hughes had O.K.'d every step of the negotiations, Rogell talking with Skirball by day and with Hughes by night. Finally, after Hughes, through Rogell, had got Skirball sweated down to a lower price, the deal was closed, verbally, and publicity released —all on Hughes's instructions. But nothing definite happened on *Appointment* until months later when Skirball pressed Hughes for action (Rogell having long since departed). He was told the movie was dead and to get off the lot. In the resultant suit, adjudicated in 1953, Hughes testified, *in absentia:* "I at no time told Mr. Rogell to close the deal. I at no time told him to discuss the deal on terms of $125,000 plus 20 percent [of the profits] with or without Gregory Peck. I at no time told him to make or close an oral production-distribution agreement with Mr. Skirball or anyone else." Rogell's testimony was in direct refutation. Judge Joseph Vickers, observing there was "no comparable case in the industry," decided there had been an agreement, and awarded Skirball $375,000 damages plus interest.[2]

Enter the "wonder boys"

Rogell's successor at RKO was Sam Bischoff, an independent producer of long experience. Bischoff had come to the film colony back in the Twenties, subsequently brought out *Murder in the Clouds* for a lithe $80,000; Harry Warner had proudly carried the cost sheets around in his pockets for days. Hollywood noted that Bischoff went into a smaller, lower-down office than the one Rogell had had and surmised that Hughes was after bigger game. The quarry he had a bead on was the team of independent producers, Jerry Wald and Norman Krasna.

After two months of ardent negotiation, Hughes finally bought the Wald-Krasna contract from Warner Brothers and signed up the team for five years with RKO. It was one of the biggest deals Hollywood had ever seen: between August 1950 and the same month in 1955, the "wonder boys" would make $50 million worth of feature pictures for RKO release; rate of production was to be twelve films a year, financed 40 percent by Howard Hughes and 60 percent by Pittsburgh's Mellon Bank and New York's Bankers Trust Company; compensation: weekly salaries of $2500 apiece for Wald and Krasna, plus 50 percent equity in the forthcoming films and 50 percent of their earnings.

The occasion was celebrated at a huge press conference, thoughtfully staged in RKO's Budget Room. Wald and Krasna, still steaming with exhilaration, had a hard time getting all the words out. They were going to assemble under one roof "the smartest people since the Greeks." One publicist would be assigned to each picture. Teams of newspaper reporters would scout the world for story material. Nine pictures were all lined up:

[2] In contending that RKO didn't make verbal agreements, Hughes had apparently forgotten his testimony in another suit just a short time before. On that occasion RKO, in court with actress Jean Simmons, insisted on the validity of an oral commitment.

(1) *Stars and Stripes,* the U.S.O. story, with Al Jolson, (2) *Behave Yourself,* a story about teen-agers, (3) *Size Twelve,* a Jerome Weidman story about a dress model, (4) *Country Club,* a social document and comment on Midwest society and prejudices, (5) *The Strong Arm,* a modern crime drama, (6) *Call Out the Marines,* a story of the beginning of the Marine Corps, (7) *Mother Knows Best,* a picture full of "clean-dirty stories," starring Mae West and, naturally, Jane Russell, (8) *Easy Going,* a Danny Kaye musical "about Hollywood," (9) *The Harder They Fall,* the Budd Schulberg novel that RKO owned. "In Hollywood," shouted Krasna, "20 percent of the people carry the other eighty. Twenty percent of the people are real hot." Hughes? "Mr. Hughes," said Wald, grandly, "is busy with big war contracts. I mean really big important—" "This [deal]," he continued, "could only be done in a time of disaster [in the industry]. Everybody's frantic. Mr. Hughes is taking a big look at the thing and he took the jump." The final duet: "We'll have even more autonomy than Zanuck."

Sharecropping with Howard

It might have been supposed that Howard Hughes, back in his offices at the Goldwyn studios, was nervously fingering their contract and wondering if he were still boss of RKO. By the very nature of their agreement with a studio, independent producers have substantial autonomy: really sharecroppers, they sign up labor on the studio's property, use its own personnel, receive its aid in financing, and when the crop is harvested split the profits fifty-fifty. Indeed, some studios like Twentieth Century-Fox will not tolerate this shift of control over output from the studio to the independent, preferring to have production handled exclusively by producers on their payroll. But RKO was desperate, and Hughes had been diligent in seeing that whatever appearances might be, he had just about as much control over Wald-Krasna as he'd had over Rogell. Although Hughes did guarantee to make his decisions in every case within a week, and regardless of the merits of the finished product to release it within ninety days, he had reserved for himself basic approval over all stories, stars, and scripts. In addition, he had the say-so on every film that cost more than $900,000.

Four months of Wald-Krasna, however, could hardly put the studio in the black. RKO Pictures was down with another thumping deficit— $5,800,000—for the year 1950. On December 31, RKO Theatres, Inc., was split off from the movie-making company, pursuant to an antitrust ruling, leaving behind $10 million to pay off the studio's bank loans.[3] This, though it strengthened RKO's financial position, did not get production off dead center.

Cherchez la femme

The twelve months of 1951 recorded another dismal struggle to make movies. Wald-Krasna's *High Heels* tripped over Hughes's star approval. He wanted Terry Moore, for whom he had an enthusiasm, in the feminine lead. Wald-Krasna refused. Hughes turned thumbs down on other candidates; no picture. Moreover, the wilted team seemed unable to deliver on anything else in the quantity expected. Over a million dollars was spent in abortive attempts to get projects rolling. Item: five directors were put on the payroll, and finally released without anything getting on film. Item: of eight scripts, only two were found suitable for filming, the others were described by gloomy staffmen as a "total loss." An ex-producer estimated that RKO's overhead went up to 60 percent.

Two pictures, *The Blue Veil* (cost: $1,100,000) and *Behave Yourself* ($900,000), were finally released and two more (*Clash by Night* and *Lusty Men*) put in production to meet the minimum contractual obligation of four pictures a year. That was a long way from the promised twelve. But RKO just *had* to show a profit. It did, and in quite a fertile way. The 1951 annual report read "net profit for the fifty-two weeks": $334,626.87. In the back was a footnote to the effect that in 1951 a decision had been made to delay a film's amortization until twenty-six weeks after the date of the domestic release. Result: "Had the same method of amortization been used in 1951 as was used in 1950, the net profit for the year and the inventory of released productions, less amortization, would have been decreased by approximately $957,000." A bookkeeping gimmick was all that had put RKO into the black.

Whether this final humiliation decided Howard Hughes to try and sell his RKO holdings is unknown, but sometime during 1952 he did entertain a dozen offers. And none too soon. Matters that year went from bad to worse. The first nine months ended in a $4,800,000 deficit. The loss would have been even greater had not RKO dusted off the nineteen-year-old

[3] Stockholders of the divided RKO Corporation got one share of stock in each of the new, independent companies. Majority stockholders had a choice of keeping their stock in *one* of the companies and either putting their holdings of the other company in a nonvoting trust or selling them. Odlum had an option to buy Hughes's theater stock, if for sale, by meeting a legitimate offer.

King Kong (estimated gross: $2,500,000), and had not "a hunt for Communists" temporarily eased the crushing burden of studio costs by a three-month shutdown.

So dismal a performance, coming after four years of failure, raises the question of why somebody didn't step in and stop the demolition of RKO. One reason was that the company's stock was widely scattered among fifteen thousand stockholders. Few of them had the economic incentive, the resources, or the information either to wage a successful proxy fight or to bring suit. The main reason, however, was that nobody wanted to tangle with Howard Hughes. His substantial investments, reaching into aircraft, electronics, the oil industry, transportation, beverages, tools, and movies, were diversified enough to suggest a large area for reprisals. To this must be added the fact that Hollywood, from whose citizens the expert testimony would have to come, was essentially a company town. Most of the employment of actors, directors, and producers was with the particular studio that held their contract, but a good bit of it was the result of innumerable side deals, really subcontracting, which their movie company made with another one. Under a system where back-scratching was the regular order of business, the head of a major studio had a strong enough trading position to make *any* critic feel his displeasure even though that critic were on somebody else's payroll.

Faith, hope, and $13,500,000

In September, Howard Hughes said au revoir, if not good-by. He sold his stock (1,013,420 shares of his common plus 36,000 shares of Depinet's) for $7,345,940 to a five-man syndicate.[4] There is considerable doubt as to whether the purchasers were ever permitted to see the books, but they had probably been titillated, as others before them, by hints of what the company held in store. Examples: RKO's main studio, carried at $600,000, would probably be worth $5 million to Paramount on whose lot it abuts; the studio's ranch, carried at $67,000, would be worth a million as a real-estate development. To stimulate further salivation, Hughes guaranteed to lend RKO $8 million (main purpose: to pay off a $5-million demand bank loan) and make the purchase payments easy: $1,250,000 down and the remaining $6 million over two years. The extraordinary thing about the

---

[4] The five: Ralph Stolkin; Stolkin's father-in-law Abraham Koolish; Ray Ryan; Edward G. Burke, Ryan's partner in an oil company; and Los Angeles movie-theater owner Sherrill C. Corwin.

deal was that penny-pinching Howard Hughes agreed to lend almost $14 million to a group of individuals about whom he apparently knew very little.

A formula for profits?

Hughes's reasons for the sale, as supplied through interpreters, were interesting. The studio was just a small part of his investments, which included the Hughes Tool Company and control of Trans World Airlines, yet he had had to spend 85 percent of his time at RKO. It was a puzzle just what to think: on the 15 percent, T.W.A. and the Hughes Tool Company had managed very well indeed; while RKO, on 85 percent of Hughes's time, looked like a sea of red ink.

The best speculation on what the Stolkin group intended to do with RKO was to "spin off" (sell) some of its assets, particularly the backlog of films, which would be valuable to television, and either operate with the rest or get out. In the meantime there was to be a brave show of conventional studio operation. An ambitious young lawyer, Arnold Grant, who has a lucrative practice as attorney and tax adviser to many motion-picture people, was put in as chairman of the board. Grant hired his cousin, Arnold Picker, an experienced distribution man (United Artists), to become executive vice-president. Heads began to roll among the tattered platoons still hanging on, the dismissals being punctuated by official reports that RKO was losing money at the rate of $100,000 a week. Then the news about the background of Stolkin, Koolish, and Ryan broke. Had somebody tipped off the newspapers? You can find wise money in Hollywood willing to bet that Hughes himself did. Who knows?

As Hughes might have put it, the syndicate was in "a fix." Any sale now was sure to bring on a stockholders' suit. On the other hand, they couldn't very well operate it by themselves. The best thing to do, obviously, was forfeit the down payment to Hughes and get out. But the contract required that to return the stock the syndicate also had to return an untenanted board of directors; and Arnold Grant, shocked by the denouement, was bent on sticking until he had exhausted all efforts to save the company. Grant was given the treatment: every nominee he brought up to replace the directors he had forced to resign was vetoed by the two still on the board. He, too, resigned. After a fruitless effort to salvage their investment, the syndicate gave back the stock and left, their pockets turned inside out. Howard Hughes, who had merely been off in the wings, climbed on stage again and took over RKO. He was $1,500,000 richer; almost everybody else, including the stockholders, had been taken to the cleaners.

Howard comes high

It is almost impossible to estimate the damage done RKO by Howard Hughes. Where is the accountant who can set a figure on the hundreds of intangible losses that came from Hughes's inability to produce enough movies? With adequate production, RKO would have been able to develop stars of its own rather than "buying" them from other studios at fancy prices. Sufficient production would also have enabled it to call the tune in negotiating with independent producers, instead of having to accept unfavorable terms just to get its costly distribution system something to distribute. Distribution, in fact, was in such a sorry state that Disney's *Peter Pan* and Goldwyn's *Hans Christian Andersen*, two of 1953's biggest box-office attractions, could only ease RKO's losses. Altogether these intangibles were expected to culminate in a highly tangible deficit: at least $12 million for 1953.

What needs to be done at RKO is as far-reaching as its trouble. The principal remedy, of course, must be a last-ditch drive to get production started again. A studio of its size should make at least three movies a month. (From the beginning of June 1951 to the end of January 1952— seven months—three were started.) This calls for careful planning and a full schedule by several independent producing units. It also calls for a chief executive who believes, along with the rest of Hollywood, that "a movie company is a kind of factory—you can't fall in love with each individual film." Other remedies will depend on who eventually takes over the studio and what they expect to do with it. For RKO, despite its difficulties, could still be pulled together by the right people. Some potential buyers think the distribution system should be sold. In their book it is both a considerable expense (roughly $200,000 a week) and an unnecessary one; Hollywood is now in a strong position vis-à-vis the exhibitors, good films virtually selling themselves. More sweeping proposals include the merging of RKO with another movie company. A suitable merger, say with Columbia, would enable it to get the talent resources necessary for casting important pictures and at the same time would provide working capital through the sale of superfluous facilities.

What's being done is something else again. Hughes's hand-picked president, James R. Grainger, and Grainger's son Edward, put in charge of the studio, are supposed to have ended the eight-month shutdown by starting a picture in March. Its title: *Second Chance*. Five others were to follow by mid-May, all using the bright new toy Three-D. More likely the Graingers and RKO's fifteen thousand stockholders are simply waiting word from the sardonic, disheveled man in the Goldwyn studios. Rugged individualism, which made some great fortunes in the nineteenth century, can cost a lot of people a lot of money in the twentieth.

Epilogue

RKO never did recover from the years of mismanagement at the hands of Howard Hughes. All that came out of the studio during twelve months of operation by the Graingers were three films and nine others released by it but independently produced. In October of 1953 some stockholders finally filed suit for receivership, charging that the corporation had lost $6 million so far that year and Hughes's "whims, caprices, improvidence, waste and negligence" were responsible for losses estimated at $38,500,000. But this action and others produced no change for the better at RKO; on the contrary, they simply hastened the day of its dissolution.

Under the pressure of the suits, Hughes offered to buy all the assets of the corporation for $23,489,000 cash. Ironically for one so given to delay and procrastination, he made his offer conditional on acceptance by the board of directors within eight days, and by a majority of the stockholders in less than two months. He won acceptance nevertheless; everyone was so anxious to get shut of the mess they accepted well ahead of schedule, and on April 2, 1954, he became the sole owner of RKO's studios, stages, properties, films, and other assets.

In the next year Hughes spent a week in bizarre negotiations with Tom O'Neil, vice-president and son of the founder of General Tire & Rubber. The culmination, reached at 6:30 A.M. in a Las Vegas hotel, was a $25-million deal whereby O'Neil bought everything but the cash in the till of the parent company. The package: a distribution network, the Gower Street and Culver City production facilities, the film exchanges, and 750 old and new films (including the unreleased *Jet Pilot* and *The Conqueror*, which the unfathomable Howard bought back a month later for $12 million).

O'Neil swore he'd dust the cobwebs out of RKO's movie lots—it was the only production company then not making money—and he actually

got thirteen new pictures in the cans during 1956. But they were a disappointment at the box office and the problems of returning RKO to
health were beyond him. The Gower Street studio was closed in 1957,
along with the 101 film exchanges, and Culver City was rented out to
independent producers and packagers for TV. The ultimate sale of RKO's
real estate to Desilu Productions in 1957 simply made irrevocable what
had been plain for some time: RKO was out of the motion-picture business. The years of neglect and mismanagement had dissipated its value as
a producing unit beyond any hope of recapture; it had become merely a
corporate derelict to be salvaged as profitably as possible. Today the enterprise's name is perpetuated only in the title of a General Tire subsidiary:
RKO General, Inc., owner and operator of radio and TV stations in
eight cities. Howard Hughes? The losses RKO sustained under his control constituted a valuable tax-loss carryback; he offered stockholders
six dollars a share for their interest in the corporate shell (what was left
after the assets were sold in 1954), eventually brought about what was
then an advantageous merger of this shell with Atlas Corporation, getting
four shares of Atlas for five and a quarter of RKO.

CHAPTER III

General Dynamics: A Crisis of Control

Prologue

Seldom has a corporate crisis been compounded of so many errors of commission and omission as General Dynamics' $425-million troubles with its 880 and 990 jet-transport planes. G.D.'s top management failed to recognize that this age requires not only technological superiority but management superiority as well. It failed to establish a detection apparatus that would have signaled trouble in time. It failed to permit only programs in each unit which would not threaten the whole company, and failed to stop one enterprise when its failings became apparent. Instead it kept sending good money after bad in the hope that one lucky coup would square all accounts. This, in short, is the story of how a great corporation got out of control.

The present chapter tells how and why the jet-transport program was started at G.D.'s Convair Division, and some of the setbacks immediately encountered. Shortly after the program was launched, the board voted to displace the dying founder of General Dynamics, Jay Hopkins, with Frank Pace, the Arkansas lawyer who had been Director of the Budget and Secretary of the Army. Pace had never run a business. Yet on becoming chief executive officer in 1957 he was confronted with the manifold problems of a decentralized industrial empire operated by strong-minded divisional heads and turning out a diversity of products ranging from Atlas missiles to hi-fi sets. Chapter IV follows the fortunes of General Dynamics and Chairman Pace from 1957, when the consequences of the unwise decision to build jet transports began to materialize, to the climax of the crisis in 1961.

*　　*　　*

Over the two-year period 1960–62 General Dynamics incurred the biggest product loss ever sustained by any company anywhere. The jet-transport program it built around the Convair 880 and 990 airliners cost the corporation far more than the $121-million licking Lockheed took on the Electras and even overshadowed Ford's $200-million disaster with the Edsel. By the end of 1961, General Dynamics had to write off some $425 million of jet losses. Not only did this wipe out all profit on G.D.'s total sales of close to $2 billion a year—but, even with the tax credit, it put the company $27 million in the red for 1960, $40 million in the hole for the first nine months of 1961. And the end was not yet. Here is the way the situation looked in early 1962, when this story was written, and when Chairman Frank Pace had been forced to concede that his company still could not "fully identify all remaining costs of the jet-transport program."

General Dynamics is being run under the corporate equivalent of martial law. An executive committee of seven directors took charge of the crisis last July; the banks, alarmed because G.D.'s earned surplus had been nearly wiped out, moved in the next month with an armful of circumscriptions. These have included bank scrutiny of the company's divisional budgets, the pledging of its government accounts receivable, a bank veto on sale or leaseback arrangements, an end to further borrowing, and a two-year moratorium on dividends. The executive committee's hope now is that it can provide enough money to keep the healthy divisions of the company expanding, while it reviews budgets, reorganizes the management, and restores General Dynamics to the strong position it once was in. Divisions like Astronautics, Electric Boat, General Atomics, and Canadair give the committee a good deal to build on.

But meanwhile the Convair debacle has excited the close interest of the business community, the investing public, and Washington; G.D. is the biggest private manufacturer of weaponry in the world. And it had been a profitable one. Net earnings had risen from $599,000 on sales of $31 million in 1947, the year founder John Jay Hopkins made his first big acquisition, to the profit peak of $56 million on sales of $1.7 billion, the year Hopkins died (1957). What could have gone so spectacularly wrong?

The story has many episodes. They include the overriding episode of the jet-transport program—the "fantastic" underestimating of costs, to employ Chairman Pace's adjective, the gross miscalculation of the market, the entanglements with the capricious Howard Hughes; the tragic death at a critical moment of the company's founder, Jay Hopkins. Many people shared in the responsibility for the disaster: chiefs and subchiefs of the huge Convair plant, a number of whom have since resigned; General Dynamics' own board of directors; Jay Hopkins himself; and Frank Pace, who succeeded Hopkins in 1957 as chief executive officer and who will depart from the company in April ("if the company has turned the corner") and return to public life, which he now says "is my forte."

But the story has implications for American business beyond the errors that can be made in engineering or in negotiating a contract. General Dynamics is an example (probably the most extreme one) of a kind of corporation that has loomed on the industrial scene—a congeries of companies, decentralized, loosely directed by a small and remote group of financiers, lawyers, and (occasionally) professional managers. There is a certain rationality in the concept of such corporations, as there is in the structure of General Dynamics itself. All but one of General Dynamics' divisions is engaged in work requiring a high degree of engineering and technological skill; the exception, Material Service, deals in gravel and cement and thus provides a hedge against the uncertainties of defense business. There is also plausibility to the theory that such a corporation can supply its divisions with support when one of them gets in trouble, and that every one of the divisions is stronger by virtue of the association. But the question posed by the General Dynamics story is whether or not effective techniques have yet been developed to manage these aggregations. (There might also be a question whether American business is developing the managerial talent for such complex jobs. An observer gets the impression that in times of corporate trouble almost all any board can think of is to reach for Ernest Breech, who at Ford and TWA established his claim to the title of top corporation executive, which inspires the question, "Isn't there anybody around but Ernie Breech?")

Pace describes the quandary he has been in at General Dynamics in these terms: "When you have a company, employing 106,000 people, made up of nine different divisions, each a corporation really in its own right, most of which were separate enterprises before they joined the organization, and headed by men who were presidents of corporations, with their own separate legal staffs, financial staffs, etc., all of these highly competent men—the only way to succeed is to operate on a decentralized basis. Our total central office in New York City was something like two hundred people, including stenographers. This group can only lay out broad policy. Your capacity to know specifically what is happening in each division just cannot exist. If you did try to know everything that was hap-

pening and controlled your men that tightly, your men would leave you
or would lose their initiative which made them effective."

One is led to conclude that G.D.'s top management failed to recognize
that the new age of advanced technology demands advanced management
techniques. It failed to establish the intelligence system that would have
given accurate and timely warning of danger. It failed to limit divisional
programs to those that would not imperil the whole enterprise and failed
to call a halt on one such program even when it appeared to be in grave
danger. Instead, it pursued a "double-or-nothing" policy, risking greater
and greater losses in the hope that one more commitment would square
all accounts. This, in short, is the story of a great corporation that got out
of control.

Jonah swallows a brace of whales

The story begins with Jay Hopkins. He was a man of almost oppressive
energy, with a bottomless capacity for alcohol, who could stay up all night
drinking, then in the morning lucidly present a complicated program to
his board of directors. Though trained as a lawyer (Harvard Law '21),
he was best known for his brilliance and audacity in finance. The grand
design he brought to fulfillment was the creation of a diversified defense
empire; it was to be capable of turning out weapons for virtually all the
armed services so that G.D. would prosper whatever the budgetary vicis-
situdes of any individual service. Thus he had almost singlehandedly par-
layed a venerable builder of submarines, Electric Boat, into a company
that could also make bombers and fighters and missiles. He went ahead
with the acquisition of two major airframe manufacturers, Canadair in
1947, and Convair in 1954, undaunted by the fact that it was a case of
Jonah swallowing a brace of whales. Hopkins' admirers insist that the
sense of symmetry that compelled him to deliberate over the proper posi-
tioning of his socks in an overnight bag or to realign an ashtray when its
use by a visitor altered the accustomed pattern of his desk top was decisive
in the way he put General Dynamics together. But the truth of the matter
was that he built the company as much for size as for sense and ran it to
suit himself. He kept posted on what went on in each division, questioning, admonishing, encouraging, vetoing with the red pencils he reserved
as his exclusive trademark around G.D., at the same time managing to
make each division head feel he was free to run his own show. In
short, management control was a highly individualized affair at General

Dynamics and worked reasonably well so long as Jay Hopkins was around
to make it work. But unhappily he wasn't around very often, at least
not at the headquarters office. Golf was a passion with him for one thing
(he founded the International Golf Association); for another, he much
preferred irregularly riding circuit through the divisions to keeping regular
office hours.

An association of opposites

Thus, in 1953, Frank Pace was brought in as executive vice-president and
director of General Dynamics. Said a member of G.D.'s board, an old
friend of Hopkins: "The truth was Jay was drinking too much and Washington had lost confidence in him. We had to get somebody in there who
would restore that confidence." Commented Hopkins himself to a golfing
companion in California: "Well, I just bought myself a show window. It
cost me $75,000 complete with secretary. They give me hell because I'm
never in the office, and I've got to have somebody there to answer the
phone."

That was certainly not all the job meant to Pace, who had declined
several other offers in order to accept it. Nor was this the way Hopkins
represented it to him, Pace says. "Jay told me when he hired me, 'I'll turn
over the operation to you. I will not second-guess you, but I will make
the ultimate decisions.' He made broad policy and ultimate decisions of
importance but left operations to me." If "answering the phone" meant
handling General Dynamics' relations with Washington, few men then
available were better equipped for that than Pace. He had a sharp mind,
an excellent education (Princeton '33, Harvard Law '36), had served as
Director of the Budget under Truman in 1949, became Secretary of the
Army just before Korea and was responsible for that service's rapid wartime expansion. He was equally at home quoting Disraeli or some home-
spun philosopher of his native Arkansas, and he shot golf in the low
seventies. But aside from golf, the law, and the high order of intelligence,
Pace and Hopkins were complete opposites: Pace temperate in all things,
oratorical, deliberate, anxious to be liked, a product of the federal staff
system, prone to rely on his second-in-command in the making of decisions; Hopkins volatile, creative, earthy, intuitive, ingrowing, willing to
listen but unwilling to share the making of decisions with anybody, a loner
more likely to give the world the back of his hand than to extend the palm
of it. "Hopkins thought he was both omnipotent and omniscient," said

an admirer by way of emphasizing the ultimate difference. "He just exuded confidence in the correctness of his opinions. He believed there was nothing he couldn't do. Frank Pace does not in any way think he's either omnipotent or omniscient." Indeed, so far as Chairman Hopkins could see at the time, he had not hired a potential successor but an able assistant for a specialized assignment: Hopkins considered the real drive of Pace's ambition to be political (he had his eye on the Democratic vice-presidential nomination) rather than corporate.

The wayward course of empire

So in 1955, Hopkins was making the broad decisions when G.D. first considered going into the jet-transport program. The original idea, however, was not his. It came from Convair, the great California division that was separated from G.D.'s New York headquarters by roughly equal amounts of geography and autonomy. Convair spoke with a loud voice in the councils of the corporation at that time, and for good reason. It was a virtual empire within an empire, making B-58 bombers at its Fort Worth plant; Terrier missiles at Pomona, California; the Atlas, jet-powered fighter planes, and propeller-driven transports at San Diego. Three dollars out of every four taken in by General Dynamics in 1956 (the total: $1 billion) came from Convair. The sprawling division was headed up by General Joseph T. McNarney with John V. Naish as executive vice-president. Tough-minded Joe McNarney, ex-chief of U.S. forces in Europe, had always been pretty much a law unto himself, while Jack Naish wore his fifteen years' experience in the airframe industry like Killarney green on St. Patrick's Day. The division had already pulled off a successful commercial-transport program; the propeller-driven 240's, 340's, and 440's were world-famous. But what prompted Convair to consider making the formidable move into jet transports was a suggestion of Howard Hughes's.

It might be said that Convair should have been prepared for almost anything in any dealings with Hughes. The division had already gone through weird proceedings with Howard in trying to sell him some 340 transports back in 1950. To preserve the privacy Hughes habitually insisted on, negotiations for the aircraft had to be conducted by flashlight during the small hours of the night, out in the middle of the Palm Springs municipal dump. Then when Hughes and Convair's Sales Vice-President Jack Zevely were writing the contract some days later in Pasadena, Ralph

Damon of T.W.A. called up and told Hughes he had already committed T.W.A. to buying the Martin 404. That was that.

The memory of this episode was still fresh when Hughes asked Convair to build a jet—a big, long-range transport. Like most first customers he insisted on taking a hand in the plane's design. By early 1955 Convair had gone through the preliminary design of two such aircraft—one with six engines and one with four. But Hughes, as Jack Zevely describes it, "kept us in a position where the plane was basically a T.W.A. design, and he could never make up his mind what the design was to be." Indeed, Hughes was still stalling and Convair still studying more than six months later when Boeing and Douglas came out with their preliminary designs for the 707 and DC-8. Boeing had already had a leg up on long-range jet transport—the 707 had been flight tested and sold to the Air Force as the KC-135 tanker—while Douglas had simply gone for broke with the DC-8, a "paper" plane. What this meant was embarrassingly simple. Convair had permitted Hughes's procrastinations to ruin its chances in the long-range market; confronted by the actuality of Boeing and Douglas models, it abandoned all plans for a competing long-range aircraft.

Now, still determined to get into jets, though the most lucrative market had gone glimmering, Convair had to choose between two alternatives. It could go for a short-distance aircraft (six hundred to seven hundred miles) or venture into the intermediate range (up to eighteen hundred miles). Since the division then held worldwide pre-eminence in the field of short-range propeller-driven transports with its 240's, 340's, and 440's, one might have supposed it would choose to make its play for the short-range jet market. General Dynamics' explanation of why it didn't is that it had no suitable engine at the time (all aircraft are designed around an engine) and that a poll of the airlines in 1956 showed no interest in short-range jets. It could be argued, however—and subsequent events would bear out this point—that airlines have a way of changing their minds rapidly if offered something more tangible than a questionnaire: the opportunities Convair abandoned in the short-range market were capitalized on by the French, who have sold 150 of their short-range Caravelles. As for a suitable engine, Convair would have had to wait, to be sure, but the wait would have made a lot of sense. No one could have beaten the division to it when one did become available, as least not in the opinion of experts like Arthur Raymond, designer of the DC-8 and Douglas' chief engineer until his retirement in 1960. "They would have had the world by the tail," he says. "The short-range 727 Boeing now has under construction would not have been built and the medium-range Boeing 720 would not have been competition for a short-range plane. Boeing and Douglas, because of their commitments with the large planes, could not have come into the short-range plane market." Boeing itself thinks it would have been tough to compete against Convair if the latter had moved into the short-range field. Richard Fitzsimmons of Boeing's preliminary design group recalls: "Our biggest concern when we came out offering the 707 —because we were the first—was that the competition might come out with something revolutionary—like the French Caravelle."

Forever Howard

In any event, Convair decided its best prospects lay in the medium-range market, and the key elements in that decision were three. First, its studies concluded the next market to open would be the medium, mainly because it expected the new long-range jets, the 707's and DC-8's, to downgrade piston planes like the DC-6 into short-range use; second, the Air Force was making a suitable engine available, the J-79 of the B-58 bomber (which Convair makes); third, Convair's engineers believed that with one and a half year's lead time in their favor neither Boeing's big 707 nor Douglas' DC-8 could be economically transformed into a plane able to go after the medium-range market.

When Convair had first proposed putting out a short-to-medium-range jet the idea got an immediate and enthusiastic response from Howard Hughes. "I'm your first customer," he said. "I'll buy thirty planes." But the most consequential backer of the venture was Joe McNarney. He was personally sold on the jet program as a hedge against what the then emergent "peace offensive" might do to Convair's military business. Nevertheless, he had gone through his usual procedure of calling the division's key executives together for a final polling of opinion. Jack Zevely, Engineering Vice-President R. C. Sebold, and General Manager B. F. Coggan of Convair's San Diego division had been for going ahead with the medium-range jet. If their estimates were sound, the prospects certainly looked great: 257 aircraft, over $1 billion worth, could be sold within a ten-year period for a possible profit of $250 million; at worst G.D. could lose only $30 million to $50 million in the venture. But there were Convair men against the program too. One of them was Thomas Lamphier, vice-president in charge of Convair's military business, who objected on grounds that the commercial program would crimp Convair's $650-million military program. Furthermore, in his experience the cost estimates and breakeven points of engineers and estimators just couldn't be relied upon: he had always had to double whatever estimates they gave him. Another who opposed the program was Jack Naish, Convair's executive vice-president. Naish argued that it did not make sense for Convair to undertake a program which would increase sales only a modest 5 to 10 percent, while requiring 50 to 60 percent of McNarney's, Coggan's, and his own time. Moreover, he felt that the odds were against making money on commercial-transport ventures, particularly jet transports. But at the end of the discussion it was clear that McNarney was still solidly behind the venture. He smilingly remarked to everyone, "Well, we're going through with the program," and then took off for the March 1956 executive-committee meeting in New York, where the final decision still had to be made.[1]

How much of a gamble was the program the committee now had up for consideration? In the cold light of the hundreds of millions of dollars worth of losses that eventually piled up, it was obviously a terrific gamble. But even if one forgoes "the advantages of 20-20 hindsight"—the phrase in current usage around General Dynamics—it was still quite a gamble. The following circumstances were all present at the time of the executive committee's final deliberations:

Convair was well aware that its first and sole customer, Howard Hughes, again spelled trouble. That is indicated in a recent comment of Earl Johnson, General Dynamics president, about the Hughes deal ("We knew right along it was going to cost us a pile of jack")—but if G.D. was going to get into the jet business at all, it had to start the program with Hughes, or give up the whole thing. As an ex-Convair vice-president put the predicament: "We were all worried as to whether Hughes would pay us [on schedule], even before the contract was signed, but at that late date in jet development, Hughes was Convair's only prime customer."

Convair had itself done much to destroy the original premise that the 880 would get no competition from Boeing or Douglas. By the time the division's engineers finished with the design, the short-to-medium-range jet had become a medium-to-long-range one. It was now not much shorter in range than the 707 (3400 miles vs. 3600 miles) nor so much smaller in size that the Boeing 707 couldn't be chopped down to its dimensions and made highly competitive.

Convair had limited the market possibilities of the 880 by making the

[1] The executive committee acted for the board of directors in approving many important ventures, including this one, which never came before the full thirty-two-man board. The committee, then made up of twelve members, was chaired by Jay Hopkins and included a banker, two investment bankers, two oilmen, and five lawyers.

fuselage too narrow to suit United, one of the three remaining prime customers for such an aircraft. United had already got Douglas to widen the fuselage of the DC-8 before ordering them in 1955, and throughout its discussions with Convair, United had insisted that for its purposes the proposed 880 should be wide enough to accommodate six seats abreast. But the aircraft Convair thereupon designed was too narrow to permit more than five-abreast seating. Such a seating arrangement, as Convair's Executive Vice-President C. Rhoades MacBride explained it in the fall of 1961, "was not based on passenger considerations, but was an aerodynamic decision to satisfy the antithetical requirements of transcontinental capability and short-field landing requirements." However this might be, the effect was to blight Convair's chances of selling United the forty 880's so hopefully listed in its market forecast.

The sliding breakeven point

None of these discouraging considerations appears to have carried much weight with General Dynamics' directors. The executive committee to a man voted for the program on the assumption it would make money after sixty-eight planes were sold, that potential sales of 257 aircraft could be realized, that the maximum possible loss was only $30 million to $50 million.

By this time three airlines—T.W.A., Delta, and K.L.M.—had already taken options to buy the 880. Now the committee instructed Convair to go ahead and get letters of intent from them within the next fortnight. The committee laid down only three conditions in authorizing the program: first, that G.E. guarantee the engines they'd produce for the 880; second, that the ability of the airlines to pay for the jets be investigated by an *ad hoc* committee of Pace, Naish, and Financial Vice-President Lambert Gross; third, that management was not to go ahead without orders in hand for 60 percent of the estimated sixty-eight-plane breakeven point.

The last proviso proved to be quite flexible. The breakeven point on the 880 had been understated: after closer figuring, Convair raised it to seventy-four planes in May, up six planes in two months. Then when K.L.M. did not pick up its option, the executive committee indulgently dropped its 60 percent condition, allowing Convair to go ahead with only 50 percent of the breakeven point assured. The new figure was made to fit the fact that by this time Convair had only forty firm orders (ten from Delta and thirty from Hughes).

These forty firm sales may seem on the surface to have been a reasonably strong beginning, but the circumstances under which they were made caused considerable anxiety in some offices at Convair. Because of an agreement with Hughes, Delta was virtually the only other airline G.D. was free to sell to for a whole year. One Convair executive says that "we were told if we sold the plane to anyone else but Delta, Hughes would get some of his money back. The 880 was an advanced plane with a better engine than any other at that time. Hughes wanted to keep it from T.W.A.'s competitors. So people who might have bought the 880 if we had been allowed to sell it to them, bought the DC-8 or the 707 instead."

Just who exercised the crucial influence in getting the jet program through was not too clear at the time, and it is certainly no clearer now when nobody wants to be singled out for fathering a failure. As a Convair vice-president recalls it, Pace's role was more than passive: "When McNarney came back, he told us that one of the reasons, not the prime reason, but one of the reasons the company was going ahead with the program was because Pace felt this was his baby, whereas everything else Dynamics was doing was a Hopkins program." As Frank Pace remembers the circumstances, Joe McNarney made it plain he'd look on disapproval of the venture as a vote of no confidence in his administration at Convair. A Hopkins man declares that the program had Hopkins' active support. And what Hopkins wanted, his directors unfailingly gave him.

A dying man's vision

Unfortunately for General Dynamics, just about the time it was launching the greatest gamble in its history, the man who had made things work as well as they had for a decade was nearing the end of his road. Jay Hopkins had been operated on for cancer in 1955, and understood the surgeons had "gotten it all," but now he suspected it might be incurable. In the late fall of 1956 he took a house at La Quinta, near Palm Springs, California, and there began to work on a five-year plan for the future of General Dynamics. His deliberations were necessarily colored by the fact that he always looked on the company and himself as one and the same thing, indeed, used his own name and the corporation's as synonyms. Hopkins had run General Dynamics out of himself, as an extension of his own personality, setting its standards and giving its people a sense of destiny. That destiny, as he saw it, was to be as big, or bigger, than the biggest corporation of them all, General Motors. But he was also aware that corporations, like trees, sometimes lose their foliage in the growth cycle, and he was determined that no winter would come to General Dynamics simply because one had come for him. More billions in sales must be added to the billion G.D. had attained for the first time that year (1956). At this point he made two decisions: to streamline the board of directors, cutting it from an unwieldly thirty-two to a compact fifteen. This meant risking his control of the company during his last days, for many of the men being dropped were his own old cronies. The second decision was to find someone to step into his shoes as chief executive officer.

He had some long and thoughtful discussions with his best friend and personal adviser, Ellsworth C. Alvord, brilliant lawyer and a General Dynamics director since 1954. Alvord was a large stockholder then, and he still controls twenty thousand shares of G.D. Much of the discussion concerned what to do about Frank Pace—still executive vice-president—whom Alvord had originally "sold" to Hopkins. Neither Alvord nor Hopkins, says Alvord, had any confidence in Pace's ability to do much more than take care of the Washington end of the business. In Hopkins' book his successor as chief executive officer should be an experienced businessman with a flair for finance and stockholder relations and the ability to talk shop—wages, salaries, programs, plans—with the divisional chiefs. Almost all these chiefs had been presidents of the companies that were now G.D. divisions, making it difficult for even the best top executives to ride herd on them.[2]

Beginning in 1955, when the jet program was first being considered, both Hopkins and Alvord, acting for Hopkins, had told Pace that if he wanted to become president—not chief executive officer—he should pick a good general vice-president and a good financial vice-president to make up for the business and financial experience he lacked. Alvord says: "I finally told Pace he had had plenty of time to look and that if he couldn't find the people he needed, I would." Pace had answered pleasantly and asked for more time.

Now, as Alvord remembers it, Hopkins and he felt that time had run out

[2] Ironically Hopkins' difficulties in finding a suitable replacement in 1956 are the same that G.D.'s emergency executive committee faced in the hunt it began in 1961 for a new chief executive to replace Pace. As committeeman Donald McDonnell of Blyth & Company recently put it: "You just can't find the people of the national stature needed. You can't put Mickey Mantle over Carleton Shugg [of Electric Boat], Geoffrey Notman [of Canadair], Charles Horne [of Pomona], or James Dempsey [of Astronautics]. You can't put in a man they don't respect."

and all they could see Pace had done by the fall of 1956 was to get in an old friend, Earl Johnson, comrade-in-arms from World War II, ex-Assistant Secretary of the Army (under Pace), ex-president of the Air Transport Association, a man whose business experience was fourteen years in the management of an investment-counseling firm. Alvord says that this wasn't enough to satisfy Hopkins, who decided not to promote Pace to the presidency but to keep him where he was and find someone else as his own successor in the top job. Alvord discussed three names with Hopkins that fall, and began actually negotiating with one candidate, an automobile executive. Then came an indication that Jay Hopkins in his sparring for time with Death and his board of directors might get crowded into a corner.

In February of 1957, General Dynamics' board met at the date ranch of Floyd Odlum, once owner of Convair. Odlum had offered his house in Indio, California, to spare his old friend and neighbor a trip east. Hopkins was then going through periods of great pain, but was as iron-willed as ever about carrying through his five-year plan for the corporation. Hopkins slipped into his seat early so no one could see the agony of his movements, and ran the meeting with his usual brilliance. He put through his personally selected slate of directors (cutting the board's membership from thirty-two to fifteen) and received from the survivors their promises of continued personal support for him in whatever he wished to do. Then, while everyone else was enjoying a steak fry on the front lawn, he quietly slipped away to his own place at La Quinta. But the plane that carried some of the board back east had hardly left the ground when director Clifton Miller mentioned to Alvord that Hopkins had looked very badly indeed and maybe the new board had a problem. Alvord dismissed the observation with "Jay knows what he's doing" and nothing further was said.

By late April, Hopkins, to the amazement of his doctors, was still alive. "I think that guy has invented something," said one of them, and in a way he had. Cancer patients characteristically are sustained right up to the end by the belief that the cure that will save them will turn up in time, but with Hopkins there was something more. It was almost as if he had managed by the terrible intensity he always put into everything to stand Death off. And so long as he was alive, he was going east just to show everybody he could. He would attend the annual stockholders' meeting on April 25. Then, as G.D.'s president, chairman, and chief executive, he would preside over the newly elected board—and the doctors be damned.

He had had a Convair 440 specially remodeled for this all-important trip and fitted out with an elevator which would raise his stretcher from the ground to the plane's cabin. But the evening of the twenty-fifth found him exhausted and in bed at his Washington apartment. In the end he had been too weak to make the annual stockholders' meeting at Dover, Delaware, which earlier that day had approved his hand-picked slate of directors. Now he was husbanding his strength for the morrow when his new board would meet to vote in the corporate officers. Nothing at all had occurred at the annual stockholders' meeting to arouse any suspicion that his grip on his company was not complete. Criticism of management at such meetings usually foreshadows bitter struggles for power within the board; but not a critical voice had been raised. That night, however, Clifton Miller, Donald McDonnell, and a third G.D. director paid a surprise call on Ellsworth Alvord in Washington.

Apparently word had got back to some directors that Hopkins was shopping around for a new chief executive, a situation that promised further unsettlement of a board that had just lost over half its membership at Hopkins' hands. Moreover, those directors who hadn't been aware of Hopkins' trouble before the Indio meeting had certainly become aware of it when they had seen him there. A number of them felt that the company was in urgent need of a new chief executive officer and that the only man available was Frank Pace. Alvord's three callers wanted him to persuade Hopkins to have Pace elected chief executive officer at the board meeting next day.

Alvord was completely taken by surprise. He indignantly refused the committee's request. Moreover, he expressed the belief that "this cabal," as he termed it, didn't have the votes to put Pace in. But the committee was insistent and he finally challenged them to muster all directors favoring the proposal at his offices next morning, before the board officially met. When he heard the news from Alvord, later that night, Hopkins was equally indignant and equally convinced the challenge to his power would come to nothing. "Hell," he growled, "that's *my* board. I picked every man on it."

On the morning of the twenty-sixth, however, a disturbingly large number of directors turned up in the law offices of Alvord & Alvord. The fight began then and there, went on into the meeting that day and next, and carried over into the following week. After one of these stormy board meetings, Pace came to tell Alvord: "I want you to know I had nothing to do with this," and he has since declared that he held himself completely aloof from the whole procedure.

During the struggle, Alvord argued that the company was running well and every division was prospering. Why not let Hopkins die in peace, he asked; even the most optimistic doctors gave him only six months to live. Moreover, he insisted Pace was not qualified to run the company. Pace's supporters argued that from what they had observed of him as executive vice-president he was well qualified and his succession should not be delayed: plenty of trouble could come to a company whose chief executive officer was under sedation. As Hopkins' slender support withered away, Alvord turned to parliamentary strategies to block the proceedings, but at the end of the final board meeting (April 29) Frank Pace was voted in overwhelmingly as president and chief executive officer.

When Hopkins, white as the pillow under his head, heard the news he couldn't believe it. He went down the list with Alvord, ticking off the names of old friends and associates, men like Donald McDonnell to whom he said before the Indio meeting: "You're going to be kept on the new board as my personal friend." Then he gave a great sigh and said, "Well, after all, it's the board's responsibility. My usefulness is gone." The next day, April 30, Hopkins went to the hospital. "A man has to have a lot of fight to live with cancer," said Alvord, "and this took all the fight out of him." On May 1 it was officially announced that Frank Pace had been elected president and chief executive officer. On May 3, Jay Hopkins was dead.

End of an era

Hopkins' death marked the end of an era for General Dynamics. The genius was gone and with him the inordinate attention to detail, the capacity to do everything himself that had made it possible for General Dynamics to get along with the same control system it had had as a company twenty-five times smaller. The time had come to institute managerial reforms that would both compensate for the loss of Hopkins and finally do what he had failed to achieve in his lifetime: give the billion-dollar enterprise the degree of control and communication such a corporation required.

The huge, sprawling Convair Division needed to be broken up into smaller, more manageable units, each reporting directly to New York instead of channeling everything first to divisional G.H.Q. at San Diego, which might or might not send it on east, depending on how it felt inclined. The surprise checkups Hopkins used to make on the division chiefs ("Expect me when you see me") needed to be augmented by an intelligence system that would give top management timely and automatic warning of trouble. Some cross-fertilization of divisional personnel was needed so that General Dynamics would develop a top management with intimate knowledge of the workings of the most important divisions. G.D.'s entire budgeting system, a hodgepodge of procedures carried over by each division from the days when it was an independent enterprise, required an overhaul, divisional budgets needed to be standardized and subjected to point-by-point review from New York so no divisional manager could get off target.

All these problems faced Frank Pace, ex-Director of the Budget, and ex-Secretary of the Army. He still believes today that he moved effectively to meet some of them. But Financial Vice-President Richard Knight, who was brought into the company from General Electric in June 1960, says a unified budgeting system was not established until September 1961, which puts it four years from the time Pace took over the company, and not until the spring of 1961 did Pace finally move to split up Convair. Indeed, one of Pace's first acts was to permit the divisions, particularly Convair, *more* autonomy than they ever enjoyed under Hopkins. Convair, which used to occupy three-fifths of Hopkins' time, seldom saw the new chief executive officer. "Convair resisted all along any attempt by General Dynamics to do anything," said Pace recently. "There is not the slightest bit of doubt that the effort of General Dynamics to dominate Convair was completely resisted. The number of times I personally sat down with Jack Naish [McNarney's successor as chief of the division] did not exceed seven or eight in a period of three years."

Thus the stage was set for disaster. When costs began to get out of hand at Convair, when critical production delays developed, when key sales were lost, General Dynamics' management was unable to cope with the crisis. What then occurred, and how management is now trying to solve its problems, we shall see in Chapter IV.

CHAPTER IV

General Dynamics: A Crisis of Control

(*Continued*)

The year 1957 was a disquieting one within "the Rock," the huge concrete monolith in San Diego from which Convair's top management bossed the 880 jet-transport program, for it was then that the first glimmerings of disaster began to appear. No doubt most Convair executives had accepted the 880 venture with the same stoicism recently expressed by Rhoades MacBride, General Dynamics executive vice-president: "No new-plane program is less than difficult and dangerous because of the amount of dough these poker games require. The 880 was a horrendous decision, but all new-plane programs are horrendous." Even such stoicism, however, did not prepare the company for what was to transpire.

Both the Convair assistant division manager, Allen Morgan, and B. F. Coggan, the division manager, had informed management back in 1956, at the time thirty planes were sold to Howard Hughes, that the 880 was underpriced. Their conclusions were ignored then because of the difficulty of substantiating their cost estimates at so early a date. But now a year had elapsed, the 880's design was frozen, and components had been ordered preparatory to starting up the production line. So the cost of the aircraft could be figured with precision; it was an amalgam of money that *had* been spent on research and development and money that *would* be spent on materials, fabrication, and assembly. Usually about 70 percent of the material costs of an aircraft is represented by items bought from outside suppliers—the engines, pods, stabilizers, ailerons, rudders, landing gear, autopilots, instruments, and so on—with only 30 percent of the total material costs being allocated to the airframe manufacturer himself. The 880 ratios followed this general pattern. But when an engineer in Convair's purchasing division began totting up the various subcontracted components, he came to a startling conclusion: outlays for the vendor-supplied components of each 880 totaled more than the plane was being sold for (average price: $4,250,000). He took his figures up the line, pointing out that when research and development costs of the aircraft (they totaled some $75 million) were added in, along with the 25 to 30 percent of the material costs allocated to Convair itself, nothing could be expected of the 880 program but steadily mounting losses. He recommended that Convair abandon the whole venture, even though the loss, according to his estimates, would be about $50 million.

Whether the engineer's recommendation and his supporting data ever reached New York headquarters is something of a mystery. In any event, when the engineer persisted with his analyses, Convair decided he was a crank and fired him—he was reinstated two years later after time had confirmed the accuracy of his judgments.

Target No. 1: United Air Lines

The sales problems that confronted Convair in 1957, however, were something that couldn't be sloughed off with the firing of a critic. At the start of the 880 program in March 1956 the potential market had been estimated at 257 planes. By June of that year Convair had raised the figure to 342, in September it was down to 150 after an on-the-spot appraisal had let the air out of the sales estimates for European airlines. These gyrations gave substance to an industry rumor that the division undertook a thorough-going market analysis only *after* commitment to the 880 program, but at least one point was clear about the "final" forecast of 150. The bulk of that number, as General Joseph McNarney, Convair's president, said at the time, had to be sold before July 1, 1957, or the 880's production line could not be economically maintained. The trouble was that the understanding with Howard Hughes had kept Convair from selling the 880 to anybody but T.W.A. and Delta for a whole year. This had already caused the loss of customers who preferred a 707 or DC-8 in the hand to an 880 twelve months down the road. So in the spring of 1957, when Convair was at last free of the commitment, it had still sold no more than the forty 880's (to T.W.A. and Delta) that started off the program. The success of that program, with only a few months to go before McNarney's July 1 deadline, now hinged on selling the remaining major airlines, American and United.

Convair's first target was United, which it had listed as a prospect for thirty aircraft. For a time things seemed to be going Convair's way in its pursuit of this critical $120-million sale. Boeing, Douglas, and Convair were all in competition for the United contract, but Convair had the edge with its 880, for it was then the only true medium-to-long-range jet aircraft being offered. All Boeing could offer was essentially the long-range 707, too big and, for its seating capacity, 50,000 pounds too heavy to suit United. The size could be reduced, of course, and some of the weight chopped out, but not 50,000 pounds unless Pratt & Whitney could substantially lighten the engines, the JT3C-6's used on the 707 aircraft. With Pratt & Whitney unwilling to make this effort, United's board decided in favor of the 880 on September 27, 1957, subject to a final going-over by United's engineers.

Soon thereafter, United's President William Patterson called G.D.'s Executive Vice-President Earl Johnson, whom Pace had put in over-all charge of the jet program, out of a board meeting to tell him Convair was "in." But perhaps the most consequential call was one Pratt & Whitney's Chairman H. Mansfield "Jack" Horner then made on Patterson himself. Spurred on by Boeing, Horner had been galvanized into action, and now he wanted to know whether something couldn't be done about getting Boeing back in the competition, if Pratt & Whitney could come up with a lighter engine. Patterson referred him to United's engineers, who made encouraging noises. They themselves had been pushing Pratt & Whitney for just that. Both Boeing and Pratt & Whitney then went into a crash program, the former to scale down the 707, the latter to develop a lighter engine than the JT3C-6.

At around that time, G.D. director Ellsworth Alvord, who made it his business to keep watch over the 880 venture, happened to see a squad of United Air Lines executives in Seattle, where Boeing is located, and surmised something significant was going on with the airframe manufacturer. He promptly called Johnson and told him the United deal might not be so solid as they'd all thought. After all, there was a substantial amount of old-school tie between Pratt & Whitney and United Air Lines, left over from the days when both were divisions of United Aircraft. Johnson, however, was blandly reassuring. Just why he was is hard to understand, since Horner had himself told Johnson that Pratt & Whitney had started working hard to lighten the JT3C-6 engine. But apparently neither Johnson nor anybody else in G.D. considered that Boeing could come up with a new medium-range aircraft before Convair signed United on the dotted line.

On or about October 10, 1957, Convair's Sales Vice-President Jack Zevely and United's Financial Vice-President Curtis Barkes had happily worked out eighteen articles of a nineteen-article contract and in a few minutes more would have finished the nineteenth, merely a statement of where the notices were to be sent, when a call came through for Barkes. As Zevely recalled the incident: "He came back, shaken, and said, 'Sorry, Boeing's back in the competition.'"

It was indeed. Pratt & Whitney engineers had managed to get 750 pounds out of the JT3C-6 engine by removing unneeded strength and using titanium. Boeing engineers had shortened the fuselage of the 707, reduced the weight of such heavy items as the landing gear, and improved its cost per mile. Within a few weeks Boeing had come up with a new medium-range aircraft—the 720—45,000 pounds lighter than the 707. United then invited Boeing and Convair to cut their prices and both did, though Convair refused to cut below what Pace recently described as "the bare minimum." In November, United's chief engineer John Herlihy compared Convair's 880 and Boeing's 720 and then strongly recommended the latter. His reasoning: the commercial performance of the G.E. engine was an unknown quantity, while "we had the Pratt & Whitney engines in our other jets and wanted to regularize our engines if we could"; moreover, the narrower fuselage of the Convair 880 permitted only five-abreast seating, a shortcoming United had vigorously protested back in 1956 when Convair had first solicited its opinion of the 880 design; the Boeing 720, on the other hand, was wide enough for six-abreast seating, a difference of as many as twenty-five passengers at full load in the tourist section of a combination first-class-tourist airliner. This meant, in Herlihy's view, that the 720 with its lower operating costs per passenger-mile was a better buy than the 880 with a $200,000 cheaper price tag. On November 28, 1957, United's board approved purchase of eleven Boeing 720's, with options for eighteen more.

"Merely a modification"

The loss of United meant a sharp reduction in the market potential of the 880, dropping it from 110 to 80 planes. Worse than this, Convair had a powerful new competitor in what had been its private preserve, the medium-range field. Boeing was now going to make it tough for Convair to sign up American Airlines just at the time when Convair expected to sell the airline thirty planes, nearly half of the 880's dwindling market potential. Discussions with American had been going on for some months, though pressure had naturally increased after United chose the Boeing 720 in November. But in January 1958, American notified Johnson, who was in over-all charge of the negotiations, that it too was going to pass up the 880 for twenty-five 720's.

In February, however, Convair was able to reopen discussions with American on the basis of a revolutionary new engine General Electric had just developed. Called a turbo fan-jet, it required 10 to 15 percent less fuel than a conventional jet to do the same job (under flight conditions) and provided 40 percent more power on take-off. The aircraft that Convair intended to use with these new engines, later designated the 990, was billed as "merely a modification" of the 880. If so, it was a modification to end all modifications.

The 990 had a bigger wing area than the 880, a fuselage ten and a half feet longer, weighed over 50,000 pounds more, required enlarged empennage, a beefed-up landing gear, greater fuel capacity, stronger structural members, and was supposed to go twenty miles per hour faster. Many of these changes were imposed by American's hard-bargaining C. R. Smith, whose talent for getting what he wanted out of an airframe manufacturer was already visible in the DC-7. But Smith hadn't stopped with just designing the 990; he designed the contract, too, using all the leverage Convair's plight afforded him. In it he demanded that Convair guarantee a low noise level for the plane, finance the 990's inventory of spare parts until American actually used them, and accept, for American's $25-million down payment, twenty-five DC-7's that had been in service on American's routes. The DC-7 was then widely regarded as an uneconomical airplane, 12 percent less efficient to operate than the DC-6, and, as Convair discovered, it could not be sold for even $500,000 in the open market. When General Dynamics reluctantly accepted this down payment, worth only half its face value, American signed up for twenty-five 990's with an option for twenty-five more.

"We had to go ahead"

Looking back, director Alvord recently commented on the whole affair: "Earl Johnson brought back a contract written to American specifications with an American delivery date, but the plane was not even on paper. It was designed by American and sold to them at a fixed price. There was not even any competitive pricing." What is more, Alvord says, "the 990 was signed, sealed, and delivered without board approval. It was just a *fait accompli*. An announcement was made to the board that there would be a slight modification of the 880." Pace himself believed at the time that the 990 was only a slight modification. He now says, "If we had known at the outset that major changes would be needed, deeper consideration would have been given it."

The decision to go ahead on the 990 was an important turning point in the fortunes of Convair and of General Dynamics itself. The reasoning behind it has been stated by Pace: "When the Boeing 720 took away our sale to United, we found ourselves in competition with a plane just as good as ours. This is just what we wanted to avoid. The 880 seemed doomed. We had to go ahead with the 990 or get out of the jet business. American had not bought any medium-range jets. . . . When the fan engine was developed, they told us, 'We will buy your plane if you produce a plane like the 990.' It was absolutely vital for us to follow American's wishes. We had to have another major transcontinental carrier. I thought I was taking less of a gamble then than I did entering into the 880 program."

But what this amounted to was that G.D. had now committed itself to a double-or-nothing policy, gambling that the success of the 990 (beginning with the American sale) would make up for the failures of the 880. The nature of this gamble is worth specifying, in view of the fiasco that eventuated:

The plane had been sold at a price of approximately $4,700,000. Yet nobody knew how much it would cost because its costs were figured on those of the 880, which were still on the rise and unpredictable.

The number of planes Convair must sell to put its jet-transport program in the black had gone up sharply. The breakeven point on the 880 had been sixty-eight planes at the start (March 1956), a figure that by 1958 should have seemed impossible of fulfillment. Nothing but dribs and drabs of sales to lesser airlines could be expected of the 880, for the "majors" (T.W.A., United, American) had already been sold or refused to buy. Convair's commitment to the 990, which had a breakeven point of its own, meant the division must sell 200 of the 880's and 990's to keep out of the red.

The success of the 990 depended largely on its being the sole plane on the market with a fan-jet engine. When it built the plane around the G.E. engine, Convair was confident that Pratt & Whitney would not make a fan jet. Barred from making a *rear* fan jet—G.E.'s licensing agreement prevented this—Pratt & Whitney simply built a *front* fan engine. Boeing used this for the 720-B, which took away a good deal of the 990's potential market.

The 990 was to be built without a prototype, or advance model. G.D.

had "lucked out," to use President Earl Johnson's phrase, on the 880 without testing a prototype.[1] So now the company was again going to gamble that it could take a plane directly from the drawing board into production without any major hitches. Said Rhoades MacBride, by way of fuller explanation: "Our time for debugging the 990 was severely compressed because we wanted to take advantage of being first with the fan-jet engine. If we had built a prototype and flown it, we would have minimized our advantage in having the fan engine before Pratt & Whitney had it. We realized that if everything went right, we would be way ahead. If the 990 didn't fly as stated, we would be in terrific trouble."

"Our basic mistake"

Yet if ever a plane needed a prototype and plenty of time for testing, it was the 990. As Earl Johnson himself conceded recently: "Our basic mistake in judgment was that we did not produce a prototype to fly to virtual perfection. From a management standpoint we should have said, 'If you haven't the time to build a prototype then you shouldn't get into the program.'" The 990 was an extremely fast aircraft, with short-field characteristics and a brand-new engine. The decision to go it without a prototype meant that Convair had committed itself to attaining the very high speed demanded by C. R. Smith—635 miles per hour—the first crack out of the box.

The odds against fulfilling these speed specifications right off the drawing board were recently assessed by a G.D. senior vice-president. "In piston aircraft," he said, "it is perfectly simple to predict the performance. You just plot the power available and the power required and where they intersect you get your maximum speed. But with jets, trying to guess the intersection of these curves is very difficult, and missing by forty or fifty miles per hour is easy and makes a fantastic difference. One way to avoid this is to have a lot more wind-tunnel testing. But when you've already underpriced the plane, you're not willing to spend too much money on wind-tunnel testing. So you try to guess, and you make bad guesses." As it turned out, a lag of only six minutes in the 990's flying time on a

[1] On one test flight over the Pacific late in 1958, however, a big chunk of the plane's tail fell off. Happily for G.D., a courageous pilot decided against ditching the aircraft and was able to fly it back to San Diego. There the trouble was remedied by beefing up the tail and installing yaw dampeners. The 880 is now considered a fine plane by Delta and other purchasers.

transcontinental run of twenty-five hundred miles was to result in C. R. Smith's canceling his contract because American wouldn't be able to bill the 990 as the "fastest airliner in the world."

"The furnace treatment"

Just before Convair undertook the 990 program, General McNarney retired, and the division got a new president, hard-driving John Naish. Naish's succession clearly indicated that Convair was still an empire within G.D.'s empire and would likely remain so. Pace had wanted the Convair job for Earl Johnson, the old Army buddy he'd made his No. 2 man. McNarney wanted Naish; McNarney got Naish. And the new Convair chief had soon made plain his confidence he could handle anything that came along—if left strictly alone. As he said at the time: "The company has a great many people who like to solve their own problems. It believes in the furnace treatment—you throw people in the fire and you can separate the good metal from the dross very quickly."

Naish had already got a taste of the furnace treatment at Convair, for troubles were piling up on all sides. Total orders for the 990 were only thirty-two, while those for the 880 were still stuck at forty-four. Overhead on the jet venture had risen as production of the Convair-made F-106 fighter dwindled and the Atlas program, which also shared the San Diego facilities, had had to be moved to another plant, on orders from the Pentagon. But these were just first-degree burns in comparison to the furnace treatment Convair's new head was about to get from Howard Hughes over the 880.

Hughes's vagaries had already caused Convair plenty of lost sales and missed opportunities, as set forth in Chapter III, and the contract negotiations with him on the 880 had been bizarre. Sales Vice-President Zevely even maintains the 880 was not named for its eighty-eight seats but for the eighty-eight conferences he had had to go through with Howard; on one that lasted until three in the morning, Hughes had brushed aside Zevely's plea of extreme fatigue and insisted a movie was all the Convair man needed to get him back in the pink. Hughes then made a few phone calls and, with the groggy Zevely in tow, went out to a studio projection room. There they were treated to a showing of *Jet Pilot*, Hughes having thoughtfully got the movie's star, Janet Leigh, out of bed to provide a running commentary on the film.

When the 880 got to the production stage, the Hughes group—T.W.A.

engineers and executives—had quietly set up shop in an abandoned lumberyard near Convair's San Diego headquarters and for a time Hughes caused more mystification than trouble. A Convair engineer would be told to appear for a conference with him at a Las Vegas nightclub, only to spend the evening sitting in solitary splendor at the huge table the erratic Howard had reserved; Hughes never did show up. As 1959 wore on it became increasingly difficult to get Hughes to commit himself on the final configuration (styling and arrangements) of his 880's. Such a situation, of course, raised hob with the Convair production line, delaying the 880's and making it certain that overtime would have to be used to meet the tightly scheduled delivery dates of the 990's—they'd been promised to American for the spring of 1961—if their dates could be met at all. As a matter of fact, in September (1959) Sales Vice-President Zevely was already notifying the airlines the 990 would be late.

Convair let more precious months slip by trying to humor Hughes before it came to a shattering conclusion: all his stalling on the final configuration of his 880's had its roots in the fact that he hadn't the money to pay for them on delivery. Indeed, in the fall of 1959, when it came time for Convair to fly his first two 880's out for delivery, Hughes blocked the move. These and the next two planes, said a G.D. vice-president, "were actually impounded by Hughes and placed under bailment, then moved off the Convair property, and put in a locked hangar guarded by his men."

Convair could have made an issue of this, but chose not to. Nevertheless, a fateful decision had to be made. The division could move Hughes's uncompleted planes into a boneyard and resume work on them when he solved his financial problems or it could finish the planes and sue him upon delivery. The latter course had been successfully followed by Boeing when Hughes made the same sort of difficulties with his 707's and it had got paid without even having to resort to the courts. But Convair chose to pull his 880's off the line and put them out on the field. What made this decision so fantastic was that thirteen of the planes were in different stages of completion. Now the economics of an aircraft production line are geared to "a learning curve," which simply means that labor costs go down as each production-line worker becomes familiar with his particular phase of putting the plane together. On the first 880 the learning curve was at its peak with labor costs of roughly $500,000; on the fortieth or fiftieth plane, labor costs were designed to drop below $200,000. Thus, removing Hughes's thirteen 880's from the line in *different stages* of completion meant that the learning curve for them would have to be begun again at the top—to the cost of Convair not of Hughes.

"It's not a baby any more"

This disastrous decision was made by Jack Naish, with an O.K. from Frank Pace and Earl Johnson. But even then New York was far from on top of the situation. Pace maintains he never knew the 880 was in serious trouble until *after* the Hughes decision: "We knew we had problems, but there were no major difficulties as far as we knew. The information that came to us fiscally, in a routine fashion, through Naish and substantiated by Naish, would not have led us to believe the extent of the losses that were occurring." Earl Johnson is not even sure just when he himself became alarmed over the jet program. "It's difficult to answer that. It's like living with a child—when do you notice it's not a baby any more?"

The sad truth was simply that General Dynamics was still being run as a holding company with no real control from the top. Its headquarters staff had been kept at two hundred, and this, in Pace's view, "automatically recognizes that it is impossible to police the operation of the divisions." But even if there had been a will, the means of policing seem slender indeed. Pace had established no reporting system that could tell him quickly when a division was in trouble; the key figures were buried in pages of divisional operating statements. G.D.'s Financial Vice-President Richard Knight is still overhauling the system of auditing the divisional books so as to prevent any doctoring of the figures to make a divisional president look good. In short, millions of dollars of publicly owned money could be on its way down the drain at Convair before New York was aware of it.

In a letter of May 10, 1960, addressed to General Dynamics' stockholders, Pace reported jet-transport charges of $91 million (as of March 31, 1960) but added "[We] have every reason to believe [the program] will be one of our most successful ventures." By mid-August, however, Pace's springtime optimism began to show the signs of an early frost. From the very beginning the 880 had been grossly underpriced in relation to its material costs; now Convair had virtually given up trying to keep those heavy costs within the budgeted amounts. For almost a year San Diego had been abuzz with rumor that losses on the 880, "the sweet bird of our economy," as local citizens called the 880, might reach $150 million. Some 880 components had overrun their original estimates by as much as 300 percent.

On the 25th of August, G.D.'s worried board of directors met to decide (1) what should be done about Convair, (2) whether to cut the upcoming dividend. Director Henry Crown, the company's biggest stockholder, had been told the week before of Pace's "disappointment and surprise" at Convair's mounting losses, but Crown, an astute businessman, had an uneasy feeling that further bad news impended. If so, he reasoned that any dividend cut the board voted then might have to be repeated later on. "I told Pace not to take two bites of the cherry," he recollected. "If we did find further losses, and the dividend had to be eliminated entirely, then I thought it should be done all at once." Pace agreed to get in touch with Naish and satisfy himself that no further jet write-offs would be necessary.

This he did, and on his appraisal of Convair's situation the board halved the dividend at the September 1960 meeting. On September 22, at the same time that Pace informed the stockholders of the dividend cut, he also released a special report on the jet program. With program charges up $34 million in six months, the directors had decided to write off all *anticipated future losses* (based on sales of ninety-four 880's and 990's, for which firm orders were then in hand). This write-off, $96,500,000 pretax, $46,300,000 after taxes, meant that the planes should now be on a break-even basis, each new sale bringing in a profit.

It was a wise move, but General Dynamics was far from out of the woods. Four months later (January 1961) Hughes got his financing and Convair was confronted with the problem of completing his aircraft. And some problem it was. Since no two planes were in exactly the same stage of completion, they couldn't be put back on the production line. They had to be hand-finished on the field, at costs many times those prevailing on the line. Moreover, engineering changes had to be made—some Convair's and some Hughes's.

"It took a real expert," explained a vice-president of General Dynamics, "to diagnose the exact state of completion of each plane, plus what engineering changes should be made. For instance, he had to work with a stack of blueprints to decide whether the wiring was nearly finished, just begun, or had to be completely changed. Do you continue the wiring? Do you rip it out? Additionally, there was some water damage from the months the planes had been sitting out on the field. Since the production line had been cut back, some of the trained people had been let go, others had to be retrained, and all this was terribly expensive. Hughes did agree to pay for the excess completion costs on the four planes he impounded, but we had to pay for most of the others."

A $40-million discovery

By February of 1961, General Dynamics was beginning to reap the economic consequences of the disastrous Hughes decision. New York "discovered" that Convair had not only failed to write off all jet losses the previous September but had incurred additional ones. These, amounting to $40 million, spelled the end for Jack Naish and for August Esenwein, the executive vice-president Pace had put under Naish to control costs. "I felt," said Pace recently, "that if I couldn't get more accurate judgments from Naish than I had gotten, he ought to go." Then he added, "Whether these problems were passed on and not properly interpreted by Esenwein and Naish, I can't tell. There are conflicting points of view now that we go back into the problem. But we in New York didn't know the magnitude of the problem."

Regardless of whether New York knew then or not, the whole business community was shortly to learn how profound was Convair's trouble. The risky decision to build the 990 without a prototype began to bear some even more expensive and sour fruit. Seventeen of American's twenty-five 990's had to be delivered during 1961, the first one in March. A flight test of this particular airplane in late January 1961, four months later than the date scheduled in a previous announcement of Pace's, disclosed wing flutter and other problems that required rebuilding the landing flaps, the leading edge of the wings, the outboard pylons. These were not too difficult to correct from an engineering point of view, but as a G.D. vice-president sadly remarked, "If you get into production with a plane whose design has to be changed, the magnitude of the troubles you then encounter becomes exponential." Moreover, these corrections now had to be made on overtime because of the tight delivery schedule to American. Ultimately this was to burden G.D. with an additional $116-million jet write-off, a source of concern to Frank Pace, not to say considerable personal embarrassment. For now "a second bite of the cherry" would have to be taken and in June, after twenty-five years, the dividend omitted.

The burning question, of course, is why *didn't* New York know the magnitude of the problem. Naish maintains he leaned over backward, because of his initial opposition to the jet program, to clear important decisions with either Johnson or Pace. In the fall of 1961 a member of G.D.'s executive committee, still puzzling over why New York had been so much in the dark, for so long, pressed Pace on the point. He wanted to know why, even if Naish's information had been suspect, Convair's controller hadn't told Pace of the losses, or why he hadn't learned of them from MacBride, whom Pace had sent out early in 1961 to investigate, or from Earl Johnson, whom Pace had given over-all responsibility for the jet program and sent to Convair in late 1958 and early 1959 when the division was plainly in trouble. Pace, at a loss to explain, wondered whether he ought to resign. No, said the director, and Pace needn't make any apologies. After all, he wasn't trained as a businessman. He (the director) made no apologies for not being able to walk into an operating room and perform like a surgeon. So Pace shouldn't feel badly about not being trained as a businessman.

Pace, of course, does feel badly. He remarked to the author, "If you don't think it twists my insides to see what has happened to General Dynamics, you are very wrong. You must know what this kind of a defeat does to a man who has been successful." But the enormity of his defeat would appear to have been due to something more than a lack of business experience. Pace himself has stated that his primary interest and, indeed, his forte are in public service. Business has been of secondary importance.

The wages of sin

Unhappily for General Dynamics, the departures of Naish and Esenwein did little to lighten the corporation's load of trouble. Nor was Rhoades MacBride, G.D.'s No. 3 man whom Pace put in as acting president of Convair, able to bring the division under control (after ten months he too was to be washed out of office). There had simply been too many sins of commission and omission to be cured by chopping off heads in San Diego; a corporate reorganization was called for.

In May of 1961, General Dynamics was split into two grand divisions: MacBride was put in charge of the Western Division, essentially the old Convair broken up into five parts, and Executive Vice-President Werner Gullander was assigned the Eastern Division. Both reported to President Earl Johnson, who made San Diego his headquarters. But then the company's creditors began to talk of calling the $150 million in notes G.D. had outstanding. This new crisis called for redoubled efforts by the executive committee of the board of directors, set up in secret six months earlier to try to set things to rights. Under the chairmanship of Henry Crown, the committee had been reviewing all divisional budgets, trying to persuade Prudential and the banks to substitute a $200-million revolving

credit for their prime-rate loans, and scouting around for a new chief executive officer. By August the committee had obtained its $200-million credit
under rigid conditions: no dividend declarations for two years, no unap-
proved incurring of debt or sale of assets, working capital to be kept above
$140 million.

This was no sooner settled, however, than G.D. ran into trouble with
American over the 990. The gamble, mentioned earlier, that Convair's
engineers could guess the jet power needed to meet the speed and fuel
requirements in the American contract had failed. In addition, the 990
was already six months late, so in September 1961, Smith canceled his
order. Now the G.D. board was confronted by two choices, both bleak. It
could turn back the uneconomical DC-7's Smith had induced it to accept in lieu of a $25-million down payment, then with the $25-million
cash reimbursement as a cushion, cut the price of the 990 and try to sell it
to other carriers; or it could try to get a new contract from Smith. A few
audacious directors, including Crown, were for trying choice No. 1, but
the opinion of the majority, as epitomized by one member of the board,
was: "Now let's not get C.R. mad. Earl Johnson knows him. Let's go and
appeal to him."

The upshot was that Pace, Johnson, and Henry Crown paid a call on

General Dynamics: Its Other Parts (1962)

*The Convair plant in San Diego is one of twelve G.D. divisions, which all
together do $2 billion worth of business. Here are estimates of how the other
divisions are doing:*
Astronautics Division (Atlas missile)—It is G.D.'s biggest, most profitable
division (estimated pretax 1961 earnings: $15 million), but has recently lost
out on contracts for Apollo and Saturn.
Canadair (aircraft)—Licensed manufacturer of the Lockheed fighter, the
F-104, which is its mainstay. High hopes had been pinned on CL-44, a
turboprop cargo plane, but only thirty were sold over the past two years,
which may lead to substantial cuts in Canadair's payroll of ten thousand
workers. Probable pretax earnings: $10 million.
Electric Boat (submarines)—Didn't do too well on low-priced submarine
contracts of 1961, has got better ones in 1962. Expected to earn $10 million
pretax 1961, but capacity for future growth is limited by capital for new
building ways.
Fort Worth (B-58 bomber)—This year's output will be a little over half of
1961's with B-58 scheduled to phase out in 1963. Unless it gets contract for

Smith. There Colonel Crown related a little story about his having let a construction company off the hook even though, legally, he had had every right to hold them to a disastrous contract. Smith made no comment, but when Pace and Johnson pursued the same thought he finally said: "I understand your problem, but I have stockholders. You told me, Earl, that the plane would go a certain speed." A new contract was signed with American and it was a tough one. The airline cut its order from twenty-five to fifteen planes, with an option to take five more if Convair could get the speed up to 621 miles per hour. Upwards of $300,000 was knocked off the price of each aircraft. With wind-tunnel tests completed, chances were good that Convair would be able to meet the 621-miles-per-hour specification.

But the end of General Dynamics' jet travail is not in sight. Howard Hughes canceled his order for thirteen 990's, an order that, surprisingly enough, Convair had accepted during the period when Hughes couldn't even pay for his 880's. S.A.S. and Swiss Air have cut their original order from nine 990's to seven. Moreover, the market is just about saturated in so far as additional jet sales are concerned, even for a fine plane like the 880. As for the 990, it too has missed its market. By mid-January 1962 only sixty-six 880's and twenty-three 990's had been sold, which put Convair

---

joint Navy–Air Force fighter, the TFX (see Chapter IX), will have to shut down facilities.

General Atomic (nuclear development)—Very promising future but no income expected for several years to come.

Liquid Carbonic (liquefied gases)—"It isn't losing money," says one G.D. director, "but it isn't ever going to make anything substantial." Estimated 1961 pretax earnings: $5 million.

Electrodynamics (electric motors)—"It's usually in the red, or a little in the black, but it never really makes a dime."

Pomona (electronics plus Terrier and other missiles)—"Doing very well," with 1961 earnings of approximately $7,500,000.

Stromberg-Carlson (telephones, electronics)—Under reorganization after disclosure of $17 million in excess inventory. "The telephone business is doing excellently [$8 million], the rest you can have."

General Aircraft and Leasing—Leases or sells used planes received as trade-ins for jets. Business is poor.

Material Service (building materials, coal mining)—Good, steady earner, though tied to building construction, which Henry Crown says will be off in 1962. Earnings for 1961: $9 million to $10 million pretax.

well behind Boeing's 120 sales in the medium-range market. Small wonder that when somebody suggests selling off Convair, a G.D. vice-president ruefully remarks: "Would $5 be too much?"

"This has hurt us in Washington"

The failure of General Dynamics' management has had some serious collateral effects. As a member of the executive committee observed, "The public has lost confidence in us. This has hurt us in Washington. We have to inject people of stature into the management." The company recently lost out on two of the three big defense contracts (the $400-million Apollo spacecraft contract went to North American, Boeing got the $300-million Saturn S-1 booster system). Its executive committee has also failed to find a new chief executive officer, a job which called for "a man forty years old with one hundred years of experience" as John McCone remarked in turning it down, and this has further delayed G.D.'s much-needed reorganization. Indeed, with MacBride's departure, the company abolished General Dynamics East and General Dynamics West and reverted to its old regimen of having all divisions report to New York.

For the near term, however, G.D.'s financial prospects are somewhat brighter than before (see the rundown on each division, "General Dynamics: Its Other Parts"). The losses of 1961 did drop working capital below the $140-million minimum, a default on its banking agreement that technically could have started the company down the road to receivership. But the banks quietly assented to the establishment of a new working-capital minimum of $100 million. G.D. believes it will have no difficulty staying on the sunny side of this figure. Moreover, Colonel Crown expects that the company will earn $50 million pretax during 1962, a decided improvement over the $60 million loss estimated for 1961. The great imponderable, of course, is whether any more jet losses will have to be written off. Says Colonel Crown: "Jet write-offs for 1962 should not exceed $5 million to $10 million."

Though the great losses are now a matter of history, the subject of what went wrong with the company will no doubt be discussed for as long as there is a General Dynamics. "It's a grave question in my mind," said one of the company's senior vice-presidents, "as to whether General Dynamics had the right to risk this kind of money belonging to the stockholders for the potential profit you could get out of it. All management has to take a certain risk for big gains. But I don't think it's right to risk so much for so small a gain."

There are, however, larger questions of management's responsibility for the well-being of the corporation. That responsibility, in the jet age, is to keep management techniques developing at the same pace as the technologies they must control. Moreover, G.D. and other decentralized companies need to understand fully the basic limitations of decentralization. No amount of decentralization can put the head of a corporate division in the same situation as the head of an independent company—no matter that he once headed such a company. The division head may be rightly encouraged to take initiative, but the ultimate responsibility for avoiding failure cannot rest with him. For under decentralization his inhibitions against risk have been lessened while his initiative has been sustained. Under these circumstances the top management of G.D. and other conglomerate corporations have to assume the "watch your step" function that formerly balanced the decision of the independent company chief.

Frank Pace, of course, has his own ideas on the whole fiasco. "Nothing ever occurs without human error," he mused, looking from his Rockefeller Center window as the rush of the Hudson seemed to be carrying the twilight out to sea. "Disraeli said, 'Circumstance is beyond us, conduct is within human control.' We have been subjected both to human error and a remarkable series of circumstances."

Epilogue

On February 22, 1962, Roger Lewis was brought in as president of General Dynamics, succeeding Frank Pace as chief executive officer. A little over two months later Pace resigned the chairmanship, as he had said he would "if the company turned the corner." Unhappily, G.D. had not turned the corner in April, nor was it likely to do so for many months to come. No matter that it was able to absorb $425 million worth of jet-transport losses, this was hardly the evidence of "strength" some optimists proclaim; it is rather a gauge of enormous problems still to be resolved.

The corporation, financially weakened by the ordeal, must now (as this is written in 1963) shoulder a debt structure of $350 million. In addition, G.D. must keep its divisions under the tightest control if they are to produce the profits so urgently needed for debt service and long-range development. Finally, G.D. will have to develop important additional sources of revenue or become a much smaller company. The backlog of

$2.5 billion it possessed in 1959 was sadly in need of replenishment by the winter of 1962—it had dwindled to roughly half the former amount.

Interestingly, this latter problem was looked upon as containing the seed of G.D.'s regeneration, at least by one body of opinion within the company. In their view, the most logical policy was to recognize that General Dynamics was going to be a $750-million company and not a $2-billion one. They'd drop down to the $750-million level quickly, scrapping one of the two manned-aircraft divisions, cutting back at Astronautics, and selling off so-so enterprises like Liquid Carbonic or even a real money-maker like the telephone business (Stromberg-Carlson), because of its ability to command a good market price. The rationale was a simple one: maintaining big plants with big overheads could quickly plunge the company into trouble again; if G.D. were to cut back deliberately, with a definite plan of consolidation, more of the real strength of the enterprise could be preserved than if it had to lose an equivalent amount of ground unwillingly and piecemeal. In sum, the better part of wisdom was to retreat to a defensible position, establish firmly there, and with that footing start an offensive to regain the lost revenues.

But Roger Lewis has followed a different course. He gambled, successfully, that the winning of one huge government contract, that for the TFX, a joint Navy–Air Force fighter plane (see Chapter IX), would keep G.D. a giant and buy him the three to four years' time he'd need to make it a healthy one. Revenues from this are now expected to bring G.D. roughly 40 percent of a ten-year program estimated to total $7 billion. Such a windfall will certainly save the Fort Worth Division from shutting down (because of the phasing out of the B-58) and do much to make up for declining production at Astronautics, G.D.'s prime profit earner, until that division can find something to replace the Atlas and Centaur rockets. But however much winning the TFX might reduce some of the financial pressures within the corporation, it can hardly be considered a cure for what ails General Dynamics. The new president must still remedy the root causes of the recent crisis—poor organization, poor information, too much autonomy, too little control—and as he himself realizes, no quick and easy cures are possible. Unlike General Electric, which also went too far with decentralization but could return to the centralized control system of the past, G.D. has had nothing to return to. It was built as a promotional enterprise, a loose collection of companies, and will remain one, regardless of lucrative government contracts, until top management gets about the formidable job of reorganization.

CHAPTER V

General Electric: A Crisis of Antitrust

Prologue

Antitrust actions like the shocking electrical conspiracy cases of 1960–61 are usually an indication of something seriously amiss in the companies concerned, something of which the conspiracy is but a symptom. In the instance of General Electric the crisis came about because top management made the mistake of piling on the pressure for profits without keeping itself adequately informed of how the recipients of that pressure, the department and divisional managers down the line, were reacting to it.

This chapter reveals how the lower echelons did react. It takes the reader inside one cartel, showing why collusion had become a corporate "way of life," and goes on into the ruinous days of the 1954–55 "white sale," the bitter meetings, the regimen of concealment.

The succeeding chapter is devoted to how the Antitrust Division finally broke the case and what went on at General Electric from the time a principal conspirator realized the game was up until the corporation threw in its hand, fourteen months later.

*　　*　　*

As befitted the biggest criminal case in the history of the Sherman Act, most of the forty-five defendants arrived early, knocking the snow of Philadelphia's Chestnut Street from their shoes before taking the elevator to federal courtroom No. 3. Some seemed to find it as chill inside as out, for they kept their coats on and shifted from one foot to another in the corridor, waiting silently for the big mahogany doors to open. On the other side of those doors was something none of them relished: judgment for having conspired to fix prices, rig bids, and divide markets on electrical equipment valued at $1,750,000,000 annually. The twenty indictments, under which they were now to be sentenced, charged they had conspired on everything from tiny two-dollar insulators to multimillion-dollar turbine generators and had persisted in the conspiracies for as long as eight years.

As a group, they looked like just what they were: well-groomed corporation executives in Ivy League suits, employed by companies ranging in size from Joslyn Manufacturing & Supply Company, whose shop space is scarcely larger than the courtroom itself, to billion-dollar giants like General Electric and Westinghouse.

There was J. E. Cordell, ex-submariner, sales vice-president of Southern States Equipment Corporation, pillar of the community in a small Georgia town, though his net worth never exceeded $25,000, and urbane William S. Ginn, G.E. vice-president at $135,000 a year, a man once thought to be on his way to the presidency of the corporation. There was old, portly Fred F. Loock, president of Allen-Bradley Company, who found conspiring with competitors quite to his taste ("It is the only way a business can be run. It is free enterprise"), and G.E.'s Marc A. deFerranti, who pocketed his repugnance on orders from his boss. There was M. H. Howard, a production manager of Foster Wheeler, who found it hard to stay in the conspiracy (his company's condenser business ran in the red during two years of it), and C. H. Wheeler Manufacturing's President Thomas, who found it hard to quit—he'd been told his firm couldn't survive if he left the cartel.

At nine-thirty the courtroom doors opened and everyone trooped in. It was a huge room, paneled in mahogany with carved pilasters that reached up thirty feet or more to a white ceiling; yet big as it was it very soon filled with tension. What the defendants were thinking of was not hard to guess: the possibility of prison; the careers ruined after decades of service; the agile associates who weren't there, the ones who had saved their hides by implicating others.

Shortly after ten o'clock, Judge J. Cullen Ganey, chief judge of the U. S. District Court, entered the courtroom. He had earned a reputation in his twenty years on the bench for tolerance and moderation. But it was clear almost immediately that he took a stern view of this conspiracy: "This is a shocking indictment of a vast section of our economy, for what is really at stake here is the survival of the kind of economy under which this country has grown great, the free-enterprise system." The first target of his censure were the twenty-nine corporations and their top management. He acknowledged that the Justice Department did not have enough evidence to convict men in the highest echelons of the corporations before the court, but in a broader sense the "real blame" should be laid at their doorstep: "One would be most naïve indeed to believe that these violations of the law, so long persisted in, affecting so large a segment of the industry and finally involving so many millions upon millions of dollars, were facts unknown to those responsible for the corporation and its conduct. . . ." Heavy fines, he said, would be imposed on the corporations themselves.

Next he turned a cold blue eye on the forty-five corporation executives who had not escaped the nets of Antitrust. Many of the individual defendants he saw "torn between conscience and an approved corporate policy . . . the company man, the conformist, who goes along with his superiors and finds balm for his conscience in additional comforts and the security of his place in the corporate setup." The judge said that individuals "with ultimate responsibility for corporate conduct, among those indicted," were going to jail.

By midafternoon of that first day E. R. Jung, Clark Controller vice-president, was ashen under a thirty-day prison sentence and a $2000 fine. Gray-haired Westinghouse Vice-President J. H. Chiles, Jr., vestryman of St. John's Episcopal Church in Sharon, Pennsylvania, got thirty days in prison, a $2000 fine; his colleague, Sales Manager Charles I. Mauntel, veteran of thirty-nine years with the corporation, faced thirty days and a $1000 fine; Ginn of G.E. (indicted in two conspiracies), thirty days and a $12,500 fine; G.E. Divisional Manager Lewis Burger, thirty days plus a $2000 fine; G.E. Vice-President George Burens, $4000 and thirty days. "There goes my whole life," said this veteran of forty years with G.E., waving his arm distractedly as he waited to telephone his wife. "Who's going to want to hire a jailbird? What am I going to tell my children?"

By lunchtime the second day it was all over. The little game that lawyers from G.E. and Westinghouse had been playing against each other—predicting sentences and total fines—was ended. G.E. had "lost," receiving $437,500 in total fines to Westinghouse's $372,500. All told, $1,924,500 worth of fines were levied, seven jail sentences and twenty-four suspended jail sentences handed down. But sentencing, far from closing the case, has raised it to new importance.

The problems of predominance

No thoughtful person could have left that courtroom untroubled by the problems of corporate power and corporate ethics. We live in a corporate society. Big business determines institutionally our rate of capital formation, technological innovation, and economic growth; it establishes the kind of competition that is typical of our system and sets the moral tone of the market place. The streets of every city in the United States are crowded with small businesses that take their cue from great corporations, whether it trickles down from what some executive tells a crop of college graduates about free enterprise or the way he himself chooses to compete. Their lawyers pleaded that the way the electrical-equipment executives did compete was not collusion at its *worst*. To be sure, it was not so vulgar as the strong-arm price fixing of the Gulf Coast shrimpers or the rough stuff employed by a certain Philadelphia linen-supply company. But by flouting the law, the executives of the great companies set an example that was bound to make small companies feel they had similar license, and never mind the kid gloves. As Robert A. Bicks, then head of Antitrust, declared early in the proceedings, "These men and companies have in a true sense mocked the image of that economic system which we profess to the world."

This being so, it is highly important to understand what went wrong with the electrical-equipment industry, and with General Electric, the biggest company of them all and the one without which the conspiracies could not have existed.

"Security, complacency, mediocrity"

When Ralph Cordiner took over the presidency of G.E. from Charles E. Wilson in December of 1950, it was clear from the outset that the corporation was in for some teeth-rattling changes. Cordiner had spent the previous five years working up a reorganization plan that would give G.E. the new plants, the new additions to capital, and the new management setup he thought essential to its revitalization. Moreover, he had long made plain his distaste for running any big company the way G.E. had been run by his predecessors, with authority tightly concentrated in the president's office. Decentralization was a thing with him: he had never forgotten how the "layers of fat" in a centralized G.E. had slowed his own incessant drive for recognition to a point where he'd once quit to take the presidency of Schick. The simple fact was that intellectually and temperamentally a centralized organization went against his grain, whether it be run with Electric Charlie Wilson's relaxed conviviality or the clockwork autocracy of Gerard ("You have four minutes") Swope.

The corporation at large learned almost immediately what the new boss had in store for it and from Cordiner himself. Within six weeks he went from New York to Bridgeport, Chicago, Lynn-Boston, Schenectady, spreading the word to some six thousand G.E. executives. The gist of his message could be divided into three parts. First, G.E. was in sorry shape. It was dedicated principally to "security, complacency, and mediocrity." Second, decentralization and rewards based on performance were going to be relied on in the rapid transformation of this "sinecure of mediocrity" into a dynamic corporation. G.E. would be split into twenty-seven autonomous divisions comprising 110 small companies. The 110 would be run just as if they were individual enterprises, the local boss setting his own budget, even making capital expenditures up to $200,000. But with authority and responsibility would go accountability and measurement, measurement by higher, harder standards. Third, G.E.'s new philosophy of decentralized management specifically prohibited meeting with competitors on prices, bids, or market shares. Charlie Wilson's General Instruction 2.35[1] on compliance with the antitrust laws, first issued in 1946 and re-issued in 1948 and 1950, would remain very much in force.

There was good reason for stressing this last point. Antitrust was then a sore subject at G.E. In the decade just ended (1940–50), the corporation had been involved in thirteen antitrust cases, the offenses ranging from production limitation and patent pooling to price fixing and division of markets. Moreover, G.E. had long been something of a battleground for two divergent schools of economic thought. One school was straight Adam Smith and dedicated to the classical concept that corporate progress, like national progress, was best secured by freedom of private initiative within the bonds of justice. Its advocates believed that nothing was less intelligent than entering into price restrictions with competitors, for this just put G.E. on a par with companies that had neither its research facilities nor its market power. Ralph Cordiner, the company's most articulate advocate of this viewpoint, prided himself on the fact that it was at his insistence that the three G.E. employees implicated in illegal price fixing got the sack in 1949; his philosophy, at its most eloquent, has been simply: "Every company and every industry—yes, and every country—that is operated on a basis of cartel systems is liquidating its present strength and future opportunities."

The second school of thought held that competition, particularly price competition, was for the birds. Getting together with competitors was

[1] "It has been and is the policy of this Company to conform strictly to the antitrust laws . . . special care should be taken that any proposed action is in conformity with the law as presently interpreted. If there is any doubt as to the legality of any proposed action . . . the advice of the Law Department must be obtained."

looked on as a way of life, a convention, "just as a manager's office always has a desk with a swivel chair." It was considered easier to negotiate market percentages than fight for one's share, less wearing to take turns on rigged bids than play the rugged individualist. Besides, the rationale went, they were all "gentlemen" and no more inclined to gouge the consumer than to crowd a competitor. Admittedly, all of them knew they were breaking the law—Section 1 of the Sherman Act is as explicit as a traffic ordinance. Their justification was on other grounds. "Sure, collusion was illegal," explained an old G.E. hand, "but it wasn't *unethical*. It wasn't any more unethical than if the companies had a summit conference the way Russia and the West meet. Those competitor meetings were just attended by a group of distressed individuals who wanted to know where they were going."

One important reason for the strength of G.E.'s anticompetition school was a change that occurred in the electrical industry after World War II. Smaller companies were becoming bigger and they were broadening their product lines. Customers had a wider choice of heavy electrical equipment, alike in quality and design. Price, consequently, became the decisive selling point. To turn this situation to their best advantage, buyers adopted a new technique: the competitive bid. When the utilities took it up, it became so prevalent that some manufacturers came to believe certain types of equipment would be treated like commodities with prices expected to fluctuate from day to day. This produced serious instability in the market and made profit planning difficult. The conspiracies proliferated at G.E. and elsewhere because the manufacturers lacked the gumption to shift the buyers' attention from price to higher quality, better service, and improved design.

Precisely what numerical strength the anticompetition school commanded at the time Cordiner took office in 1950 is of course a controversial point. G.E. prefers to talk of it as "a pocket," while the collusionists themselves like to think nine G.E. executives out of ten shared their point of view. A fact to keep in mind is that thirty-two G.E. executives implicated themselves before the grand juries in addition to those general managers and vice-presidents, clearly involved, but not called to testify. There can be no doubt that the collusionists' influence was formidable and pervasive. And now, despite what Cordiner said about over-all company policy on cartels, under his decentralization plan the head of each of the 110 units comprising the company was being given power to set his own marketing policies and to raise or lower prices as he saw fit. Under the circumstances, anyone might have foreseen the results.

A way of life for Clarence Burke

One of the more attentive listeners to what the incoming president had to say about antitrust was Clarence Burke, a hard-driving, tenacious executive in his middle forties (who was to become the $42,000-a-year general manager of the High Voltage Switchgear Department and one of fifteen G.E. executives sentenced in Philadelphia). Burke had come to the heavy-equipment end of G.E. in 1926, fresh from the Georgia Institute of Technology (B.S. in electrical engineering), and his entire corporate life had been spent there. The heavy-equipment division was more than just the group that accounted for some 25 percent of G.E. sales; it was the oldest division, and the foundation upon which the whole company had been built. Moreover, it was the stronghold of the collusionists. All of the nineteen indictments to which G.E. pleaded either guilty or no contest in Philadelphia sprang from price fixing, bid rigging, market dividing in heavy equipment.

Burke's introduction to the heavy-equipment conspiracies was easy as falling off a log. It occurred when he reported to Pittsfield, Massachusetts, on June 1, 1945, as sales manager of distribution transformers. A month or so after Burke's arrival, H. L. "Buster" Brown, sales manager of the whole Transformer Department, called the new man in and told him he'd be expected to attend a Pittsburgh meeting of the transformer section of the National Electrical Manufacturers' Association. It was a regularly scheduled affair, held during OPA days, in what is now the Penn-Sheraton Hotel, and it was attended by thirty or forty industry people plus the N.E.M.A. secretaries from New York. But after adjournment—when the N.E.M.A. secretaries had departed—the company men reassembled within the hour for a cozier meeting. The talk this time was about prices, OPA-regulated prices, and how the industry could best argue Washington into jacking up the ceilings. Burke didn't consider this illegal, and he took part in several subsequent monthly meetings before OPA was abolished.

The convenient price *klatches* following the regular N.E.M.A. meetings continued after OPA's demise. But instead of discussing pricing under government controls, the conspirators turned to fixing prices among themselves. "In that conspiracy," Burke recalled, "we didn't try to divide up the market or prorate the sealed-bid business. We only quoted an agreed-upon price—to the penny." Nor did the post-OPA agreements seem to some of the participants like Burke to put them any more outside the law than agreements under the OPA. "We gradually grew into it. Buster Brown assured us that [the company's antitrust directive] didn't mean the kind of thing we were doing, that Antitrust would have to say we had *gouged* the public to say we were doing anything illegal. We understood this was what the company wanted us to do."

For a while this comfortable rationale sustained Burke and any conspirators who had qualms about the matter, but in 1946 it was demolished by the company lawyers. Teams of them made the rounds of G.E. departments, no doubt in response to federal probings that were to result in the successful antitrust prosecutions of G.E. two years later. The lawyers put everyone in G.E. on notice that it certainly was illegal to discuss prices with competitors, whether the public was gouged or not. Then the head office followed this up by barring anybody who had anything to do with pricing from attending N.E.M.A. meetings. Engineering personnel were substituted for people like Buster Brown and Clarence Burke. The G.E. conspirators called such enforced withdrawal from active participation "going behind the iron curtain." This situation continued for about nine months, during which everyone received a copy of Electric Charlie's antitrust admonition and during which G.E.'s competitors kept the Pittsfield shut-ins informed by telephone of their own price agreements.

Then, abruptly, the iron curtain was raised.

"Word came down to start contacting competitors again," Burke remembers. "It came to me from my superior, Buster Brown, but my impression was that it came to him from higher up. I think the competitive situation was forcing them to do something, and there were a lot of old-timers who thought collusion was the best way to solve the problems. That is when the hotel-room meetings got started. We were cautioned at this time not to tell the lawyers what we were doing and to cover our trails in our expense-account reports." Part of Burke's camouflage: transportation entries never showed fares to the actual city where the meeting was held but to some point of equivalent distance from Pittsfield.

The conspiracy operated, although sporadically, for the next several years of Burke's Pittsfield assignment (he was reassigned February 1, 1950). Every so often, the G.E. participants would retire behind the iron curtain, until it seemed necessary to bring about some general price increases. Then there would be a resumption of quiet talks with the men from other major manufacturers like Westinghouse. The antitrust-compliance directives they had all initialed? "When anybody raised a question about that, they would be told it doesn't apply now."

"I was adept at this sort of thing"

By 1951, however, at the time Burke was listening to new President Ralph Cordiner's antitrust exhortations, the Pittsfield conspiracy had closed down —to make matters simpler if, as everyone correctly suspected, Cordiner was going to clamp down on such cabals. But bigger and better conspiracies were in the offing. In September 1951, not very long after the Cordiner meeting, Clarence Burke walked into a new job at G.E.—and into membership in probably the oldest conspiracy then extant. The conspiracy was in circuit breakers[2] and it had been operative over the span of a quarter-century. Burke's new job was manager of all switchgear marketing, which included circuit breakers, switchgear, and other items of heavy electrical equipment. This particular spot was open because the previous incumbent had been troubled ever since signing a restatement of Charlie Wilson's "Policy Concerning the Antitrust Laws" the year before. As Burke got the story from Robert Tinnerholm, who interviewed him for the job: "I was to replace a man who took a strictly religious view of it; who, because he had signed this slip of paper [the Wilson directive] wouldn't contact competitors or talk to them—even when they came to his home." Burke got the job, an important step up the G.E. ladder, because he had become something of a conspiratorial wheel by then: "They knew I was adept at this sort of thing. I was glad to get the promotion. I had no objections." No objections then or subsequently, as it turned out, for he found it easy to persuade himself that what he was doing in defiance of the letter of the antitrust directive was not done in defiance of its spirit.

Burke's boss when he first went to switchgear in 1951 was Henry V. Erben, to whom Buster Brown had reported in the cozy old days at Pittsfield. Erben had risen to the No. 3 spot in G.E.—executive vice-president, Apparatus Group—and as Burke recalls, "he was saying then that he had talked to Cordiner about this policy, that Cordiner was not pleased with [the idea of getting together with competitors] but that he, Erben, had said he would do it in a way that would not get the company into trouble. And I'd been told by others that Erben had said things like this earlier than that."

Burke's initial assignment in Philadelphia was to get to know the local

---

[2] Like their household counterparts, circuit breakers are used to interrupt the flow of electricity when it reaches dangerous voltages. The industrial versions are sometimes forty feet long, twenty-six feet high, and weigh eighty-five tons.

marketing executives of Westinghouse, Allis-Chalmers, and Federal Pacific, and then to see they met the other new members of G.E.'s switchgear management. (This department had been restaffed in anticipation of being split into three parts, the separate companies called for by Cordiner's decentralization plan.) He was also expected to take a hand at indoctrination in conspiracy. "Erben's theory had been live and let live, contact the competitors. He gave us that theory at every opportunity and we took it down to other levels and had no trouble getting the most innocent persons to go along. Mr. Erben thought it was all right, and if they didn't want to do it, they knew we would replace them. Not replace them for that reason, of course. We would have said the man isn't *broad* enough for this job, he hasn't grown into it yet."

One man, ironically enough, who had not yet "grown" into the job was George Burens, the new boss of the whole switchgear operation. Burens had started out in G.E. as a laborer; he had the additional disadvantage of being a junior-high-school man in a corporate world full of college men, but during the next thirty years he had steadily risen by sheer competitive spirit. Part of his zest for competition had been acquired in the Lamp Division, where he had spent the bulk of his career. Lamps had long been noted as the most profitable of G.E. divisions and the most independent, a constant trial to Gerard Swope in the days when he tried to centralize all administrative authority in G.E.'s New York headquarters. But most of Burens' competitive spirit was simply in the nature of the man. "He had grown up hating competitors," was the way a colleague put it. "They were the enemy."

"This is Bob, what is 7's bid?"

Burens arrived on the scene in September of 1951 and busied himself solely with the job of splitting switchgear into three independent companies (high, medium, and low voltage), each with a general manager and himself as general manager of the division. Once decentralization was accomplished, he was content for a time to let his new departmental general managers like Clarence Burke run the conspiracy. And some conspiracy it was.

Roughly $650 million in sales was involved, according to Justice Department estimates, from 1951 through 1958. The annual total amounted to about $75 million and was broken down into two categories, sealed bids and open bids. The sealed-bid business (between $15 million and $18 million per year) was done with public agencies, city, state, and federal. The private-sector business was conducted with private utilities and totaled $55 million to $60 million per annum.

The object of the conspiracy, in so far as the sealed-bid business was concerned, was to rotate that business on a fixed-percentage basis among four participating companies, then the only circuit-breaker manufacturers in the United States. G.E. got 45 percent, Westinghouse 35, Allis-Chalmers 10, Federal Pacific 10. Every ten days to two weeks working-level meetings were called in order to decide whose turn was next. Turns were determined by the "ledger list," a table of who had got what in recent weeks, and after that the only thing left to decide was the price that the company picked to "win" would submit as the lowest bid.

Above this working-level group was a second tier of conspirators who dealt generally with the over-all scheme of rigging the sealed bids but whose prime purpose was maintenance of book prices (quoted prices) and market shares in the yearly $55 million to $60 million worth of private-sector business. Once each week, the top executives (general managers and vice-presidents) responsible for carrying out the conspiracy would get the word to each other via intercompany memo. A different executive would have the "duty" over each thirty-day period. That involved initiating the memos, which all dealt with the same subject matter: the jobs coming up that week, the book price each company was setting, comments on the general level of equipment prices.

The conspiracies had their own lingo and their own standard operating procedures. The attendance list was known as the "Christmas-card list," meetings as "choir practices." Companies had code numbers—G.E. 1, Westinghouse 2, Allis-Chalmers 3, Federal Pacific 7—which were used in conjunction with first names when calling a conspirator at home for price information ("This is Bob, what is 7's bid?"). At the hotel meetings it was S.O.P. not to list one's employer when registering and not to have breakfast with fellow conspirators in the dining room. The G.E. men observed two additional precautions: never to be the ones who kept the records and never to tell G.E.'s lawyers anything.

Where to cut throats

But things were not always smooth even inside this well-oiled machine, for the conspirators actually had no more compunction at breaking the rules of the conspiracy than at breaching the Sherman Act. "Everyone ac-

cused the others of not living up to the agreement," Clarence Burke recalled, "and the ones they complained about tried to shift the blame onto
someone else." The most constant source of irritation occurred in the
sealed-bid business, where chiseling was difficult to detect. But breaks in
book price to the utilities in the open-bid business also generated ill will
and vituperation. Indeed, one of the many ironies of the whole affair is that
the conspiracy couldn't entirely suppress the competitive instinct. Every so
often some company would decide that cutthroat competition outside was
preferable to the throat-cutting that went on in the cartel; they would
break contact and sit out the conspiracy for a couple of years.

What prompted their return? Chronic overcapacity, for one thing, overcapacity that put a constant pressure on prices. Soon after he went to
Washington as defense mobilization chief in 1950, Electric Charlie Wilson
announced that the nation's electric-power capacity needed to be increased 30 percent over the next three years. The equipment industry
jumped to match that figure, and added a little more as well. Thus an
executive, who ebulliently increased capacity one year, a few years later
might join a price conspiracy to escape the consequences of that increase.
"This is a feast or famine business," summed up Clarence Burke. "At
one time everybody was loaded with orders, and ever since they wanted
to stay that way. When utilities decide they need more generating capacity, they start buying and we have three years of good business—and
then three years of bad. The decision to build capacity was delegated down
to the managers [under decentralization]."

A more human explanation of why the conspiracy snarled on for eight
years was corporate pressure, the pressure to perform. "All we got from
Lexington Avenue," said Burke, "was 'get your percentage of available business up, the General Electric Company is slipping.'" Cordiner himself has
remarked: "I would say the company was more than slightly nervous in
1951–52–53."

Certainly corporate pressure no more exculpates an executive who en-
ters into an illegal conspiracy than the relatively low pay of a bank clerk
justifies his dipping into the till. But that is not to say it didn't carry
weight with the conspirators from G.E. For the company was not only experiencing the increased pressure that goes with new presidents but was
adjusting to a whole new organizational setup. Said one observer of the
scene, Vice-President Harold Smiddy, G.E.'s management expert: "Some
thought . . . that he was going too fast. But Cordiner's asset is stretching
men. He can push them and he did." Said another observer, G.E. Director

Sidney Weinberg: "If you did something wrong, Cordiner would send for you and tell you you were through. That's all there would be to it."

Down the line, where the pressure must have been intense, Clarence Burke had this to say of it as a factor in continuing the conspiracy: "We did feel that this was the only way to reach part of our goals as managers. Each year we had to budget for more profit as a percent of net sales, as well as for a larger percentage of available business. My boss, George Burens, wouldn't approve a budget unless it was a 'reach' budget. We couldn't accomplish a greater percent of net profit to sales without getting together with competitors. Part of the pressure was the will to get ahead and the desire to have the good will of the man above you. He had only to get the approval of the man above *him* to replace you, and if you wouldn't cooperate he could find lots of other faults to use to get you out."

Cordiner takes the plunge

By May of 1953, Clarence Burke had been promoted to general manager of one of the three new switchgear departments (high voltage), a post that made him in effect the president of a small company with some $25 million worth of sales. He felt he had a bellyful of the cartel because "No one was living up to the agreements and we at G.E. were being made suckers. On every job someone would cut our throat; we lost confidence in the group." So he got out.

The G.E. boycott of that cartel continued on through 1954. To be sure, Westinghouse, Allis-Chalmers, and the other competitors would still call Royce Crawford, Burke's marketing man, to tell him the price that the high-level group had decided on, and express the heartfelt hope he would honor it. Crawford did honor it pretty much, though maintaining a free hand to go after all the business available.

This was the situation when, in mid-September 1954, Ralph Cordiner replaced the Wilson directive of antitrust compliance with a stronger one of his own. Far more explicit than Wilson's directive, Cordiner's Directive Policy 20.5 went beyond the compliance required by law and blanketed the subject with every conceivable admonition.

But 1954 was a bad year for the industry and for G.E. The company's sales slumped for the first time since Cordiner had taken the helm, dropping almost $176 million. Moreover, profits as a percent of sales were still well below the 8 percent achieved by Charlie Wilson in 1950. The result was that Cordiner and Robert Paxton, executive vice-president for industrial products, began putting more heat on one divison after another.

"We were told," as one general manager remembered it, "that G.E. was losing business and position because our prices weren't competitive." Then, in the latter part of 1954, Paxton heard a report that moved him from words to the action his blunt Scottish temperament favored. Westinghouse had beaten G.E. out of a big turbine order and had done it at considerably off book price. Determined that no more of the big ones were going to get away, Paxton decided he'd instruct the fieldmen personally. Thus, when the next big job came along, a $5-million affair for transformers and switchgear with Ebasco, the New York district manager knew he was not to let the competition underbid him. But Westinghouse and the others were hungry too, and the price breaks came so fast it was difficult to keep track of them: one day the price was 10 percent off book, the next 20 percent, finally 40 percent.

So began the celebrated "white sale" of 1954–55. Before it was over, the electrical industry was discounting price as much as 40 to 45 percent off book. Delivery dates began stretching out, got as far as five years away from date of sale. This of course meant that the impact of 1955's giveaway prices was not confined to that one year; the blight they put on profits persisted down to 1960.

Mixing conspiracy with golf

General Electric, with its broad product lines, was not hit as hard by the "white sale" as some of its smaller competitors, but it was just as anxious as anyone else to call a halt. The word went out from headquarters on Lexington Avenue that prices had to be got back up, and stability restored. Sales responsibility was being returned to the general managers. They certainly welcomed the news, for all during the period that Paxton had taken over sales nobody had relieved the general managers of the companion responsibility of turning in the profit demanded. Now with power over sales restored, they could strike a better balance between the irreconcilables of getting more market and getting more profit.

At the Switchgear Division, the pressure was so great that George Burens, the lifelong believer in tough competition, underwent a remarkable conversion. He called department manager Clarence Burke into his office and told him the old cartel was going to be cranked up again. More than that, Burens was going to do the job of re-establishing it himself.

Shortly thereafter, he and Burke trotted off to mix in a little conspiracy with a little golf in Bedford Springs, Pennsylvania. Burens and Burke formed a foursome with Landon Fuller and J. B. McNeill, key men in sales at Westinghouse. They concluded that it might take more than the combined market power of G.E. and Westinghouse (some 70 to 75 percent) to get things back to normal; other companies would have to be brought in. Fuller agreed to contact Allis-Chalmers and Burens agreed to get in touch with I-T-E Circuit Breaker—but only at a high level. Everyone was concerned at the danger of low-level contacts and rightly so, for, as Burke remembers what happened subsequently: "It got so that people who worked for people who worked for me knew about pricing arrangements."

About January 1956 another high-level meeting was held in Cleveland. Fuller's call on Allis-Chalmers had been successful; he had Joseph W. McMullen in tow. But at I-T-E, George Burens, trying to keep the contact at a high level, apparently hadn't got to the right man. Joe McMullen, however, had his eye on somebody in I-T-E (Harry Buck, as it turned out) and volunteered to bring him into camp. Then there was a round of golf and a couple of rounds of drinks and the conspirators went their separate ways, after agreeing to keep in touch by memorandums. Every month that year one company conspirator would initiate a memorandum to the others (who now included I-T-E's Buck), listing every pending job whether sealed bid or open and stating what the calculated book price would be. Then the conspirators would reassemble and compare calculations to forestall any chiseling from the agreed-upon book. There were nine such meetings in 1956, held in various hotel suites. These and the memorandums worked fairly well, until the first part of 1957. Then a one-man gang named McGregor Smith lighted the fuse that blew them up.

The malign circle

"Mac" Smith, chairman of the Florida Power & Light Company, personally handled some of the buying for his dynamic utility. As he went into the market for equipment, it struck him that the manufacturers had set artificially high profit goals for themselves, had priced their products accordingly, and then had got together to see that the prices stuck. In other words, a malign circle of manufacturers was short-circuiting what Ralph Cordiner liked to call the "benign circle of power producers and power consumers." Smith was buying a lot of transformers, switchgear, and other equipment in 1957, but the manufacturers were defending book price as if life depended on it and, despite heavy pressure from Mac Smith and his purchasing agents, were giving little in the way of discounts.

Then one Monday, Smith closed his transformer purchases with a number of companies, including G.E. and Westinghouse; on Tuesday Clarence Burke got a worried report from one of his switchgear salesmen in Miami: Westinghouse had proposed to Florida Power that it add all its circuit-breaker order (about a million dollars' worth) to its order for Westinghouse transformers. In return, Westinghouse would take 4 percent off circuit-breaker book and hide the discount in the transformer order. Telling his man to be sure of the facts first, Burke gave him authority to meet the Westinghouse terms. A grateful Mac Smith then decided to split the circuit-breaker order, half to Westinghouse, which had broken the price, and half to G.E., which had matched the break.

This unexpected turn of the wheel brought the Westinghouse salesman boiling into Florida Power's executive suite. There he raised Mac Smith's hackles to a point where the latter called G.E. and asked it to do him the favor of taking the whole order. G.E. naturally obliged.

Retaliation was not long coming. "Westinghouse went to Baltimore Gas & Electric," says Burke, shaking his head in recollection of the chaos that ensued, "and said they'd give them 5 percent off on switchgear and circuit breakers, and a week later Allis-Chalmers gave Potomac Electric 12 percent off. A week after *that*, Westinghouse gave Atlantic City Electric 20 percent off, and it went on down to much worse than the 'white sale'—in the winter of 1957–58 prices were 60 percent off book."

That was the end of that cartel. It did not, of course, mean the end of the other conspiracies G.E. was involved in. Far from it. Each general manager of a division or department took a strictly personal view of his participation in any cartel. Thus while circuit breakers was at daggers drawn, industrial controls was enjoying an amiable conspiracy. Indeed, W. F. Oswalt, general manager of G.E.'s industrial-control department, seems to have accomplished the neat trick of fulfilling the purpose of that conspiracy—to fix prices—while at the same time remaining true to Cordiner's antitrust directive, in a fingers-crossed sort of way. He regularly attended meetings from 1953 to 1955, then stopped upon receiving the assurance of the other conspirators that they would keep him informed of what went on. In August of 1956, for example, Oswalt was lounging comfortably in his cabin at North Bay, Ontario, physically removed from the cabin down the road where the cartel was busy hammering out a price rise. Nevertheless, the resultant 10 percent boost in prices was really his contribution: a representative of one of the smaller companies had panted back and forth between him and "the boys," carrying his strong recommendations to that effect.

Cordiner's "pieces of paper"

G.E. was involved in at least seven other conspiracies during the time the circuit-breaker cartel was inoperative. The one in power transformers (G.E. Vice-President Raymond W. Smith) was going, for G.E. had yet to develop the "black box" (a design breakthrough using standard components to produce tailor-made transformers), which two years later would enable it to take price leadership away from Westinghouse. The one in turbine generators (G.E. Vice-President William S. Ginn) was functioning too. In the fall of 1957 it was agreed at the Barclay Hotel[3] to give G.E. "position" in bidding on a 500,000-kilowatt TVA unit.

The question that naturally arises, the cartels being so numerous, is why didn't G.E.'s top management stop them? Cordiner has been criticized within the company, and rightly so, for sitting aloofly in New York and sending out "pieces of paper"—his 20.5 antitrust directive—rather than having 20.5 personally handed to the local staff by the local boss. But there was also a failure in human relations. A warmer man might have been close enough to his people to divine what was going on. According to T. K. Quinn (*I Quit Monster Business*), the G.E. vice-president who had helped him up the ladder, Ralph Cordiner, was "first class in every aspect of management except human relations."

After the conspiracy case broke, the question of top-level complicity came up. G.E. hired Gerhard Gesell of the Washington law firm of Covington & Burling to come to a conclusion one way or another as to whether Cordiner, Paxton, or any other member of the Executive Office had knowledge of the cartels. No corroborated evidence ever came to light that Cordiner knew of them; quite the opposite. As Clarence Burke himself put it: "Cordiner was sincere but undersold by people beneath him who rescinded his orders."

Robert Paxton, however, is something else again. The fifty-nine-year-old G.E. president, who subsequently resigned for reasons of health, was in

[3] On February 2, 1960, the hotel jocularly described its *spécialité de maison* in a small New York *Times* ad: "Antitrust-corporation secrets are best discussed in the privacy of an executive suite at the Barclay. It's convenient, attractive, and financially practical."

the unenviable position of having worked most of his corporate life in those vineyards of G.E. where cartels thrived. He was in switchgear for twenty-one years, five of them as works manager, went to Pittsfield with his close friend Ray Smith (later one of the convicted conspirators), and eventually became manager of the Transformer and Allied Product Division there. A conspiracy had started before he got to Pittsfield and one was operating (first under Ginn, then under Smith) after he left. Paxton was not then *responsible* for marketing, as G.E. points out, but he has always shown a lively interest in the subject: "I found myself, even as a very young engineer working for General Electric, dealing with the very practical daily problem of how to minimize cost and how to maximize profit."

Lawyer Gesell discovered there was violent disagreement within G.E. about Paxton and the cartels: "Things were said about his having knowledge. I interviewed Ray Smith and made every effort to pin down what he thought he had, but it was always atmospheric. The government investigated and didn't have any better luck."

Judge Ganey, however, expressed a more definite view: "I am not naïve enough to believe General Electric didn't know about it and it didn't meet with their hearty approbation." In Ganey's opinion, Directive 20.5 was "observed in its breach rather than in its enforcement." To say the least, there was a serious management failure at G.E.

Cold turkey and the pressure for profits

In 1958 the circuit breaker–switchgear conspiracy started up again. George Burens and his three departmental general managers, Burke, H. F. Hentschel, and Frank Stehlik, were all dead set against resumption. But the pressure was too great. Pressure had already produced some profound changes in Burke. "He used to be hail fellow well met," said a colleague who witnessed the transformation over the years, "until he was put under that great pressure for profits. Then he simply shrank into himself; everything got to be cold turkey with him—without any warmth at all." Now the pressure was redoubling, as it always did after the market went to pieces. Burens and some of the other apparatus executives were summoned to New York in 1958 for a talk with the boss, Group Executive Arthur F. Vinson. This affair became known to Burens' subordinates as the "Beat Burens" meeting, for at it were aired angry complaints by G.E.'s customers that, with switchgear selling at 40 to 45 percent off book, other G.E. departments should be offering their products at substantial discounts. The solution: stablize switchgear prices; in other words, get back in the cartel.

Burens returned to Philadelphia, battered but unshaken in his resolve to keep clear of the cartel. He expected to do it by keeping up quality and efficiency, and by pricing the product so that there was a fair profit. Ironically enough, in view of his subsequent indictment, he was firmly of the belief that, given six months time, he could bring prices up in the free market without messing around with any conspiracy. But at the annual business-review meeting of apparatus people, held on July 30 and 31 in Philadelphia, he underwent a further hammering from other divisional general managers about the way switchgear prices were hurting them. He seemed morose at the following banquet, held in a private dining room at the Philadelphia Country Club; indeed, he got into a heated argument about prices with Paxton, who had succeeded Ralph Cordiner as president that April.

What happened next to change George Burens' mind about getting back into the conspiratorial rat race is a matter of great controversy. It concerns whether he got a direct order to rejoin the cartel from his superior, Arthur Vinson. If Vinson did so instruct Burens, and others, then General Electric's complicity extended to the highest corporate level, for Vinson was a member of the fifteen-man Executive Office, a group that included Cordiner and Paxton. This key issue will be examined at length in the next chapter, which discusses Arthur Vinson's indictment as a conspirator and the government's eventual quashing of that indictment.

Suffice it to say here that Burens did rejoin and was confronted by a delicate problem of face. He didn't want to have to crawl back, particularly after having given everyone such a hard time when he quit. But as matters turned out, G.E. was holding its quadrennial Electric Utility Conference in California that fall and there Burens ran into Fischer Black, the amiable editor of *Electrical World*. Black reported that a lot of people in the industry were sour on G.E. in general and Burens in particular because Burens had refused to go along with new pricing agreements. To end this insalubrious state of affairs, Black would be happy to set up a meeting— if Burens would just attend. The latter agreed.

On October 8, 1958, the cartel set gathered at the Astor Hotel in New York. The G.E. contingent was there, headed by Burens and Burke, Landon Fuller for Westinghouse, Harry Buck for I-T-E Circuit Breaker, Frank Roby for Federal Pacific. L. W. "Shorty" Long had called in to say he couldn't make it but anything they decided was O.K. with Allis-Chalmers. Black himself popped in to chirp that he was paying for the suite and to be sure and order up lunch. Then he left them to business. Not much of it was transacted. There was a lot of crape-hanging over what had happened in the past and a number of hopeful ideas for the future were discussed. The net of it was that everybody agreed to go home, check his records, and come up with proposals on November 9, at the Traymore Hotel in Atlantic City.

A party for Burens

Whatever watery cordiality prevailed at the Astor vanished into the steam of conflict at the Traymore. Circuit-breaker prices had been dropping alarmingly ever since September, so much so that G.E., Westinghouse, Allis-Chalmers, and Federal Pacific extended options to some utilities to purchase large numbers of circuit breakers at 40 to 55 percent below book. Moreover, I-T-E Circuit Breaker had got into the business via the purchase of Kelman Electric and wanted a slice of the sealed-bid market; Federal Pacific had a slice but wanted a fatter one.

Deciding what to do about prices was not particularly trying; an agreement was reached to keep them substantially identical at book. The real trouble came over changing the percentages of sealed-bid business. G.E., Westinghouse, and Allis-Chalmers knew that anything done to accommodate the demands of Federal Pacific and I-T-E would have to come out of their hides. But at the end of ten hours of angry argument they decided the only way to get the cartel going again was to submit to the knife: General Electric's percentage was sliced from 45 to 40.3, Westinghouse's from 35 to 31.3, Allis-Chalmers from 10 to 8.8. I-T-E was cut in for 4 percent and Federal Pacific got a 50 percent boost, its percentage of the market was raised from 10 to 15.6.

So began the final circuit-breaker cartel, born in recrimination and continued in mistrust. George Burens struggled with it for the next three months, in a round of meetings at the old hotels and several swanky new places. Circuit-breaker prices inched up. Then in January 1959, Burens was promoted out. It was a gay party that celebrated his departure to head up G.E.'s Lamp Division, and nobody was gayer than Burens, the tough competitor returning to free competition. Paxton was on hand with an accolade; the Lamp Division, he said, needed Burens' admirable talents to get it back where it belonged.

But there was no gay party for the incoming general manager of switchgear. Lewis Burger was simply told his job was "at risk" for the next two years. If he performed, he could keep it and become a vice-president to boot. If he was found wanting, he wouldn't be able to go back to his old job. He'd just be out. Burger promptly joined the circuit-breaker conspiracy. But the day was not far off, indeed it was only nine months away, when a phone call would set in motion the forces that would shatter the conspiracy and send Burger along with Burens off to prison.

CHAPTER VI

General Electric: A Crisis of Antitrust

(Continued)

Shortly before ten o'clock on the morning of September 28, 1959, an urgent long-distant call came in to G.E.'s vast Transformer Division at Pittsfield, Massachusetts. It was for Edward L. Dobbins, the divisional lawyer, and the person on the line was another attorney, representing Lapp Insulator Company. He just wanted to say that one of Lapp's officers had been subpoenaed by a Philadelphia grand jury and was going to tell the whole story. "What story?" said Dobbins pleasantly, then listened to an account that sent him, filled with concern, into the office of the divisional vice-president, Raymond W. Smith.

At that time Vice-President Smith was a big man in G.E., veteran of twenty-eight years with the corporation, and one of President Robert Paxton's closest personal friends; he was also a big man in Pittsfield, where the Transformer Division employs six thousand people out of a population of fifty-seven thousand, director of a local bank, active member of the hospital building board. Smith heard Dobbins out, his six-foot-five frame suddenly taut in the swivel chair and a frown deepening on his forehead; he got up and began pacing back and forth. "It's bad," he said, "very bad." Then he added, shaking his head grimly, "You just don't know how bad it is!"

The story Dobbins had, which the man from Lapp was about to spill before a Philadelphia grand jury, was that Paul Hartig, one of Ray Smith's departmental general managers, had been conspiring with Lapp Insulator and a half-dozen other manufacturers to fix prices on insulators. Such news was unsettling enough to any boss, but Smith's alarm had its roots in something deeper than the derelictions of a subordinate. He was himself "Mr. Big" of another cartel, one involving $210 million worth of transformers a year, and he didn't need the gift of prescience to sense the danger to his own position. Nevertheless, Smith concluded that he had no choice but to report the trouble to Apparatus Group Vice-President Arthur Vinson, in New York.

That very night Vinson flew up to Pittsfield. A cool, dynamic executive, boss of G.E.'s nine apparatus divisions, Vinson was used to hearing the word "trouble" from his general managers, but the way Smith had used it permitted of no delay, even for a storm that made the flight a hazardous one. He had dinner with the Smiths at a nearby inn, and then, back in Smith's study, heard the story. Vinson's concern centered immediately on the extent of G.E.'s involvement. His recollection today is that after discussing Hartig, he asked Ray Smith whether the Transformer Division was itself involved in a cartel and received assurances to the contrary. Hartig's case appeared to be just that of a young manufacturing executive whose inexperience in marketing matters had got him compromised.

By sheer coincidence G.E. Chairman Ralph Cordiner showed up in Pittsfield the next day. He had come, ironically enough, to hear an account of the new market approach by means of which Smith's Transformer Division expected to beat the ears off the competition, foreign and domestic. G.E. had worked out a method of cutting the formidable costs of custom-made transformers by putting them together from modular (standard) components. Westinghouse, long the design and cost leader in the transformer field, had been put on notice only the previous month that new prices reflecting the 20 percent cost reduction were in the making.

Told of Hartig's involvement in the insulator cartel, Cordiner reacted with shock and anger. Up until then he had reason to think his general managers were making "earnest efforts" to comply with both the spirit and the letter of the antitrust laws; he had so testified in May before a congressional antitrust subcommittee. When the Tennessee Valley Authority had complained that it was getting identical bids on insulators, transformers, and other equipment, and the Justice Department had begun to take an active interest in this charge, he had sent G.E.'s amiable trade-regulation counsel, Gerard Swope, Jr., son of the company's former chief executive, to Pittsfield. Swope considered it his mission to explore "a more dynamic pricing policy to get away from the consistent identity of prices." He had, however, ventured to say, "I assume none of you have agreed with competitors on prices," and when nobody contested this assumption, he came away with the feeling that any suspicion of pricing agreements boiled down to a competitor's voicing a single criticism at a cocktail party. Cordiner had been further reassured by a report from G.E.'s outside counsel, Gerhard Gesell of Covington & Burling, who had burrowed through mountains of data and couldn't find anything incriminating. Gesell's conclusion, accepted by the top brass, was that G.E. was up against nothing more than another government attack on "administered" prices such as he and Thomas E. Dewey had beaten off earlier that year in the Salk vaccine case.

It was no wonder, then, that Cordiner was upset by what he heard about the insulator department. And this was only the beginning. G.E.'s general counsel, Ray Luebbe, was brought into the case, and within a matter of days Paul Hartig was in Luebbe's New York office implicating Vice-President Ray Smith. Smith made a clean breast of things, detailing the operation of the transformer cartel (bids on government contracts were rotated to ensure that G.E. and Westinghouse each got 30 percent of the business, the remaining 40 being split among four other manufacturers; book prices were agreed upon at meetings held everywhere from Chicago's Drake Hotel to the Homestead at Hot Springs, Virginia; secrecy was safeguarded by channeling all phone calls and mail to the homes, destroying written memoranda upon receipt).

Then Smith implicated a second G.E. vice-president, William S. Ginn. Head of the Turbine Division at forty-one, Ginn was considered a comer in the company. Unfortunately for him, he was just as much of a wheel in conspiracy, an important man in *two* cartels, the one in transformers, which he had passed on to Ray Smith, and the one in turbine generators, which only the year before had aroused the suspicions of TVA by bringing about some very rapid price increases.

The involvement of divisional Vice-Presidents Smith and Ginn put G.E.'s whole fifteen-man Executive Group—a group including Cordiner and Paxton—in an understandable flap. By now, the corporation was plainly implicated in four cartels, and an immense number of questions had to be answered, questions of how to ferret out other conspiracies, what legal defense to make, whether there was any distinction between corporate and individual guilt. For the next few weeks—from early October to late November—the executive office was to devote itself almost exclusively to searching for dependable answers.

Big fish in small companies

The Justice Department was also looking for answers. It had got started on the case because of TVA's suspicions and because Senator Estes Kefauver had threatened an investigation of the electrical industry, putting the executive branch of government on notice that if it didn't get on with the job, the legislative branch would. Robert A. Bicks, the most vigorous chief of Antitrust since Thurman Arnold, certainly had plenty of will to get on with the job, but the way was clouded. The Antitrust Division had once before—in 1951–52—tried to find a pattern of collusive pricing in the maze of transformer bids, but had wound up with no indictments. Now, as Bicks and William Maher, the head of the division's Philadelphia office, moved into the situation, proof seemed just as elusive as ever.

The tactics of the Antitrust Division were based on using the Philadelphia grand jury to subpoena documents, and then, after study of these, to subpoena individuals—the corporation executives who would logically have been involved if a conspiracy existed. The ultimate objective was to determine whether the biggest electrical manufacturers and their top executives had participated in a cartel, but the approach had to be oblique. As Maher put it: "Even if we had proof of a meeting where Paxton [president of G.E.] and Cresap [president of Westinghouse] had sat down and agreed to fix prices, we would still have to follow the product lines down through to the illegal acts. You have to invert it, start with what happened at a lower level and build it up step by step. The idea is to go after the biggest fish in the *smallest* companies, then hope to get enough information to land the biggest fish in the biggest companies."

In mid-November a second Philadelphia grand jury was empaneled, and Justice Department attorneys began ringing doorbells across the land. As more of these rang and the trust busters took more testimony (under grand-jury subpoena), a sudden shiver of apprehension ran through the industry. The grapevine, probably the most sensitive in American business, began to buzz with talk that the feds were really on to something—moreover, that jail impended for the guilty. Everyone by then was only too well aware that an Ohio judge had just clapped three executives behind bars for ninety days for participating in a hand-tool cartel.

Cordiner's command decision

Back at G.E., meanwhile, Cordiner had issued instructions that all apparatus general managers, including those few who had so far been implicated, were to be interviewed by company attorneys about participation in cartels. Most of the guilty lied, gambling that the exposures would not go any further than they had. Cordiner, accepting their stories, began to formulate what he thought would be G.E.'s best defense. It would have two principal salients: first, the company itself was not guilty of the conspiracies; what had occurred was without the encouragement or even the knowledge of the chairman, the president, and the Executive Office. G.E.'s corporate position on antitrust compliance was a matter of record, embodied in Directive 20.5, which Cordiner had personally written and promulgated five years before. Furthermore, illegal conduct of any individuals involved was clearly beyond the authority granted to them by the company, and therefore the company, as distinguished from the individuals, should not be held criminally responsible. Second, those employees who had violated Directive 20.5 were in for corporate punishment. "Stale offenses" were not to be counted, but a three-year company "statute of limitations" would govern liability (the federal limitation: five years).

Punishment of necessity had to go hand in hand with a corporate not-guilty stance. If G.E.'s defense was to be that the conspiracies had taken place in contravention of written policy (Directive 20.5), then unpunished offenders would be walking proof to a jury that 20.5 was just a scrap of paper. On the other hand, here was a clear management failure on the part of the Executive Office—a failure to detect over a period of almost a decade the cartels that were an open secret to the rest of the industry.

As G.E. was to learn to its sorrow, lots of people who approved of punishment for the offenders did not think this permitted G.E. to wash its hands of responsibility. Westinghouse's president, Mark W. Cresap, Jr., spoke for many executives both inside the industry and out when he stated his position in January 1961: "Corporate punishment of these peo ple . . . would only be self-serving on my part . . . this is a management failure."

But aside from the moral question, the legal basis of G.E.'s not-guilty stance was also shaky. Its lawyers felt bound to inform the Executive Office: "The trend of the law appears to be that a business corporation will be held criminally liable for the acts of an employee so long as these acts are reasonably related to the area of general responsibility entrusted to him notwithstanding the fact that such acts are committed in violation of instructions issued by the company in good faith. . . ." Under the decentralization policy, distinguishing between an "innocent" corporation and its "guilty" executives would be tough, for Cordiner himself had given the general managers clear pricing powers.

The Cordiner position had another weakness: it was based on the assumption that G.E. was involved in only four cartels—at the most. Yet wider involvement could reasonably have been expected by G.E.'s top management. That very month general counsel Luebbe (who retired on October 1, 1960) had been warned by one of the general managers, who had confessed, that collusion would be found to have spread across the whole company front. ("I tried to tell Luebbe to stop the investigation," reflected the general manager, "and try to make a deal with the government. I told him in November 1959 that this thing would go right across the board. He just laughed at me. He said, 'You're an isolated case—only you fellows would be stupid enough to do it.'") Thus when wider involvement actually did come to light—the four cartels multiplied into nineteen and accounted for more than 10 percent of G.E.'s total sales—the company found itself in the ludicrous position of continuing to proclaim its corporate innocence while its executives were being implicated by platoons.

The ax falls

But vulnerable or not, G.E.'s posture was officially established in November, and management moved to put it into effect. Ray Smith was summoned to Arthur Vinson's big, handsome office and told he was going to be punished. His job was forfeit and his title too. There was a spot for him abroad, at substantially less money, if he wanted to try to rebuild his career in General Electric. Smith was stunned. Once implicated, he had leveled with the company to help it defend itself, and there'd been no hint of punishment then or in the succeeding two months. He decided he'd had it, at fifty-four, and would just take his severance pay and resign.

It was probably a wise move. Those conspirators who didn't quit on the spot had a rough go of it. Initial punishment (demotion, transfer, pay cuts) was eventually followed by forced resignation, as we shall see. But the extra gall in the punishment was the inequality of treatment. William Ginn had been implicated at the same time as Ray Smith, and his case fell well within G.E.'s statute of limitations. Yet he was allowed to continue in his $135,000 job as vice-president of the Turbine Division—until he went off to jail for that conspiracy, loaded with the biggest fine ($12,500) of any defendant.

Widespread resentment over this curious partiality to Ginn and over the meting out of discipline generally was destined to have its effect: willing G.E. witnesses soon began to turn up at the trust busters' camp; among them was an angry Ray Smith, who claimed he had been acting on orders from above. His mood, as a govenment attorney described it, was that of a man whose boss had said: "I can't get you a raise, so why don't you just take five dollars out of petty cash every week." Then the man gets fired for it and the boss does nothing to help him out.

There was, however, an interval of some three months between Smith's resignation in November and his appearance in Philadelphia with his story. And eventful months they were. The first grand jury was looking into conspiracies in insulators, switchgear, circuit breakers, and several other products. The second grand jury was hearing four transformer cases and one on industrial controls. With a score of Justice men working on them, cases proliferated, and from December on lawyers began popping up trying to get immunity for their clients in return for testimony. Scarcely a week went by that Bicks and company didn't get information on at least two new cases. But what they still needed was decisive data that would break a case wide open. In January 1960, at just about the time Ralph Cordiner was making an important speech to G.E.'s management corps ("every company and every industry—yes, and every country—that is operated on a basis of cartel systems is liquidating its present strength and future opportunities"), the trust busters hit the jackpot in switchgear.

"The phases of the moon"

Switchgear had been particularly baffling to the Antitrust Division, so much that in trying to establish a cartel pattern in the jumble of switchgear prices the trust busters got the bright idea they might be in code. A cryptographer was brought in to puzzle over the figures and try to crack the secret of how a conspirator could tell what to bid and when he'd win. But the cryptographer was soon as flummoxed as everyone else. One of the government attorneys in the case, however, had made a point of dropping in on a college classmate who was the president of a small Midwestern electrical-equipment company. This executive didn't have chapter and verse on the switchgear cartel but what he did have was enough for Justice to throw a scare into a bigger company, I-T-E Circuit Breaker. Indicating that subpoenas would follow, antitrust investigators asked I-T-E's general counsel, Franklyn Judson, to supply the names of sales managers in specific product lines. Judson decided to conduct an investigation of his own. When the subpoenas did come, a pink-cheeked blond young man named

Nye Spencer, the company's sales manager for switchgear, was resolutely waiting—his arms loaded with data. He had decided he wasn't about to commit another crime by destroying the records so carefully laid away in his cellar.

There were pages on pages of notes taken during sessions of the switchgear conspiracy—incriminating entries like "Potomac Light & Power, O.K. for G.E." and "Before bidding on this, check with G.E."; neat copies of the ground rules for meetings of the conspirators: no breakfasting together, no registering at the hotel with company names, no calls to the office, no papers to be left in hotel-room wastebaskets. Spencer, it seems, had been instructed to handle some of the secretarial work of the cartel and believed in doing it right; he'd hung onto the documents to help in training an assistant. But the most valuable windfall from the meticulous record keeper was a pile of copies of the "phases of the moon" pricing formula for as far back as May 1958.

Not much to look at—just sheets of paper, each containing a half-dozen columns of figures—they immediately solved the enigma of switchgear prices in commercial contracts. One group of columns established the bidding order of the seven switchgear manufacturers—a different company, each with its own code number, phasing into the priority position every two weeks (hence "phases of the moon"). A second group of columns, keyed into the company code numbers, established how much each company was to knock off the agreed-upon book price. For example, if it were No. 1's (G.E.'s) turn to be low bidder at a certain number of dollars off book, then all Westinghouse (No. 2) or Allis-Chalmers (No. 3) had to do was look for their code number in the second group of columns to find how many dollars they were to bid *above* No. 1. These bids would then be fuzzed up by having a little added to them or taken away by companies 2, 3, etc. Thus there was not even a hint that the winning bid had been collusively arrived at.

With this little device in hand, the trust busters found they could light up the whole conspiracy like a switchboard. The new evidence made an equally profound impression on the grand juries. On February 16 and 17, 1960, they handed down the first seven indictments. Forty companies and eighteen individuals were charged with fixing prices or dividing the market on seven electrical products. Switchgear led the list.[1]

[1] The other six: oil circuit breakers, low-voltage power circuit breakers, insulators, open-fuse cutouts, lightning arresters, bushings. Each indictment covered one product and listed all the corporations and individuals charged with conspiracy to fix prices on that product.

A leg up from Allis-Chalmers

These initial indictments brought about two major turning points in the investigation. The first was a decision by Allis-Chalmers to play ball with the government. This move came too late to save L. W. (Shorty) Long, an assistant general manager—he was one of the eighteen already indicted—but the trust busters were willing to go easier on Allis-Chalmers *if* the company came up with something solid. It did. Thousands upon thousands of documents were turned over to the government. Further, the testimony of Vice-President J. W. McMullen and others was so helpful (attorney Edward Mullinix had coached them many hours on the importance of backing up allegations with receipted hotel bills, expense-account items, memorandums, telephone logs, etc.) that a number of new cases were opened up. Only two of those first seven indictments retained their Justice Department classification as "major" cases. To them were added five new major indictments—power transformers, power switching equipment, industrial controls, turbine generators, and steam condensers—culled from thirteen to follow that spring and fall.

The second major turning point came through a decision in March by Chief Federal Judge J. Cullen Ganey, who was to try all the cases. That decision concerned whether the individuals and companies involved in the first seven indictments would be permitted to plead *nolo contendere* (no contest) to the charges. The matter was of vital importance to the companies, which might well be faced by treble-damage suits growing out of the conspiracies. (A G.E. lawyer had advised the Executive Office: "If a criminal case can be disposed of by a *nolo* plea, the prospective damage claimant is given no assistance in advancing a claim; it must be built from the ground up.") The matter was also of great importance to a determined Robert Bicks, who argued that *nolo* pleas would permit the defendants "the luxury of a 'Maybe we did it; maybe we didn't do it' posture. 'Oh, yes, technically before Judge Ganey we admitted this, but you know we weren't guilty. You know we didn't do this.'"

Actually, in the opinion of one veteran antitrust lawyer, everybody in the industry and 99 percent of the government thought the court would accept *nolos*. Indeed, the Justice Department was so worried about the matter, and so anxious to forefend such a development, that for the first time in the history of the department an attorney general sent a presiding judge an affidavit urging rejection of *nolos*.

"Acceptance of the *nolo* pleas tendered in these cases," William Rogers deposed to Judge Ganey, "would mean [that] . . . insistence on guilty pleas or guilty verdicts would never be appropriate in any antitrust case— no matter the predatory nature of the violation or the widespread adverse consequences to governmental purchasers. This result would neither foster respect for the law nor vindicate the public interest. These interests require, in the cases at bar here, either a trial on the issues or pleas of guilty."

But Judge Ganey didn't need to be impressed with the seriousness of the cases. He ruled that *nolo contendere* pleas were inacceptable (unless, of course, the Justice Department had no objections). The corporations and individuals would either have to plead guilty or stand trial. At the arraignment in April, Allis-Chalmers and its indicted employees promptly pleaded "guilty"; most others, including G.E. and its employees, pleaded "not guilty." They intended at that time to take their chances before a jury, no matter how bleak the prospects.

The trails to Arthur Vinson

Around the time of Judge Ganey's eventful decision, Bicks and company got what seemed to be another windfall: two potential leads to the very summit of power at G.E. The first came from Ray Smith. He and a St. Louis lawyer had registered at a Philadelphia hotel that February and got in touch with the local Justice Department office. The attorneys there refused to see Smith personally—he was on the way to being indicted in the transformer conspiracy and they were afraid that talking to him might be construed as pressure—but he did get his story to them via a series of notes, with the St. Louis lawyer as the go-between. The gist of it was eye-popping. In June of 1958 two top officials of G.E. and two from Westinghouse had got together during the Electrical Equipment Institute convention in Boston. The meeting had taken up the matter of stabilizing prices in transformers, among other products. That cartel was not only to be kept alive; it was to be revitalized.

At first blush Smith's charge looked like the answer to a trust buster's dream. But under careful checking some serious flaws arose: Smith could only attest to what Arthur Vinson, allegedly one of the two G.E. officials at the Boston meeting, had told him of the top-level get-together. Any account by Vinson to Smith of what the other parties had said or done was hearsay. Moreover, in the face of Vinson's expected denial that any such meeting had ever occurred it would be just Smith's word against Vinson's

—unless, of course, corroborating evidence might come to light in the course of the investigation. None ever did, apparently, for nothing came of the charge.

The second lead to top-level executives, however, was based on the evidence not of one man but four. Vice-President George Burens, head of G.E.'s Switchgear Division, and his three departmental general managers (Clarence Burke, H. F. Hentschel, and Frank Stehlik)—all of whom had been indicted in switchgear that February—trooped down to Washington and claimed the government had missed the key man: their boss, again Group Executive Arthur Vinson.

Needless to say, Antitrust was fascinated. On top of Smith's charges, here were four of the company's general managers, one a vice-president, now prepared to swear that Vinson had authorized them to rejoin a price-fixing conspiracy sometime in the third quarter of 1958. Moreover, their story was a clear-cut account, with few of the ambiguities the Justice Department had come to expect from G.E. witnesses.[2]

The luncheon in dining room B

The story, as Clarence Burke told it to the Justice Department, to the grand jury, and, in April of 1961 to this writer, began with a 1958 visit by Vinson to the Philadelphia works. Burens had been under heavy fire from other apparatus general managers, because, they said, his cut-rate switchgear prices were bringing complaints from their customers, who considered they should be getting similar discounts on other G.E. equipment. Now, according to Burke, Vinson himself was taking up the cudgels to get a reluctant Burens to raise switchgear prices by reactivating the cartel.

According to Burke's account of the episode: "I got a call from Burens to drop by his office [in Philadelphia]. Arthur Vinson was there and Burens, looking like the wreck of the Hesperus. Burens said 'Tell Art your experience contacting competitors, particularly Westinghouse.' So I said, 'Art, we've been in and out and we've tried it so much but they only try to make monkeys out of us, particularly Westinghouse. They get us to agree to book prices and then they chisel.' Art said that that wouldn't take

[2] "I think part of G.E.'s management course must be how to double-talk," commented a government attorney, ruminating about the investigation. "They were always 'gathering' that such and such was said." Indeed, a story of such circumspection going the rounds at the time of the trial concerned a G.E. employee who told his boss, a member of the Executive Office, that he intended going to Canada on vacation. Said the boss: "I am *told* you will have a good time."

place any more, that it had all been squared away. I said I had heard that before, then they say they hadn't had enough control over their field. Vinson said, 'I have assurance of it from Montieth [Westinghouse vice-president]; they don't want to be leaders, they just want to make money.' Burens said, 'See, that confirms it—we don't have to be in.' Vinson said (with some vehemence), 'I told you I've got it all set up.' So Burens said, 'All right, we'll re-establish contacts.' Then he said something like 'I know you're in a hurry, Art. I've called the two other managers and we'll have a quick lunch.'

"As we came out of Burens' office, I saw Stehlik coming down the corridor toward us and noticed that he'd reach the turn which led down to dining room B after we did, so I dropped back and waited for him. He remembers this, and on the way down to the dining room I briefed him on Art's having ordered us to re-establish contacts.

"All during lunch we talked about price stability and I tried to get Art to say the same thing he had in Burens' office, but he wouldn't volunteer anything. Finally, I said, 'Art, these competitors of ours have been calling us up recently.' He looked as if he could have hit me, and Burens said quickly, 'Yes, Art, what do you think we ought to do?' Vinson said again we ought to talk to them, but he said don't let it get below the general managers' level."

Burke's best recollection was that the Vinson order occurred between the end of July and September 13, 1958. In independent testimony, Burens set it in August or September; Stehlik, between mid-August and October, Hentschel, the latter part of August. The dates were highly important, in view of subsequent events; they were also highly illuminating. They fitted in nicely with Ray Smith's story of the top-level Boston meeting that June, the meeting reported to him by Vinson where Westinghouse and G.E. had allegedly decided to bury the hatchet and get together again on prices.

As a result of this information, Vinson was indicted. Clarence Burke's name was dropped from the new switchgear indictment in consideration of his testimony against Vinson, although he continued to be charged for conspiracy in circuit breakers. Then a few weeks later the government chestily filed a voluntary bill of particulars, which included Cordiner, Paxton, and the board of directors among those charged with the illegal switchgear actions. In the same bill the government volunteered the time and place of Vinson's alleged instruction of Burens *et al.* to reactivate the switchgear cartel "in or about July, August, or September, 1958, at General Electric's plant in Philadelphia."

The bill of particulars had been intended as a tactical move to impress

G.E. with the strength of the switchgear case and influence the corporation to change its not-guilty plea. It had just the opposite effect. The company lawyers realized that if Group Executive Vinson went down, their whole corporate defense (no authorization) would collapse at the same time. Moreover, they were by then familiar with "the Vinson lunch," having got wind of it in April during some re-interviews with Burke and others. Vinson had denied the whole affair. More than that, he had come up with records of his whereabouts during 1958. Now that the government had particularized the time, place, and individuals, all Vinson had to do was prove he'd never even been in Philadelphia during July, August, and September of 1958.

A talk with Bicks

Necessarily, the Vinson case had a vital bearing on how G.E. would plead on its own indictments, but the issue was also important to the other corporate defendants. The one thing nobody wanted was a trial where the dirty linen of the conspiracies would be washed every day in the public press. If one company, or even an employee of one company, chose to stand trial, everyone else might just as well too, for all the juicy details of their involvement would surely come out. But the problem of settling the case without trial was complicated by the fact that the companies involved were of different sizes and degrees of guilt. Five companies, for example, had had no part in any conspiracy save steam condensers; they were understandably opposed to any package deal on the twenty indictments that committed them to a guilty plea instead of the *nolo* plea they might otherwise have been allowed to make.

G.E. and Westinghouse, however, were both convinced by now that rapid settlement was essential. G.E.'s own hopes of a successful not-guilty plea had been trampled to death under the parade of grand-jury witnesses, and were interred by a decision in the Continental Baking case that summer.[3] Moreover, Bicks still had the grand juries going full blast; at the rate these were taking testimony any delay in settling might dump a half-dozen additional indictments on top of the twenty already handed down. Judge Ganey was certainly willing to speed up the proceedings and

[3] Said the U.S. Court of Appeals (Sixth Circuit): "The courts have held that so long as the criminal act is directly related to the performance of the duties which the officer or agent has the broad authority to perform, the corporate principal is liable for the criminal act also, and must be deemed to have 'authorized' the criminal act."

suggested all defendant companies have an exploratory talk with Robert Bicks.

On the 31st of October the lawyers of almost all the affected companies crowded into a Justice Department conference room and from nine in the morning till seven that night worked at hammering out a package of guilty and *nolo* pleas. On thirteen "minor" cases, where only corporations had been indicted, Bicks was willing to accept *nolos*, but he insisted on guilty pleas in the seven major cases. And he wanted pleas (guilty or *nolos*) on all twenty indictments at the same time. But one thing stood in the way of the package deal: G.E.'s insistence on trial or dismissal of the Vinson indictment in switchgear, a major case.

Early the next month Vinson himself made a move that for cool nerve commanded the respect of even Justice Department attorneys. He offered to let the government see the evidence supporting his alibi. If the evidence failed to convince Bicks that his indictment should be dismissed, then he'd be at a serious disadvantage, having given the government that much more time to poke holes in his alibi. Bicks accepted the offer with alacrity; in his office on Sunday night, November 6, the curtain rose on one of the strangest incidents of the whole affair.

Eight fateful days

Vinson's attorneys had got recapitulations of the testimony about the luncheon in the Philadelphia plant from the executives concerned. That luncheon allegedly took place in company dining room B, so it had to occur on a working day. There were fifty-odd working days in July, August, and September, but only eight when Burens, Burke, Hentschel, and Stehlik were all at the plant between the hours of eleven and one. For those eight days, said Vinson's lawyers, his expense accounts showed no Philadelphia trip, and Vinson was a man who put the smallest items on that account. There was no entry in the company-plane log showing a Philadelphia flight for Vinson in the eight days, though he was an inveterate flyer, nor any such entry in the executive-limousine log. On one of the eight days the head of a fund-raising committee at Michigan State had a toll slip on a telephone call to Vinson in New York at close to noon, Eastern standard time. On another, a Manhattan banking transaction had been stamped at a late morning hour. For two days Vinson could prove he had been with some Little Cabinet officers in Washington. There was a Pinnacle Club luncheon check testifying he'd had a noon meal in New York with an executive from another company and other checks from G.E.'s executive dining room, consecutively numbered and countersigned by the waitress. And so it went.

Bicks was impressed. The next day the expense-account records of the Four (Burens, Burke, Hentschel, and Stehlik) were examined and Bicks made a disquieting discovery. There was no item showing a group luncheon with Vinson in the records of the Four. Vinson had been indicted without an expense-account item to help corroborate the conspiratorial meeting. This led Bicks to wonder whether the whole Vinson charge might not be a self-serving fabrication, to support a plea of corporate coercion. He summoned the Four to Washington, and they volunteered there to go through lie-detector tests.

It was a grueling experience, considering the perjury charges hanging on the outcome, but certainly a dramatic one. The procedure was to establish the "lie pattern" of each individual by recording his uncertainties under casual questions and then compare this pattern with his response to sudden queries about the Vinson lunch. Clarence Burke's lie pattern was established early when he hesitated on being asked if he'd ever been arrested ("I was wondering if 'arrest' meant being nabbed by a traffic cop"). Then the FBI man asked unimportant things like where he'd lived and worked and sensitive things like whether he'd ever cheated on his income tax (he said he had) and whether Vinson was in Philadelphia between July 31 and September 13 (he reiterated that Vinson was). The machine showed Burke to be telling the truth; Burens, Hentschel, and Stehlik also came through their lie-detector tests with flying colors.

There was now no doubt in the minds of the trust busters about the veracity of the Four. But corroborative evidence, not lie-detector tests, was needed to demolish the Vinson alibi. The government promptly assigned a score of agents to that job.

The impregnable alibi

As the weeks ticked off, FBI men poked Vinson's picture at Philadelphia cab drivers to see if anyone remembered driving him to the switchgear plant, examined notebooks for erasures, interviewed scores of individuals. The most likely day of their meeting, Justice figured, was September 12. Vinson's alibi for that day consisted of some phone calls and a bank deposit in New York; but G.E. records couldn't pin down the time of the phone calls and the bank deposit had been made after two o'clock. (New

York City is only ninety-plus miles from Philadelphia.) But then the investigation turned up a G.E. man who had written a detailed memorandum of his activities during that day, and they included a meeting with Vinson in the New York office just before lunch.

All weekend December 3 and 4 Bicks pondered the Vinson case. He was of half a mind to press for Vinson's trial anyhow, banking that corroborative evidence might turn up then or proof be forthcoming that the incident with the Four had occurred earlier, say in 1957, at the time Vinson became vice-president of the Apparatus Group. On the other hand, Vinson's alibi had stood up like a rock; it seemed certain to get him off the hook and might even win jury sympathy for the other switchgear defendants. Bicks decided to drop the charges.

In a carefully worded statement, government attorneys informed Judge Ganey they couldn't "argue convincingly to a jury of Vinson's guilt of the specific charges contained in the bill of particulars." At the same time, they set aside the charge in the bill of particulars that Cordiner, Paxton, and G.E.'s board of directors had authorized the switchgear conspiracy, and stated that the government did not now claim any of them "had knowledge of the conspiracies . . . nor that any of these men personally authorized or ordered commission of any of the acts charged."

So the curtain rang down on the Vinson case, and then went up on the last act of the drama. With Vinson's involvement no longer at issue, G.E. pleaded guilty to all the major indictments against it, and with the government's consent, *nolo contendere* to the thirteen "minor" ones. The other major companies followed suit. The way thus cleared, judgment was swift in coming. On February 6, executives from every major manufacturer in the entire electrical-equipment industry sat in a crowded courtroom and heard Judge Ganey declare: "What is really at stake here is the survival of the kind of economy under which this country has grown great, the free-enterprise system." Seven executives went off to a Pennsylvania prison; twenty-three others, given suspended jail sentences, were put on probation for five years; and fines totaling nearly $2 million were handed out.

Twenty-nine companies received fines ranging from $437,500 for G.E. down to $7500 each for Carrier Corporation and Porcelain Insulator Corporation. The others, for the record, were: Allen-Bradley Company, Allis-Chalmers Manufacturing Company, A. B. Chance Company, Clark Controller Company, Cornell-Dubilier Electric Corporation, Cutler-Hammer, Inc., Federal Pacific Electric Company, Foster Wheeler Corporation, Hubbard & Company, I-T-E Circuit Breaker Company, Ingersoll-Rand Company, Joslyn Manufacturing & Supply Company, Kuhlman Electric

Company, Lapp Insulator Company, McGraw-Edison Company, Moloney Electric Company, Ohio Brass Company, H. K. Porter Company, Sangamo Electric Company, Schwager-Wood Corporation, Southern States Equipment Corporation, Square D Company, Wagner Electric Corporation, Westinghouse Electric Corporation, C. H. Wheeler Manufacturing Company, and Worthington Corporation.

Is the lesson learned?

So ended the incredible affair—a story of cynicism, arrogance, and irresponsibility. Plainly there was an egregious management failure. But there was also a failure to connect ordinary morals and business morals; the men involved apparently figured there was a difference.

The consent decrees later hammered out by the Justice Department are partial insurance that bid rigging and price fixing won't happen again. Yet consent decrees are only deterrents, not cures. The fact is that the causes which underlay the electrical conspiracies are still as strong as they ever were. Chronic overcapacity continues to exert a strong downward pressure on prices. The industry's price problem—outgrowth of an inability to shift the buyer's attention from price to other selling points such as higher quality, better service, improved design—could hardly be worse: many items of electrical equipment are currently selling for less than in the ruinous days of the "white sale." Corporate pressure is stronger than ever on executives, who must struggle to fulfill the conflicting demands of bigger gross sales on the one hand and more profit per dollar of net sales on the other. These are matters that require careful handling if conspiracy is not to take root again in the electrical-equipment industry.

The antitrust laws also confront the largest corporations with a special dilemma: how to compete without falling afoul of Section 2 of the Sherman Act, which makes it unlawful to "monopolize, or attempt to monopolize." It will take plenty of business statesmanship to handle this aspect of the law; one way, of course, is simply to refrain from going after every last piece of business. If G.E. were to drive for 50 percent of the market, even strong companies like I-T-E Circuit Breaker might be mortally injured.

Has the industry learned any lessons?

"One thing I've learned out of all this," said one executive, "is to talk to only one other person, not to go to meetings where there are lots of other people." Many of the defendants interviewed both before and after sentencing looked on themselves as the fall guys of U.S. business. They protested that they should no more be held up to blame than many another American businessman, for conspiracy is just as much "a way of life" in other fields as it was in electrical equipment. "Why pick on us?" was the attitude. "Look at some of those other fellows."

This attitude becomes particularly disturbing when one considers that most of the men who pleaded guilty in Judge Ganey's court (to say nothing of the scores given immunity for testifying before the grand juries) are back at their old positions, holding down key sales and marketing jobs. Only G.E. cleaned house; out went Burens, Burke, Hentschel, and Stehlik, plus ten others, including the heretofore unpunished William S. Ginn. (Although the confessed conspirators at G.E. had been assured that the transfers, demotions, and pay cuts received earlier would be the end of their corporate punishment, this was not the case. In mid-March they were abruptly told they could either quit or be fired, and were given anywhere from a half-hour to a few days to make their decision.)

Disjointed authority, disjointed morals

But top executive offices of the biggest companies, at least, have come out of their antitrust experience determined upon strict compliance programs and possessed now of enough insight into the workings of a cartel to make those programs effective. Allis-Chalmers has set up a special compliance section. G.E. and Westinghouse, without which cartels in the industry could never endure, are taking more elaborate preventive measures. Both are well aware that any repetition of these conspiracies would lay them open to political pressure for dismemberment; size has special responsibilities in our society, and giants are under a continuous obligation to demonstrate that they have not got so big as to lose control over their far-flung divisions.

Over-all, the case has focused attention on American business practices as nothing else in many years. Senator Kefauver says he intends to probe further into the question of conspiracy at the top levels of management. Justice Department investigations are proliferating. Declared Attorney General Robert Kennedy in April of 1961: "We are redoubling our efforts to convince anyone so minded that conspiracy as 'a way of life' must mean a short and unhappy one."

But the problem for American business does not start and stop with the scofflaws of the electrical industry or with antitrust. Much has properly been made of the fact that G.E. operated under a system of disjointed authority, and this was one reason it got into trouble. A more significant factor, the disjointment of morals, is something for American executives to think about in all aspects of their relations with their companies, each other, and the community.

Epilogue

The most conspicuous result of the electrical conspiracy was the deluge of damage suits filed against the several companies. So great was the number —more than fifteen hundred actions had been instituted even by early 1962 —that Chief Justice Warren moved to establish special procedures for their handling lest they overwhelm the judicial system. A majority of the suits did not specify the amount of damages demanded, leaving that for the courts to determine, but a settlement between the government and General Electric in July of 1962 did pave the way for settlement of other suits and provide an insight into what this might cost the manufacturers. Some $69,600,000 worth of electrical products was involved in the government's suit against G.E.; the latter settled for $7,470,000, or a little better than 10 percent of the sales total. If settlement could be effected on G.E.'s other suits on the same basis, the cost to that company would be between $45 million and $50 million.

Less visible but more important are the internal results of the conspiracies on the two principals, G.E. and Westinghouse. There is substantial evidence that General Electric has had second thoughts about decentralization. The company, it will be remembered, was strongly centralized to begin with and Ralph Cordiner had had the good sense to retain much of its centralized control apparatus when he decentralized it, beginning in 1950. But a number of G.E. executives had long felt that he was pursuing decentralization too far, as if it were an end in itself. That drift ended with disclosure of the electrical conspiracies. The pendulum is now swinging back, with G.E. remaining a decentralized organization but with top management far more aware of what's going on in its manifold divisions and exercising tighter divisional control. At the same time, some of the pressure for profit, a prime excuse of the conspirators, has been relaxed, with the divisions being given more latitude to price according to industry conditions rather than New York's aspirations.

As for Westinghouse, President Mark Cresap had resolved he would never again be in a position of having to plead ignorance of how the company's executives were conforming to the antitrust laws. To this end he instituted a compliance system with two grand purposes. One is to demonstrate that competition, properly pursued, can produce far more consistent profits than any conspiracy. "We have to build into the organization an understanding of what competition is," he said, "and how to be competitive in a profitable way. We must change executive thinking from the old idea that the only way to protect profits is through keeping prices up, to the modern conception that we must be truly competitive in every sense of the word, not only through pricing policies. We're going to try for an understanding of the positive forces of competition, getting into new products and new markets." Beginning early in 1963 a seminar with readings in economics was set up for Westinghouse executives; by the end of the year Cresap expects to have put all his key people, some sixteen hundred men, through the course.

The compliance system's second grand purpose is to provide rapid intelligence of antitrust infractions or potential lapses. Certificates of all contacts with competitors are filled out by Westinghouse men and filed. Thus they provide a permanent record of both how the company's executives are conducting themselves and the related conduct of other manufacturers. Said Cresap: "A competitor recently called up one of our men to ask when we were going to raise prices. He also requested that no certificate be filed on the call. Our man hung up and immediately reported the conversation to the head of Westinghouse's antitrust enforcement section."

With a giant conducting itself in such fashion, conspiracy as a way of life could rapidly disappear in the electrical-equipment industry. For none but the foolhardy is going to initiate an illegal price discussion with a competitor under circumstances where a written record of his intent is readily available to subpoena by the Justice Department or Congress.

CHAPTER VII
Ingalls: A Crisis of Leadership

Prologue

A company built to become an extension of the personality of its founder may do quite well so long as the founder is around to run things. But his death or decline usually precipitates a crisis unless his successor is able and willing to make drastic changes in the character, structure, and outlook of the enterprise. Executives once prized because of their pliancy may have to be displaced by men able to make important decisions on their own and follow them through. The founder's devotion to certain programs and his prohibitions against others may have to be adjusted to the realities of the marketplace. The trouble at Ingalls Industries in the spring of 1958 (when the central section of this story was written) was that its new president, Robert Ingersoll Ingalls, Jr., had neither the opportunity nor the experience to make the necessary changes in the company inherited from his father. Old Bob had seen to it that his only son never got the training necessary to head up Ingalls. Moreover, he continued to influence corporate policy from the grave, with his widow carrying on their bitter legal battle to have Young Bob dismissed.

*   *   *

In 1951, when death ended Robert Ingersoll Ingalls' savage battle with his son for control of Ingalls Industries, one might have thought this riven family enterprise was in for a period of peace. The courts had already confirmed Young Bob's right to the decisive shares his father once so carelessly gave him, and now Old Bob's outraged voice was silenced; nothing, presumably, stood in the way of the company's getting back to the relatively tranquil business of being America's fourth-ranking shipbuilder and one of the biggest independent steel fabricators in the land.

The fact of the matter is that the father and son feud continued on, and almost as disruptively as when the elder Ingalls sacked Young Bob as president for inefficiency and Mrs. Ingalls had testimony introduced in court to try to prove their son mentally incompetent to manage the company's affairs. To all intents and purposes, Old Bob is calling the turn from the grave. The litigation goes on, continued in his name by his wife (who has even insisted on perpetuating the testimony about her son's mental condition). As for Young Bob himself, he has voting control of the enterprise and possession of the chairman's gavel, but it is his dead father who still has the say on how much of a swath he can cut in the company; the elder Ingalls' small cadre of key men continues to run basically the same sort of organization the elder Ingalls planned, and his plans gave scant latitude to the son, now forty-nine. Not surprisingly, the virtues of Ingalls Industries are not apparent to the casual eye. Indeed, the company is so plagued by internal disruptions as to suggest that its present success could only have been the result of supernatural intercession.

This may seem a singular way to explain a company whose divisions and subsidiaries—Ingalls Steel Construction, Birmingham Tank, the Southside (Birmingham) plant, and the Verona (Pennsylvania) plant—have left their impress all over the country in bridges, powerhouses, factories, blast furnaces, skyscrapers. The shipbuilding subsidiary has turned out almost two hundred ships in a generation: war vessels, tankers, liners, even submersible oil-drilling barges. Yet, to pursue the original point, what company, except a well-starred one, would have based its continuance in the tough postwar shipbuilding business on the quaint notion that the manufacture of pecan pralines would tide it over the lean years—then eventually wind up with a $228-million backlog of orders, including two new $26-million liners for Moore-McCormack and two atomic submarines? And how could any young man as different from his father as Bob Jr. jump into the old man's hobnailed boots and run up a $30-million surplus in a few years' time—unless the strongest single influence around Ingalls Industries does indeed come from the Great Beyond, specifically from Old Bob himself? Taken all together, it adds up to a story that has few parallels in fiction, probably none in American business.

The lights under the bushel

It would be a mistake, of course, to assume that simply because the situation at Ingalls is so perilously mixed the company's merits are either sparse or inconsequential. What are the merits that today have made Ingalls Industries a prospering corporation worth upwards of $60 million? A few can be ticked off quickly after analysis of the company's unpublished records and annual reports. Close estimating and cost control, a legacy from Old Bob, stand at the top of the list. The company's ability to keep direct labor costs down—a dollar cut there lops as much as $2.50 off overhead—has given it a reliable edge in the structural-steel business, where margins are narrow indeed. Though sales from this custom shop are relatively small ($26 million in 1957), it is able to compete vigorously with the industry leaders (U. S. Steel's American Bridge Division and Bethlehem's fabricating works), and at the same time keep part of its market out of general reach: the production of massive beams and girders, Ingalls' mainstay, is beyond the capability of smaller plants. The same tight estimating and cost control extends to the shipbuilding subsidiary, where Ingalls earned its reputation of being able to erect welded steel as fast and cheaply as any yard in the U.S.

Both the ironworks and the shipyard enjoy two other advantages: (1) a climate that permits them to operate virtually without interruption, and (2) a lower pay scale than their northern competitors. This last does not necessarily mean lower take-home pay per employee: efficient workers can more than make up the difference through a bonus system, but in return the company gets extra productivity out of each eight-hour day. And productivity is critical in the construction of ships, where labor can be as much as 50 percent of the cost.

Financially, the state of the enterprise is implicit in the fact that Ingalls has no bonded indebtedness and only a million dollars in a long-term loan. Earnings have been sufficient to swing a $10-million expansion between 1953 and 1958, with short-term bank loans (the 1958 total: $6 million) tiding it over such emergencies as enlargement of the shipyard labor force by three thousand men and heavy purchases of steel in anticipation of the strike in the summer of 1956. During 1957, shipbuilding and the ironworks together generated a surplus of $2,200,000, after payment of a $32.50 dividend on each of the 12,713 shares outstanding. As for the future, the company has enough business booked right now to carry it comfortably through the next three years: sales for 1958 are projected at $132 million, for 1959 at $103 million, for 1960 at $116 million.

Even so, Ingalls Industries is today facing one of the most critical periods in the firm's forty-eight-year history. Its most serious problems arise from the fact that the enterprise is still largely the sort of company Old Bob meant to perpetuate. Not that Bob Jr. prowls the office after hours as his father did, making sure no spendthrift employee has left a light on; or that the son has any relish for the paternal pastime of spotting fugitive nuts or bolts on the ground around the company's fabricating shops. The old man's fulminations against smoking no longer echo at Ingalls Shipbuilding Corporation, where he used to insist that the smoke-clouded eyes of his labor force were costing him a cool half-million in lost productivity every year. And at Pascagoula, Mississippi, when the sleek Moore-McCormack liner *Argentina* was launched in 1958 as further proof of Ingalls' entrance into big-time shipbuilding, the event was witnessed by a full fifteen hundred of the yard's employees; Old Bob wouldn't even let the launching crew watch a ship slide into the water—once she was in motion down the ways, he wanted them busy setting up the keelblocks for the next vessel to be built. No, the critical problems now confronting Ingalls have nothing to do with Old Bob's obsessive cost-consciousness. They arise rather because he built his enterprise on a narrow management base, for manipulation by one man. It has now outgrown these dimensions, the One Man is dead, and no matter that the wheels are still going round at a good clip, the weaknesses grow steadily more apparent.

A canny, bone-deep pessimism

Ingalls Industries, for example, is one of the few companies in the U.S. which are actually embarrassed by a handsome earned surplus. What *should* it do with the $30 million now in hand and the six or seven million likely to be generated in the next three years? Forward planning is a new thing around Ingalls' Birmingham headquarters: Old Bob had done all that, off the top of his head; his planning was intuitive and never reached any further than the question of immediate profitability. The senior Ingalls was chary of things getting big—it made one-man control too difficult —and he opposed expansion, sometimes with a canny, but always with a bone-deep, pessimism. A trained accountant, he was mainly interested in keeping a hawk's eye on the profits of the present rather than spying out the potentiality of the future. Yet, though *this* sort of "programing" should have ended with his death in 1951, it wasn't until 1957 that the company got around to some sort of formal financial plan for the future. As for an operational plan, one has yet to materialize, and nobody is doing much thinking about one. Ingalls executives, as many of them are quite well aware, don't have time to sit back and consider such vital questions as where to diversify, where to invest, where to expand, what sort of market forecasting should be undertaken. They're still too loaded down with day-to-day operations for that; indeed, their schedules are too heavy to let them familiarize themselves even with what is going on down the line in other Ingalls divisions and subsidiaries.

It is hard to see how Ingalls can weather the next five years without a major organizational overhaul. The present setup wasn't planned: it just grew over the decades, or rather, was pounded into shape to suit the temperament and virtuosity of Old Bob. As such the management group was thinly spread and markedly subservient, the senior people being much more accustomed to working in whatever harness Ingalls rammed them into than being given their heads. Now thanks to circumstances and some of Young Bob's inadequacies, they have been permitted a considerable amount of initiative. But though this salvages extremely valuable managerial talent at a time when the corporation needs all it can get, it simply substitutes an organization tailored to the talents of two or three men for the old one-man show.

Ingalls, in essence, has become a group of associates, not a company. Lines of authority, responsibility, and function are still so intertwined that only this year the preparation of a simple company-wide organization chart had to be abandoned after a day and a half of work. If the veterans do retire over the next five years, not only will a substantial second echelon have to be found but it will have to be instructed as to what its functions are. Thinness of management, a point of pride with cost-conscious Ingalls Sr., is now a disturbing liability. The Navy, for one, is worried about the company's being "too thin topside." It is concerned about continuity of management during a ten-year submarine-building program. But the twin problems of the second-level management and organization have broader implications than that. Unless they are corrected, a good bit of Ingalls' economic power and potentiality will wither away.

Yachts, money, status, and power

The subtlest yet one of the most pervasive of Ingalls' problems, however, is its peculiar philosophy at the summit, specifically Young Bob's image of himself as the chief executive and largest single stockholder of the corporation. This, no doubt, is compounded as much from his personal tastes as from the traumatic conflicts with his father. The younger Ingalls has always been interested in yachts, money, status, and power. Bob Sr. clamped a definite ceiling on all four. The old man tied his son to routine company jobs as soon as he got out of Columbia (engineering) and took particular pleasure in hauling him down to the office at 5 A.M. on Sunday, if he found he'd been partying late Saturday night. (Even as a youngster, Bob remembers, his grandmother would say on a Sunday, "Take the boy to church, where he can learn some religion," and his father answer, "You can't make money going to church. You've got to go over the plants on Sundays and see that people are working as they should.") The money was passed out slowly and the stock only a little faster. But by 1948, Bob, president for some seven years, had been given 4501 of Ingalls' 15,000 shares of stock (his two daughters were joint beneficiaries of various trusts, which totaled 5750 shares) and was making $45,000 a year. Power alone was lacking; he was denied the authority of experience that would have enabled him to fill a No. 2 job, and denied it by intent. Ingalls Sr. was going full blast and had no thought of grooming a successor, perhaps the more so because of his son's tactless reminders that "you're living on borrowed time." Nobody was going to be allowed to forget that Old Bob was in absolute control of the prospering corporation that he'd built up from that 1910 iron shop. "I started out in Birmingham," was his habitual boast, "with one Negro, one mule, a busted crane, and the [Twenty-sixth Street] viaduct for a roof."

"They're gonna spend my money"

The deep-seated conflict between father and son came to a climax in 1948, when Young Bob, a few months after being divorced from his first wife, decided to marry the woman who is his present one. The elder Ingalls' ostensible objection was his own childhood experience (his father had married twice) that two sets of children in one family just didn't get along together. Bob remembers retorting, "Who I marry and sleep with is none of your business," and his father, not to be outdone, replying, "By God, it *is* my business, they're gonna spend my money."

In any event, when Bob stuck to his marriage plans, he was sacked from the presidency and cut off the payroll; later the father moved to have the company purchase the son's stock on grounds that it possessed the option to do so in case of death or "retirement." But regardless of what touched it off, the resentments and bitterness of the ensuing fight came mostly from the father's fear that his son was trying to take over the company. Indeed, the setup of the various trusts established to perpetuate family control was such as to nourish the fear, for a voting switch by only one trustee, the company treasurer, would have put the mechanism for control in Young Bob's hands.

It is unnecessary to go into detail about the thirty-odd suits filed by Young Bob to retain his stock and get back into the company and counter-suits by Old Bob to frustrate these aims. What is important is the litigation's impact on the personality and outlook of the present chairman of Ingalls Industries. The company's then directors, among whom were executives Young Bob had known and worked with much of his life, turned on him and, first under his father's dictation, then at his widowed mother's behest, lent support to the allegations of incompetence and irresponsibility. Moreover, he heard himself charged with having threatened to kill his father, and with actually beating him up in front of his mother; he saw a further move by his mother, on this occasion, to have him declared mentally incompetent even to serve as a trustee of his children's trusts; he witnessed on the one hand his father's efforts to starve him into submission by cutting off his income from all sources, and on the other an insulting attempt to buy him off—$2,132,000 in greenbacks paraded before him on a bank dolly, the price Bob Sr. was willing to pay for surrender of his stock. And no doubt Young Bob's lawyer, Charles Greer, reported to him the significant conversation he had had with the senior Ingalls one morning in the empty courtroom.

The old man was pacing up and down, talking to himself, as was his custom when thinking out a business deal. As he moved past Greer's table, the lawyer heard him say quite distinctly: "I've made a mess of everything." When this occurred a second time, Greer, who had been willing to let Ingalls Sr. have Bob's stock if he'd just put him back in the company, rose and said: "Now Mr. Ingalls, it isn't as bad as all that, it's not too late —you haven't made a mess of everything. We want to effect a reconciliation. Bob wants to settle it all." The elder Ingalls fixed him with a stony eye and snorted: "You misunderstand me. I meant when I gave that young scoundrel that first share of stock!" The violence of Old Bob's feeling on this subject eventually destroyed him: on the day the suit was to be finally decided by the Supreme Court he was so confident of winning that he went aboard his houseboat to prepare for a victory celebration. When he heard the crushing news of his defeat, he suffered a stroke on the spot, died a fortnight later.

The impact of all this on Young Bob, and hence on corporate policy, is highly subjective, but in some cases unmistakable. He got himself the sort of yacht his father would never have permitted, the million-dollar *Rhonda III*, run at an annual cost to the company of $200,000. He uses her as a Miami base two and a half months of the year and considers the vessel a prime asset to Ingalls: "I figure that through personal contacts with executives, vice-presidents, chairmen, and presidents whom I entertain on her, this boat has produced $60 million to $70 million worth of business. I make almost invaluable contacts moving around as I do. Benson Ford, for instance, has been my guest on the *Rhonda*. When I do business with my friends, they will say we want you to do the job and they'll tell me how much we should quote to get it. . . . You've got to be a man that can mix and make contacts. That's where I come in—when a big job comes up I can go to their front door and rap on it and they'll say 'Come right in and have a drink and we'll discuss matters.' My business depends on the success of Bob Ingalls, Jr. I have fifteen thousand men dependent on me; if I fail them, they lose their jobs."

"I knew he'd hang himself someday"

Some of the company's senior people expressed a more restrained view of Bob's importance. "He doesn't make enough sales with the *Rhonda*," declared one, "to put in that ashtray." Another commented dourly: "Bob is the only one who doesn't work and never intended to work." Then looking at the brighter side, he added, "But he doesn't attempt to control operations, he delegates his authority to Lanier and Guest [shipbuilding] and Palmer and Anderson [structural steel]. All that he's primarily concerned with is whether there's adequate cash for the operation. . . . He gets the reports for all the subdivisions every week, sees what's going on, and finds out why in hell it isn't finished or on schedule. . . . Bob will never be a grind, he doesn't intend to, doesn't have to, as long as he has confidence in those running the business."

Yet the son certainly has the urge to crack the whip like his father and on occasion does. There is, for example, the way in which Kenneth Gayle, Jr., elected president in 1951 (after Old Bob's death), left the company. Young Bob's version of the affair was that he didn't "fire" this veteran of thirty-two years with Ingalls—four of them as operating head—because "I knew he'd hang himself someday. I went by his house one evening and saw two company trucks and company employees seeding his grass. I telephoned him and said, 'What the hell are you doing? Even I don't use company employees like that.' Gayle said he'd been told when he came down [from Ingalls' New York sales vice-presidency] that he could get all the same courtesies that my father got or he wouldn't have come in the first place. He said he had his pride and would resign. I said 'Get your resignation to me in fifteen minutes and I'll accept it.'"

But only a day after this rhubarb, Young Bob came full about and wrote to Gayle about his resignation: "It occurs to me you might wish to reconsider and I think you should have an opportunity to do so before the board is asked to act upon it." Gayle, however, had had enough.

Enter the "wrong" woman

Such an incident reveals more than Young Bob's unsatisfied hankering to run the show; it also underscores his barely concealed irritation with the older executives who really do make things go. "I tell these old men," he said recently, "they should get off the pot—they're too old to be there now anyway—and give the young ones a chance." But the young ones may also find their career under a cloud if they don't stand just right with Young Bob, if they are too wellborn or not wellborn enough, or have married the "wrong" woman. Wives do play a part in the careers of executives, but what other twentieth-century corporation chairman ever told one of his vice-presidents: "I don't care who you marry or sleep with but get yourself someone else"? Such an attitude is disquieting enough when Bob Ingalls is confiding, as he has on occasion, that he knows he's not smart enough to run the company but can get good men who will; when set against his ambitious declaration that he will be running things five years hence, it reveals how much his concept of management needs renovation.

Old Bob's own conception of management, for all its crotchets and limitations, has been responsible for a good measure of Ingalls' underlying strength. Essentially, this strength can be summed up as a sort of residual vitality that years of working hard in harness at the same jobs sometimes produce. In the structural-steel divisions, it is personified by New York's veteran sales vice-president, Ross S. Anderson, fifty-eight, and by Executive Vice-President Robert C. Palmer, fifty-two, whose wits have been sharpened to a chisel edge in almost a quarter-century of effective work for the company. In shipbuilding, Ingalls' strength is apparent in two of Bob's "old men": Monro Banister Lanier, the seventy-one-year-old vice-chairman of the board, a peripatetic ball of fire whose salesmanship keeps the yard full; and William R. Guest, sixty-five, president of Ingalls Shipbuilding Corporation, whose management keeps the yard profitable.

Lately, Ingalls' dynamism has been enhanced by several younger executives, some of whom were brought in as recently as two years ago in an effort to make up for a lost generation of management: Vice-Presidents J. Carter Hammel and Marshall H. Osburn, who have been letting light into the dark areas of corporate planning and organization; Vice-President Earl R. Hammett, a crack shipbuilding production chief; and other young men-on-the-move like Jack B. Kopp, Frank Sandner, Jr., James Moran, William R. Guest, Jr., and John P. Coakley.

Less palpably, Ingalls' strength manifests itself in the farsighted counsel of Young Bob's personal lawyer, Charles Greer, a strong voice for stability and sober second thought, and in the jungle wisdom of the company's Washington office. Recently, for instance, Ingalls' Washington representative nosed out the rumor that despite its $10-million low bid, his company was not going to get the job of building a 22,500-ton Maritime Commission tanker; a California yard would do the work, for an extra million dollars, on the grounds that this would alleviate unemployment in the area. Before very long a powerful Congressman from the House Appropriations Committee was talking to the Department of Commerce along these lines: if Maritime could really afford to pay 10 percent more than Ingalls' low bid on this particular ship, maybe the commission's whole appropriation contained enough fat to be trimmed by an equal percentage. Ingalls got the ship.

Pot along, or gamble

But perhaps the most telling test of the merit of any company is how it handles itself during major turning points in its development. For Ingalls the year 1938 was one such turning point, because at this time it had to choose between potting along as a small outfit and taking a gamble on real growth.

Young Bob, a shipbuilding buff since his early teens, had persuaded his father to take a flyer in barge construction some years before. The Decatur Barge Division and the small yard at Chickasaw, Alabama (where Ingalls built America's first all-welded tanker in 1936), had turned out more profitably than the ironworks itself. Thus the old man's eyes were opened wide enough so that by 1938, after the government had announced its bold new program of building fifty ships a year for ten years, he was ready to bid—provided, of course, it wouldn't cost him anything much.

Monro Lanier was told to prepare bids for four of the Maritime Commission's C3 cargo ships. The trouble was, it soon became apparent that if Ingalls got the bid it would have to build the ships and an adequate yard at the same time. Chickasaw was too cramped for construction of anything as big as the prospective 12,500-tonners. When Ingalls Sr. was told Lanier wanted $1 million for a new yard at Pascagoula, he responded with a characteristically emphatic "Nothing doing—you'll put me in the poorhouse!" But Lanier was a shrewd salesman even then. Enthusiastically supported by Young Bob ("If he hadn't backed me all the way, I'd never have gotten to first base"), he persuaded the boss to commit the yard at Chickasaw and the barge division at Decatur. From the former he could scrape up enough equipment to make a start at Pascagoula, and use the latter as collateral for a $1-million bank loan. Pascagoula itself could only be described as real estate: fifty acres of coffeeweed nodding beside Mississippi's "Singing River," so named by the Indians for the music it makes, particularly during the hot summer months.

Lanier got the $11-million contract for those four C3's and within the hour Bill Guest started the bulldozers and draglines clearing the ground for shipways. Around Washington, however, there was little but skepticism about the Ingalls adventure. The president of U.S. Steel's Federal Shipbuilding Company, chafing over this presumptuous intrusion, buttonholed Lanier and said bluntly: "You may start one of these ships but you'll never finish it. Keep out, Lanier, you're messing up our business. You don't know anything about shipbuilding, you'll go broke."

A windfall of people

By a stroke of luck Lanier had learned that United Shipyards (Staten Island) was about to be bought by Bethlehem. This provided him with some desperately needed personnel: a general manager, a chief naval architect, the heads of hull, machinery, electrical, and other divisions. The reason he got so many so quickly: it was Bethlehem's policy not to rehire anyone who had voluntarily left the company and all of these people had quit its Quincy yard to go to United in the first place.

At Pascagoula, keels were being laid on some ways while others were under construction and the shops themselves half built. Almost every day freight trains would rumble into the new siding, each loaded with Birmingham subassemblies, fabricated at the other end of this, "the longest assembly line in the world." And every so often Old Bob would pile off the 4:30 A.M. train from Birmingham, walk the dusty mile to the yard, clacking his gum all the way, and learn everything that was going on before the staff showed up at their desks. When he wasn't poking around personally, he was telephoning from Birmingham, or writing acrid letters. But in one way or another the ships got built, and built well. Their trail-blazing all-welded construction caused an admiring stir in the industry, though perhaps President John Slater of American Export Lines put the emphasis where it belonged. "This is the first time," he remarked as one of the C_3's slid into the Singing River, "that I ever saw a big ship launched without a shipyard." When the last of them was completed, the ship-building subsidiary owned its four ways, had paid back its $1-million loan, and put money in the bank. Ingalls? "When we were having trouble," Lanier chuckled reminiscently, "he said we'd break him; when we succeeded, why then it was 'just luck!'"

The trouble with sympathy

Nevertheless, Old Bob didn't believe in pressing his luck, as events were to reveal. He did rush everybody up to Washington—management as well as engineering—to whip up a fast bid on six of the C_1's Maritime subsequently offered, and read it attentively when it was handed to him at 2 A.M. of the day it was due. But when he finally emerged from seclusion, full of the milk of human kindness, Lanier knew something was wrong. "If Mr. Ingalls got a little rough with me, I knew I was doing all right," he recalled. "But when he got sympathetic, I was in for trouble." The barb in Ingalls' solicitude was soon revealed. He had decided not to bid. While his men were working, he had slipped up to Sun Shipbuilding at Chester, Pennsylvania, and was going to accept their advice: "Stick to C_3's, you've learned how to make those, don't try anything else."

Lanier, however, had a stunning rejoinder. "I hate to tell you this, Mr. Ingalls," he said, "but my arrangements with the commission have already committed you to taking those ships."

Happily for Lanier, Old Bob didn't believe him, and by the time he did, that agile negotiator had arranged to swap the six C_1's for four C_3's. How did he get around the legal requirement of competitive bidding on the substitute ships? Simple. The Maritime Commission's Admiral Vickery, he recollected, "just sent out telegrams saying: 'I want bids on four C_3-IN design vessels. I must have the price in ten days. You may negotiate with Ingalls for the basic design.' With Ingalls so plainly in the catbird seat and time so short, nobody bid. Then on the day for opening the bids, Vickery called a friend in the shipbuilding business and asked him to make a bid, any bid. So we got the four C3-IN's." And what was a C3-IN? When a reporter put this question to the Maritime Commission, he got an answer that made beautiful music on the Singing River: "A C3 built by Ingalls." From then on nobody was much surprised when, of the 184 vessels built in this category (1939 to 1947), eighty went down the ways at Pascagoula.

Ingalls' next turning point was a decision to break into Navy work, no matter what the cost. Lanier had been angling for a decade to hook a piece of the naval building program but his best efforts had been met with doubt and indifference. "In 1951 we finally bought our way in, you might say," he recalled, "by bidding on five LST's at below cost." Once in, however, Ingalls moved heaven and earth to minimize the expected loss. It lost heavily on the first ship, but by the time the last one had been built labor efficiency had jumped so much and costs had come down so markedly that there was actually a small black figure on the books. In addition, though everyone had expected Ingalls to finish last among the several yards building that series of LST's, it was the first to complete all its ships.

The high price of cream

Sometime in 1953, Monro Lanier took his eye off the pleasant flow of Navy business—several LSD's, some tankers, an icebreaker—and together with Guest and Hammett made a complete appraisal of the facilities at Ingalls Shipbuilding. The longer they looked the more convinced they became that the company should spend a pile of money to consolidate and expand its new position in combat vessels. Over $5 million was poured into Pascagoula during the next few years, enlarging and re-equipping its ten shipways and its shops and offices, as well as adding special equipment like heavy plate rolls ($250,000). This totaled almost as much cash as Ingalls had put into the yard from the start, but Lanier had not been content simply with expansion. A good part of the money spent was to pave the way for getting into "the cream" of naval construction, destroyers and submarines—and eventually into nuclear propulsion.

The Navy gave Lanier no commitment, either before renovation or afterward. Yet it went without saying that the department would welcome almost any newcomer who could reduce price and improve quality, with a good location from the standpoint of strategic dispersal. With this much in his favor, and an allocation of $500,000, Lanier set up a submarine and nuclear training program in mid-1955. In 1956, Ingalls got its first submarine contract, a conventionally powered ship of the *Albacore* type. A year later the yard got its first two atomic subs.

A 10 percenter?

Such an achievement was looked upon with understandable pessimism by the veterans in this lucrative but tricky business, for indeed the complications of even conventional submarines have sunk at least one experienced builder. Yet Ingalls was chesty enough to believe its streamlined construction methods could knock 10 percent off the money Electric Boat would get for building two Polaris-missile submarines.

What dimensions the U.S. submarine-construction program will assume in the future is anybody's guess. For 1958, the Navy is still holding fast to its balance-of-forces concept, in the belief that this will enable the U.S. both to handle Russian subs and to sustain the vital capability of moving masses of men and matériel the easiest way, on the surface. (As a matter of fact, Navy men are inclined to think the Russian emphasis on submarines a mistake, for if the Soviet subs were successful in sweeping the seas of American surface ships, they still couldn't exploit the advantage with large-scale surface movements of their own.) America's 1958 naval bets, consequently, are down on carriers, destroyers, missile ships, *and* nuclear submarines—with some twenty-two of the last authorized so far and an additional seven requested for fiscal '59.

On the other hand, enthusiasts like Senator "Scoop" Jackson of Washington are beating the drum for rapid construction of at least a hundred atomic subs, and it should not be forgotten that only two years ago Congress rammed an unwanted quantity of another weapon, the B-52, down the Pentagon's throat.

Where versatility counts

Ingalls Shipbuilding, in any case, feels it can afford to bide its time. In the spring of 1958, its twentieth anniversary, the yard had the biggest backlog ever. Its own design department was getting set to do *all* the drawings on five 11,000-ton freighters for the Lykes Brothers Steamship Company. Its new commercial atomic division was hard at work on the containment vessel for what may be the first nuclear tanker. Meanwhile, on its ways or tied up to its fitting-out piers was a demonstration of versatility such as few other yards could equal: two destroyers, the prospective atomic tanker, three submarines (two nuclear), a $3,500,000 mobile drilling barge (for offshore oil), a Mariner-class vessel being converted into a transatlantic liner, a pair of towboats, and a self-unloading cement carrier, plus the liners *Argentina* and *Brasil.*

Yet eerily enough, even as the *Argentina*, Ingalls' 189th ship, was sliding into the Singing River, the music was not gay enough or the bunting so bright as to dispel the illusion that Old Bob was right on hand, still the dominant influence in company affairs, still implacably bent on getting his son out of Ingalls Industries. Storm signals were flying everywhere. The company's management problem had barely missed coming to a head: William Guest, president of Ingalls Shipbuilding Corporation, had announced his intention of retiring before the end of 1958. He decided to stay on a while, however, presumably to permit Ingalls to get the replacement it had failed to find. But sooner or later the sixty-five-year-old Guest and the seventy-one-year-old Monro Lanier will leave the company. It will probably take two good men to replace Guest; and when Lanier stops selling, as a Moore-McCormack executive commented recently: "Ingalls is in for trouble."

The long arm of Old Bob

Trouble for Young Bob himself would appear to be even closer. His mother started another suit in the spring of 1958 over the 2287 shares of stock in her husband's possession at the time he died. The litigation will decide whether the company (in 1952) had, or had not, the right to buy up the shares from Old Bob's estate and retire them. If Young Bob should win, as Charles Greer is confident he will, nothing will change. But if Mrs. Ingalls should win, a great deal might change. Her lawyer is James A. Simpson, whose opinion of Young Bob ("irresponsible spendthrift") was developed while representing the father in all the suits from 1948 on. Simpson, as the co-trustee of Old Bob's estate, would be entitled to vote the stock. Charles Greer made it plain that should this occur, the situation around Ingalls would become so intolerable for Young Bob that he'd advise him to get out.

Potential buyers of Ingalls Industries (either individual companies or investment houses acting as agents) are always clamoring at the door, if Young Bob is to be believed; indeed, "they approach us three or four times a year to see if we're interested in selling." But *would* he sell? The answer trembles in the balance, tipped this way by pride, prestige, and luxurious corporate perquisites, tipped that way by a host of company problems and the inevitability, perhaps within five years, of public ownership. Sitting comfortably on his yacht on a warm spring day, Ingalls remarked that he wouldn't sell the company for less than $100 million. But perhaps he'd balk even at that figure, for then Old Bob would have won.

Epilogue

Eventually Old Bob did win, in the sense that he triumphed over his son. Young Bob proved incapable of either resolving the problems he had inherited or coping with the new ones that confronted the company. Ingalls continued to rattle along without an organization plan, a sense of direction, or a second level of management. The mainstays of the enterprise, the senior people such as William Guest and Monro Lanier, the men whom Young Bob had been arrogantly telling "to get off the pot," did retire, and the trouble the Moore-McCormack executive had predicted came with a vengeance in the next few years. What an executive described as "the breaking point for the organization" occurred soon after the shipbuilding affiliate faced up to its enormous losses on the two Moore-McCormack liners. Keen to get into passenger-ship construction, Ingalls had won the contract at a very low figure, gambling that it had a chance to break even or at worst lose a million or two. But the company had been caught in the steel strike (which made for delay), the steel price increase (it had a fixed-price contract for the ships), and a management upheaval (the displacement of Guest and Lanier). Material shortages, inept management, and outright mistakes[1] compounded the trouble until finally the shipbuilding subsidiary found itself $17 million in the red on that contract, undoubtedly a record loss on just two ships.

Such a blow quite naturally subjected Young Bob to a storm of criticism from other members of the family, particularly since the loss promised a deficit for Ingalls Industries *in toto* (it went $4 million in the hole for 1961). This might have come to nothing, for he still held the controlling interest, but his mother subsequently won a crucial victory from him in court. Mrs. Ingalls, it will be remembered, had filed suit over the 2287

[1] One of the most costly was an underestimation in the amount of lead-and-armor electric cable the ships would require. Ingalls estimated 300,000 to 400,000 feet of this expensive item would be sufficient, wound up having to install 700,000 to 800,000 feet.

shares of stock in her husband's possession at the time of his death. The litigation was to decide whether the company (in 1952) had, or had not, the right to buy up the shares from Old Bob's estate. A New Orleans court ruled the company did not have the right, and the shares, in consequence, could still be voted by Old Bob's trustees. This substantially diluted Young Bob's control and added a new set of critics to those he already had to contend with. His position did indeed become intolerable, as his lawyer had prophesied it would if he lost the suit, but just at the time the family vendetta had reached a new climax, a group of Birmingham citizens stepped in as peacemakers.

Their hope was to prevent internal dissension from destroying an important local enterprise, and they were partially successful. Young Bob was persuaded to sell out to his mother and one of the peacemakers for $4 million, and that, at least, brought an end to the battle Old Bob had been waging from the grave. But it certainly didn't bring an end to the troubles of Ingalls Industries. They were by then so serious as to defy cure. Some of the most promising younger executives threw up their jobs, convinced that the company's problems were insoluble. So did the peacemakers, after a vain attempt to get the business out of the ruck and get along with an unreasonable, immature ownership. Bob Ingalls, for his part, enlivened his retirement by a barrage of letters to public officials and Capitol Hill intimating that with his departure the light had gone out of the enterprise. As matters went from bad to worse, the Navy was induced to grant Ingalls Shipbuilding a $9-million credit. Then finally, at the end of the year, the shipbuilding subsidiary was put on the block. Its worth had been estimated at $40 million to $60 million, and $5 million worth of improvements had been added in 1953–55 alone, but the Ingallses let it go at a bargain-basement price. Litton Industries got it for $8 million.

All that now remains of Ingalls Industries is Ingalls Iron Works, a relatively small custom shop. It is, to be sure, a far cry from the broken-down crane, the single mule, and the lone Negro that Old Bob started out with fifty-odd years ago. But even he, looking at what Ingalls Industries was, and what it might have been, would likely count his ultimate victory a defeat.

CHAPTER VIII

U.S. Steel: A Crisis of Judgment

Prologue

Business decisions are an obvious cause of corporate crises, but few have ever precipitated one so quickly or so painfully as U.S. Steel's move to increase prices in April of 1962. Aside from being a public-relations gaffe of classic proportions, it was an error of economic judgment, for the company had failed to distinguish between what it *needed* and what it could expect to win in the marketplace. Here is an analysis of why Big Steel was so wrong when it was so sure it was right.

*   *   *

The afternoon of April 10, 1962, was a tranquil one in New York, mild and sunny, as if the west wind had become charged with the balm of national well-being in its sweep across the land. The specter of a steel strike had been quietly laid to rest in the agreements labor and management had been signing since April 6, and the agreements themselves, providing a package settlement of ten cents an hour, were among the most moderate in the postwar history of steel. Down on Varick Street the big Miehle multicolor presses of Lind Brothers were happily clattering away on an expression of euphoria, a lead article in the monthly survey by the Morgan Guaranty Trust Company. It began: "To a business community eager for good news, the labor agreement in the steel industry has provided the brightest word of recent weeks. . . . If it proves to set a pattern for other industries, the bargaining outcome could encourage investment spending by easing apprehensions over a further profits squeeze in industry generally and, over a period of time, could help the competitive position of U.S. goods in world markets."

Certainly nobody other than the handful of men gathered together in a big paneled room at 71 Broadway could have had any idea that the afternoon's tranquillity was about to be shattered by a sudden action on the part of U.S. Steel. The top people at Morgan Guaranty obviously didn't expect it, though bank officers had sat on U.S. Steel's board ever since the corporation had sprung full-blown from the heads of J. P. Morgan and Charlie Schwab, sixty-one years before; they learned the news over the radio that evening, after the monthly survey, embarrassingly, was in the mail. Nor was it expected by those who keep an attentive eye on the doings of the steel industry. Only the day before the *Wall Street Journal* had reported from Pittsburgh that the nation's leading steel producers were saying they didn't expect any significant improvement in business before autumn and as a result "many of them have about given up any hope of generally boosting prices this year." Nevertheless, that was what happened; U.S. Steel's executive committee voted an across-the-board price increase in the big paneled room that April afternoon. And at 5:45 P.M. Chairman Roger M. Blough handed the President of the United States a press release to put him on notice of what they had done.

So began the most mystifying episode American business had witnessed in many a year. Roger Blough has been castigated for "stupidity" and President Kennedy's angry reaction has been termed "arrogance." But these judgments divert attention from important lessons of the April crisis. Why did U.S. Steel make just the wrong decision at just the wrong time? The answer lies partly in the character of the corporation, partly in our changed economic environment with its squeeze on profits and discouragement of capital investment. But the place to begin the quest for an explanation of the mystery is with the men of U.S. Steel as they appeared at the denouement of the drama, on Friday, April 13.

A day at the Carlyle

That morning found U.S. Steel's finance-committee chairman, Robert C. Tyson, its president, Leslie B. Worthington, and Chairman Blough closeted with Labor Secretary Goldberg and Clark Clifford in Goldberg's suite at New York's Hotel Carlyle. Clifford, once special counsel to President Truman and a lawyer of broad corporate experience, had been brought in by Kennedy late on Thursday, April 12. Of the three U.S. Steel men present for the conference, Worthington was described by one of the conferees as silent ("he didn't say a word all day long"), Tyson as "terribly worried," and Blough as "amiable and tenacious" in his "exceedingly unimpressive" arguments rationalizing the general price increase. Those arguments, together with Goldberg's ripostes, took up most of the morning.

"Did we help you to get a more favorable settlement?" the Labor Secretary asked at one point, and received an assent from Blough. "Then what do you think we were in there for? Roger, there were eight to ten times during this period when all you had to say was: 'Understand we are taking part in the negotiations, but understand that no one is going to interfere with our right to raise the price of steel.' Did you ever say that?" Blough replied no, because he felt it was implicit that steel had the right to raise prices anytime it chose.

But around midday there was a change in U.S. Steel's tone of voice. Blough had admitted at his press conference the day before that the corporation might have to rescind its price increase if certain competitors didn't go along with it. Now at 12 noon New York time Inland Steel had announced it would not raise its prices and Kaiser had followed suit, as Blough no doubt learned during his frequent telephone calls from an adjoining room at the hotel.

After Inland's announcement the men in the suite at the Carlyle turned from accusations and rationalizations about the past, and focused their discussion on recision of the price increase. When offers to help him "save face" were reiterated in this context, Blough finally asked, "What excuse have we got?" Three face-saving ideas were promptly suggested: (1) U.S. Steel could announce that careful study had indicated the price boost was not in the public interest, consequently it was being rescinded; (2) U.S. Steel could say there had been a "misunderstanding" with the Administration and since the Administration felt so strongly that steel should not have raised prices, it was appropriate to remove the source of the controversy and rescind; (3) U.S. Steel could explain that some companies had not gone along with the increase, and since it was not in the best interest of the corporation to engage in this kind of intra-industry contest, it was rescinding. The last suggestion seemed to gain merit as Blough & Company pondered, especially toward midafternoon. It was then, at 3:25 P.M. to be precise, that the announcement came of Bethlehem's recision. But though it became a little clearer as time went by that U.S. Steel was ready to throw in the sponge, when Blough & Company left the Carlyle suite at 5:10 P.M. Goldberg and Clifford were still in the dark about just how U.S. Steel would explain its capitulation. They learned a half-hour later when a phone call notified them the corporation was rescinding on the ground that other companies had not gone along.

"We had a fundamental problem . . ."

Three months later many businessmen were still wondering why U.S. Steel had not foreseen both the government's reaction and the purely commercial difficulty of raising prices in a weak steel market. Quotes from three of U.S. Steel's executives offer clues to this part of the mystery. "We looked at the costs of the fourth quarter of 1961 and the first quarter of 1962," said President Worthington, "and we looked ahead to the prospects down the line. We have to invest $400 million in physical properties every year just to stay even. Adding it all up, it was certainly high time we got going. The thing was debated and it was our conclusion that we should announce a general price increase." Added Executive Vice-President Richard F. Sentner: "We had a fundamental problem. The company was not making a sufficient margin to do what we needed to do commercially. In the Commercial Department we wanted new strip mills and we were told, sure, we could have them if the company had the money. It was not anything that happened all at once. It was an accumulation of things dating from 1958 onward." Summed up Chairman Blough: "When would there have been a better time to test the market? In our judgment the cost and commercial factors all warranted it; and, from the competitive angle in a highly competitive industry, one of the best possible times we could elect to increase prices would be one not expected by the rest of the industry."

Certainly if the strategy behind Big Steel's timing was to catch the industry unawares, it succeeded. All the companies I talked to expressed astonishment over the timing, however much each of them considered that it *needed* a price increase. Bethlehem, U.S. Steel's major rival, had previously examined the market and decided against initiating any general boost for reasons that were obvious throughout the industry. Demand for the metal was still soft, as it had been for the past several years; orders were sufficient only to justify industry-wide operation at an estimated 60 percent of capacity, and that was expected to drop to the lower 50's before customers worked off the inventories they had accumulated as a hedge against a strike. Foreign competition was on the rise, nourished by highly efficient new mills and important increases in capacity. Indeed the period would have seemed more appropriate for a major producer to be adjusting itself to the disciplines of international competition. In 1955 the United States had exported 4,061,000 net tons of steel products, imported only

973,000. By 1961 exports, down to 1,989,000 tons, were passed by imports, which rose to 3,164,000. By the spring of 1962 foreign nails and staples had grabbed off 47 percent of the U.S. market, drawn wire 9 percent, wire rods 27 percent; reinforcing bars—in which competition was so intense there was no quoted price—25 percent; pipe and tubing 7 to 8 percent, shapes and piling the same proportion. As for materials in competition with steel—aluminum, plastics, concrete—the price increase could be expected only to accelerate their threatening displacement of steel in building construction, containers, automobiles, etc.

The decisive role of Inland

A compelling factor in Bethlehem's earlier decision not to initiate a general price increase was one that U.S. Steel might also have foreseen; Bethlehem had calculated that Inland Steel probably would not go along with an across-the-board boost. U.S. Steel's strategy was based in part on the premise that other companies would follow its lead because they were all in a comparable situation in so far as costs were concerned. But Inland had been able to absorb the greater part of the wage increases of the previous contract (1960–62); indeed its first-quarter net earnings in 1962 were only 6.8 percent below those of the comparable quarter of 1959. Per ton margins at Inland had dropped only $1.65 below 1959's first quarter (U.S. Steel's were down $7.90). As late as November 1961, Inland's Chairman Joseph L. Block had publicly stated his belief that under prevailing conditions an improvement in profits could best be obtained by cutting costs rather than trying to raise prices. Said he to the Controllers Institute of America: "Profits can be improved either by raising prices or by lowering costs. Of these alternatives I would much prefer the latter. Price levels which would further weaken the American steel industry's competitive position in relation to foreign producers would not be in the interest of the United States or of the employees, customers, and stockholders of the steel industry." In addition, Inland had a wary eye on the plant Bethlehem was planning to build nearby, which would considerably enhance Bethlehem's competitive position in Inland's prime market, Chicago. The company considered maintenance of customer loyalty of vital importance.

Now the character of the steel business is such that if a major producer in a major market, like Inland in Chicago, does not go along with somebody else's price increase, it is just a matter of time before that somebody has to beat a retreat. Indeed, this fundamental truth was succinctly stated in 1957 by none other than Roger Blough himself: "There isn't certainly any steel company in the first ten or in the first twenty that couldn't require us to change our prices overnight simply by taking action which is different than the action that we take." As Joe Block analyzed the situation that arose in mid-April: "Once Inland announced it would stay out, Bethlehem rescinded their price increase because they immediately recognized what would happen to them in the national market if they didn't. In the Chicago area Inland would be running at full capacity, the rest of the industry at about 50 percent. To be sure, Chicago is only a part of the national market for steel, but the impact of such action is national, and with the industry only running at 60 percent nobody could afford to lose any tonnage anywhere." There was something else. The customers that Inland, U.S. Steel, and others supply in Chicago also have operations in localities beyond the Chicago marketing area. These companies would bring heavy pressure to force prices in their areas back to the level Inland maintained in Chicago. As Block put it: "You can have a lot of different prices, say for automobiles, because styles are different. But if you are making steel for fenders for General Motors or whomever, you have to meet the specifications of the automobile company. You either have to supply to these specifications at the lowest competitive price, or you don't get the order. Steel for a particular purpose is standardized and competition forces prices of such steel to be the same at a given time throughout the industry." Logan T. Johnston, president of Armco Steel, next to Inland the steel industry's most profitable producer (1961), echoed Block: "If *we* had raised our prices and Inland's stayed put, Inland would have moved so deep into our territory we'd have to put a moat around our plant in Middletown [Ohio] to keep them out."

Size, tradition, and dichotomy

Why, then, did U.S. Steel disregard general and specific factors militating against an across-the-board price increase in the steel industry? There are at least two possible explanations, one an economic reason, the other founded in Big Steel's corporate psychology. The company's outlook on the world has been profoundly influenced by the fact that back in the Twenties it was adjudged a "good trust." This judgment, handed down by the Supreme Court in a four-to-three decision, permitted Big Steel to escape dismemberment at the hands of the Justice Department, but at the price of the aggressiveness that produced big, strong companies out of split-up empires like Standard Oil. U.S. Steel was left intact, but it was inhibited from trying to obtain a larger share of the total market for steel. This somewhat dulled the corporation's competitive instincts. In the 1930's Chairman Myron Taylor complained he was hard pressed "to find men who will leave private business [sic] and devote themselves to the corporation." In 1958 a Brookings study found U.S. Steel's pricing policy "colored by a concept of the corporation as the industry leader vested with the responsibilities and subject to the inhibitions of a public utility."[1]

In certain respects, U.S. Steel's "inhibitions" do it credit and help account for the company's survival in the face of anxieties about its vast size and power. There have been a number of occasions in the past when U.S. Steel could have raised its prices but refrained from doing so because of its special "inhibitions"; looking inward, it told itself it didn't need the money. But the other side of this "public utility" psychology has been a certain insensitivity to the market pressures that more directly affect the behavior of other companies. In the new situation this habit of thinking again led U.S. Steel to look inward and to justify a price increase on the ground that now it *did* need the money. U.S. Steel's corporate behavior pattern, in short, is partly like that of a public utility (without a regulatory body) and partly like that of a competitive enterprise. Such dichotomy was in the background of the April blunder. President Worthington's public statement defending the price increase was wholly based on U.S. Steel's "need" for more profits, and when a public utility can make a case for *needing* a price increase, one is usually forthcoming. But, to repeat, though U.S. Steel may sometimes think and act like a public utility, its price increases are not granted by some regulatory body; they must always stand the tests of the marketplace.

Leading from weakness

This other side of the corporation's position—its involvement in a competitive market—merits closer examination, for U.S. Steel did not give it adequate consideration in the price boost. Steel prices are typified by their stability—they are set at levels designed to equate supply and demand over periods of months, even years, rather than fluctuating with short-term

[1] *Pricing in Big Business* by A. D. H. Kaplan, Joel B. Dirlam, and Robert F. Lanzillotti; the Brookings Institution.

changes—and they are customarily set by the industry's price leader. That price leader, though its leadership has always been subject to challenge, has almost always been U.S. Steel. However, in 1958, the year of the last price increase, U.S. Steel made some moves that stand in significant contrast to what it did in April 1962.

In 1958 the corporation's president, in an unprecedented statement, announced U.S. Steel would not increase prices July 1 but would wait to see what might happen. Declared President Hood: "Any adjustment of sales prices can only be made in the light of all known commercial and economic factors, including competitive conditions in the steel industry, competition with other materials, underlying customer product demand, and economic climate and outlook, together with other factors. United States Steel is continuing its study of all of these factors. The only point we have reached to date is not to attempt to change our prices until the situation clarifies itself." This was interpreted in the trade press as a plea for someone else to take the pricing leadership—and Armco eventually did. It increased prices, not across the board but selectively, in a cautious probing of the market. Armco's move was followed in short order by Republic, Jones & Laughlin, then U.S. Steel. Thus on this occasion Big Steel no doubt recognized the heavy pressures price leadership would be under (the market was soft and a congressional investigation of steel prices in the offing) and adopted a new tactic: it would follow suitable selective price increases by others, though its own pattern had been to put up prices across the board at a level of its own choosing. What had made the increases of Armco *et al.* acceptable to the corporation in July of 1958, however, was their being at levels that suited U.S. Steel's needs. But in April of 1962 the situation was quite different. By then U.S. Steel could ill afford to hang back, since it would likely have had to wait for some time before other producers boosted prices. Moreover, when such increases did come they would likely have been selective, rather than across the board, and set at levels that suited the needs of those who announced them, not U.S. Steel. As such they would touch only a part of the corporation's broad product range and provide it only partial relief at that, for U.S. Steel was in worse straits than many of its competitors. The important fact was that in 1958 the corporation was strong enough to do a little experimenting in price leadership; in 1962 it was not. By then it was leading the industry not from strength but from weakness, and that weakness had been on the increase for the past several years.

Trending into trouble

From 1958 through 1961, the corporation's tonnage of steel shipped fell substantially below the level of 1950. Nor had it been able to maintain its percentage of the market—shipments dropped from 30.1 percent of the industry total in 1955 to 25.4 percent in 1961. (A drop of 1 percent in shipments in a 66-million-ton market like 1961's represented roughly a $130-million loss of sales.) Ever since Ben Fairless' testimony before a congressional committee in 1950, U.S. Steel had been on record as intending to "keep in step with the growth of our country"—i.e., finally abandon Judge Gary's old policy of letting its share of the market decline. Now Blough explains that U.S. Steel could not preserve its share of the market and at the same time have a profitable operation. But, in fact, the corporation's profits have declined along with its share of the market. In 1957 it was earning 9.5 percent net on every dollar of sales, the highest since the war; by 1961 this had dropped to 5.8 percent. On profits as a percent of net worth, the drop was from the handsome 14 percent of 1957 to a troubling 5.8 percent in 1961. On sales last year Big Steel earned no more than the average of the seven next largest steel companies, while the steady downward trend of its earnings on net worth had dropped it well below the seven's average in 1961 (5.8 percent vs. 7.1 percent). Inland alone netted $55 million in 1961 on sales of $725 million, while U.S. Steel earned only $190 million on $3.3 billion; as for the seven as a group, their profits were 1.5 times those of the corporation in the first quarter of 1959; by the first quarter of 1962 they were 2.2 times U.S. Steel's.

The reasons behind this progressive deterioration are difficult to determine with precision, especially since U.S. Steel is an admixture of steel-making facilities, ore and coal enterprises, railroads, ships, a cement company, and reticence. The best explanation is that during the Fifties the company calculated the future market for steel would be sufficiently big to justify the heavy capital expenditures, principally for raw-material plant, that it had in mind. (Such capital expenditures reached a peak of $469 million in 1952, another peak of $515 million in 1957, still another of $492 million in 1960, and in the long run may pay off.) But market volume proved to be a disappointment: steel shipments never regained their postwar high of 85 million tons (1955), fell off to 60 million tons in the recession year of 1958, stood at 66 million by the end of 1961. The

year 1957 marked the end of the sellers' market in steel and the advantage
has remained with the buyer ever since. Next the wage-price escalator
ended in 1958 (the year of the last price increase) and with it the easy-
come easy-go method of raising earnings by boosting prices above whatever
level seemed necessary to meet the wage increases. And finally the character of the market changed with a shift from low-profit heavy products
(in which U.S. Steel's capacity was concentrated) to high-profit light ones.
Inland, among others, drastically revamped its product mix to take full
advantage of the increased demand for the lighter steels (for the burgeon-
ing market in containers, appliances, and automobiles), U.S. Steel did
not; thus today only about 20 percent of U.S. Steel's capacity is devoted to
light, flat-rolled steels while Inland has committed 60 percent of its capacity to them.

The cumulative impact of all these developments on the U.S. Steel of
1962 was formidable to say the least. With its competitive edge already
dulled by a decade of inflation, it was now confronted by intensified competition both at home and abroad. It had seldom considered the small
order worth its while; now it was having to scratch for them in a buyers'
market where many buyers were still resentful at being fobbed off by Big
Steel in the past. It had obviously miscalculated the product mix of the
future, continuing to bank on the heavy steels for the capital-goods industries while the competition put its emphasis on light, flat-rolled steels;
thus in 1962, when light, flat-rolled products were expected to account for
over half of all steel shipments, up from 40 percent in 1951, Big Steel's
share was estimated to have dropped to 20 percent (from 25 percent eight
years ago).

Financially, the results have been only too visible. With its cash flow
(retained earnings plus depreciation) sliding from $509 million in 1957
to half that figure in 1959 and on down to $213 million by the end of last
year, U.S. Steel was pinched for funds. Income available for reinvestment
in the business (after payment of dividends) plummeted from $117 mil-
lion in 1960 to $2,700,000 in 1961.

No doubt the corporation had counted on relief during the first quarter
of 1962 when it had been generally assumed that U.S. Steel's share of the
market would rise as demand for steel recovered from the recession period
of 1960–61. But the outlook, as the first-quarter figures came in, was if
anything more dismal than before. The corporation's market percentage
continued its decline, at 24.9 was the second-lowest share for any quarter
in U.S. Steel's history. Profit margins were equally disappointing. They

failed to rise despite the 85-million-ton annual shipment rate the industry was running at in the first quarter; earnings were only half what they had been on the same volume in prior quarters.

Need is reason enough

Thus on April 10 many factors came together to convince U. S. Steel that an across-the-board price increase was timely. Indeed, Roger Blough has maintained to this day that nothing was wrong with the timing, that there's never a *good* time to raise prices. Considering this in the context of April 10 one can only conclude he was insensitive to the tremendous difference between facing the "normal" resistance to a price boost—the public never takes kindly to one under the best of circumstances—and choosing the *worst* possible time to raise prices. To him and a majority of Big Steel's executive committee, the corporation's need for more profits —a need that was real enough—constituted by itself a sufficient reason for the price increase. And once the increase was decided upon, there was no paving of the way, no preparatory measures to soften the shock. Indeed, Big Steel's public-relations department had only an hour to prepare the release.

Back to "the good old days"

What the timing of the price increase has to say about U.S. Steel, however, goes beyond any entries on a profit-and-loss statement. The prices it advanced on April 10 were a failure to read the clock correctly: the corporation thought it was back in "the good old days" of a sellers' market, wage-price escalation, and across-the-board increases. The April 10 increase was an anachronistic reversion to the across-the-board pricing policy the corporation had itself found unsuitable even in 1958. Very likely, economic circumstances would have forced its rapid recision, as increasing discounts and U.S. Steel's own price *cuts* in June 1962 suggested; as a matter of fact, if the corporation can take any comfort from the government's antitrust harassment and Internal Revenue pressures, it is that these abuses of federal power have drawn attention away from the basic unsoundness of U.S. Steel's commercial judgment. "Throwing a lot of prices up against the wall to see which ones will stick," as one of the company's executives reportedly explained the rationale of its across-the-board increases, could only further unsettle an already discount-ridden market; "U.S. Steel's increase," recently declared a Wall Street analyst of thirty years' specialization in the industry, "was an open invitation to other producers to start discounting the new mill-based prices. Everyone in the industry had been reconciled to living with the existing price structure, then suddenly they were handed a $6-a-ton increase to fiddle with. An unrealistic price produces all sorts of discounts and once posted prices start being discounted you probably wind up worse than when you started."

A call for cost leadership

Looking back over the whole unfortunate episode, one cannot but feel that it provides a valuable insight into a new order of things. For basic industry, the surest road to better profits now obviously lies in cutting costs rather than raising prices. Big Steel itself will have to become more of a *cost* leader—if the corporation is to improve its profitability and remove industry's growing doubts about the validity of its price leadership. Any company following a price leader whose costs are no longer low enough to permit it to meet its competitors in a given market is hardly maximizing its opportunities.

In the present noninflationary economy, across-the-board price increases in a basic industry are unlikely for a long time to come—and for the same reasons (foreign competition, a soft market, and national economic policy) that resulted in recision in the spring of 1962; selective price increases, however, are still feasible and may even materialize this fall. Prices of certain items (e.g., galvanized and cold-rolled sheet steel) might be raised if steel demand picks up, as expected, in the second half. Even so, some experts believe steel is in for a new kind of market. Steel prices are going to be more and more responsive to the marketplace: discounting will be more prevalent or the posted mill prices set will endure for shorter periods than has been the custom.

In such circumstances, common sense imposes on the government an obligation to make up in other ways for the price increases it opposes. Worthington's proposition that U.S. Steel needs more money to modernize falls apart only when he ties it to a general price increase. The difference between what the industry needs and what it can't get in the way of price increases should be made up by more favorable depreciation provisions and some tax relief.

At the same time one of the most significant lessons of the April crisis concerns this very word "need." It is simply that whenever a great company gets away from market factors and starts talking about its *need*, such talk constitutes an open invitation to government to start applying the fair-return concepts by which public utilities are regulated. How much Washington considered it an invitation is indicated by the emergency measures the President was ready to push on April 13. They would have made Big Steel a quasi-public utility—i.e., forced to announce price rises in advance and justify them in public hearings. Of course, the steel industry is not a public utility in the sense of a legal monopoly. It is—as the upshot of the April crisis demonstrated—regulated by a competitive market. That kind of "regulation" makes government price interventions unnecessary and disruptive; certainly, price decisions should be free from government harassments under the pretext of antitrust and tax investigations. But market "regulation" also requires of the price leader keener insight, better public relations, and sounder commercial judgment than U.S. Steel displayed to the nation in April.

Epilogue

As 1962 drew to a close, events failed to put U.S. Steel's abortive price move in any kinder light. Foreign competition remained intense. The domestic market remained soft, with mills continuing to operate at around 60 percent of capacity and demand not strong enough to justify selective price increases even in galvanized sheet and cold-rolled steel. On the contrary, price cuts were then the order of the day.

But, as one steel executive observed, "in our industry it takes a couple of years to get off dead center, once you decide what you want to do," and there was early evidence in the shutting down of two Pennsylvania plants that U.S. Steel did intend to become more of a cost leader within the industry. Moreover, the cutting of Big Steel's third-quarter dividend from seventy-five to fifty cents, the first reduction in nearly a quarter century, was a triumph of economics over tradition; profits had dropped to the lowest level of any non-strike-affected quarter in sixteen years. Only Roger Blough appeared unchanged. He was still insisting that business conditions would be better if Big Steel's attempt to raise prices the previous April had been successful.

CHAPTER IX

Boeing vs. General Dynamics–Grumman:
A Crisis of Competition

Prologue

The $7-billion contract that changed the rules: "A single plane is the name of the game," said a Pentagon civilian boss, and the TFX became a high-stakes project that irritated rival services, drove the aircraft companies into frantic competition, brought Congressmen on the run, and set the pattern for a new era of defense procurement.

* * *

The world of defense procurement stretches across some 10 percent of U.S. production and whole hemispheres of geography, but its fortunes rise and fall with the moves and moods of its single customer in Washington. It has only begun to feel the impact of an epochal defense contract awarded four months ago, the first step in a $7-billion outlay for design and production of a fighter plane known as the TFX, or Tactical Fighter Experimental. Nine airframe companies and three engine manufacturers were initially involved in the battle over this joint Navy–Air Force plane, before Boeing and the team of General Dynamics and Grumman were selected for an unprecedented sudden-death play-off lasting ten months. When it was over, General Dynamics–Grumman had won the airframe part of the contract (expected to reach $4.2 billion by 1970), Pratt & Whitney had run away with a potential billion-dollar order for the engines, and Defense Secretary Robert Strange McNamara had wrought a profound shift in what might be called the realpolitik, the working strategy, of U.S. weapon procurement.

For some time after taking office, McNamara had cast about for a way to drive home his concept of "value engineering" in the tradition-encrusted procurement system of the U.S. armed services. He took a dim view of the old relationships between particular services, or branches, and their suppliers. He was less than tolerant of interservice rivalry, and generally gave single-service recommendations a hard going-over no matter how heavy in rank the earnest military pleader. He believed firmly that task forces of Defense Department civilian specialists, viewing rival claims with above-the-battle objectivity, could make broader, sounder judgments in many areas. And he had a conviction that the nation could save hundreds of millions by coordinating its weapon procurement, and an equal amount through "cost-effectiveness" measurement of rival programs.

In the TFX, a multipurpose airplane that is likely to shape the future of military-aircraft development, he found a vehicle to put wings on his approach, and before the contract was awarded he had created a situation of unprecedented, and perhaps unexpected, magnitude.

The design of the aircraft was enormously complicated, as we shall see. By requiring a virtual breakthrough in the state of the art, it put the contractors under the sort of pressures that defense firms can come to expect in the day of fewer but more complicated weapon systems. Moreover, the stakes were huge. The biggest fighter-plane program since World War II, perhaps the last consequential one for manned military aircraft, it had drawn almost every major airframe company into the battle at one time or another. Total industry investment in the gamble has been estimated at $75 million (Boeing alone spent over $10 million). But much more than money was involved; Boeing, in losing, may see its great Wichita division wither on the vine for lack of work; General Dynamics, in winning, keeps its great Fort Worth division from going down the drain, a development that might have made G.D. a much smaller company in the wake of the disastrous losses of 1960-61.

The odds on a successful program were enormously long. McNamara himself was gambling—that he could get the Navy and the Air Force to accept a common aircraft (though each was prepared to go through hell and high water to win a separate, tailor-made TFX of its own). He was also gambling that he could get the contractors to design such a plane when this ran directly counter to their long-standing—and profitable— habit of giving the separate services what each wanted. Moreover, betting he could save $1 billion by having one TFX for both services, he had boldly called his shot by making that potential billion-dollar saving the showpiece of his cost-effectiveness program.

With so much money at stake, with the whole airframe industry hungry for business, and thousands of jobs hanging in the balance, politics was everywhere. A politician's choice lay in pushing the interests of his constituents or explaining why he hadn't during the next election campaign. Openly pushing for Grumman, which is located on Long Island, was Congressman Otis Pike from Long Island. Allied with him was the entire Texas congressional delegation, particularly Representative Jim Wright of Fort Worth. Also presumably in G.D.'s corner was Vice-President Lyndon B. Johnson, whose predilection for the made-in-Texas label had early prompted some Pentagon cynics to rename the TFX the LBJ. As for Boeing, it had the powerful backing of Senator Warren Magnuson, considered the best horse trader in the U. S. Senate, and of Senator Henry Jackson, whose dedication to the affairs of the Seattle-based plane maker prompted some to refer to him as "The gentleman from Boeing."

This chapter and the one following will examine the corporate strategies involved in winning and losing this memorable contract and will look into the new facts of life that will likely prevail in the world of the defense contractor for a long time to come. There are a lot of questions to be dealt with. Was Boeing unfairly done out of the contract after being judged technically far in the lead? Was the competition prejudged in favor of G.D.-Grumman? How much was politics a factor? Necessarily, the story must be told from many viewpoints, for everyone—the armed services, the airframe companies, the politicians, the engine manufacturers, the Pentagon—saw things according to his own special lights, but the start, at least, was simple enough. The TFX story began as a gleam in the eye of General F. F. Everest, in 1959 the incoming commander of the Air Force's Tactical Air Command.

"Everybody thought he was nuts"

At that time the industry itself was working on advanced fighter planes, a result of having nosed around the Air Force to see what was wanted and needed. The new commander, however, was about to put the companies on a radically different tack. On Hank Everest's mind was a fighter-bomber that would meet the new and tougher conditions that he envisioned for the mid-Sixties. The Air Force had eleven main bases in Europe, plus thirty-three others of middling quality, and fifty emergency fields "not worth a damn" to TAC. The net of it was that the best Air Force fighter, the Republic F-105, was in a vulnerable position with only forty-four suitable take-off and landing fields, and these long since pinpointed on Soviet military maps. So Everest's initial requirement for a new fighter was that it should be able to land and take off on sod fields, and on runways less than half the length necessary for a 105. Then he wanted the plane to be able to fly from the U.S. to the European bases nonstop, and to the Far East with a single refueling. Such long legs, of course, demanded a large wing area, but Everest also wanted his fighter to be able to dash in at treetop levels doing one thousand miles per hour, which a big-winged plane can't do in such rough air without putting its pilot through a buffeting of as much as three G's. On top of all this, he expected his plane to have the virtuosity of a hummingbird, able to "loiter"—at subsonic speeds for reconnaissance and ground-support missions—or do aerial combat at seventeen hundred miles per hour.

"Everybody thought Everest was nuts," says one plane builder. "He was asking for too much of a state-of-the-art advance." But Everest recruited the talent and enthusiasm of John Stack, then assistant director of NASA's Langley Research Center. Stack recognized that since "the Lord had not given man the power to change the flow laws," something special would be needed to get so many antithetical capabilities into a single aircraft, and he thought he knew what it was: a variable-geometry wing. Variable sweep was nothing new in aerodynamics; in 1951 Bell's subsonic X-5 demonstrated the principle of having wings pivot inward to reduce drag for high-speed performance, and outward when more surface was needed for the slower speeds of take-off, landing, and cruising. But the wing of the X-5 had had a serious defect: to maintain proper longitudinal stability as the wing was extended and retracted, the whole wing had to shift fore and aft. This meant a ponderous mechanism, heavy weight penalties, and inability to achieve supersonic speed "on the deck" (at sea level). Obviously needed was a wing design that would sweep back without upsetting stability.

Profit in a headstart

Stack had some definite ideas about just such a wing and plenty of manpower at his disposal. By March 1960, Stack and his crew had worked out enough of the wing's kinematics and put it through enough tests in the big Langley wind tunnel to tell General Everest that his requirements were technically feasible. Everest forwarded the Stack findings to the professional skeptics at Wright-Patterson Air Force Base and, when their initial incredulity turned to enthusiasm, felt he was finally ready to fight his fighter through the turbulent air of the Pentagon.

Every military program is in competition with every other for funds, and in the last year of the Eisenhower Administration the reigning nuclear-deterrent rationale had put conventional weapons under a particularly heavy burden of proof. Everest's evidence, however, convinced even the bomber-minded skeptics in the Air Force high command, and with top-rank endorsement he had little trouble in "energizing" the airframe industry. Essentially, Everest told the companies that the TFX was the only aircraft likely to be built in operational numbers, despite agitation for the celebrated B-70 bomber. While he couldn't promise when—or if—Congress would vote the funds ("that's the smartest thing I ever said"), here was a real business opportunity. He hardly needed to point out that advance planning on the TFX, with its variable-sweep wing, would give an airframe company a headstart on the most promising technology for a multipurpose supersonic jet transport.

Thus by late April a joint conference of the Air Research and Development Command, the Tactical Air Command, and NASA had agreed on a program for the TFX: total cost would be $2.2 billion, R. and D. cost for sixteen test aircraft $338 million, first flight May 1963, date of operational availability October 1965—all assuming a go-ahead in October 1960. The Air Force routinely approved the development plan and the operational requirement, then went through the formalities of winning verbal consent from the Defense Department's Director of Defense Research and Engineering to proceed with the selection of a source (contractor) for development of the weapon. Two Air Force-attuned companies, meanwhile, were running out ahead of the formalities—Boeing, in particular. It had worked from Stack's findings to a variable-sweep delta-wing design of its own, and by this time both Boeing and Republic Aviation had completed TFX wind-tunnel tests and were well along on full-scale mock-ups. But just at the moment when the schedule called for the go signal, all of this forehandedness was dashed by an order from Defense Research and Engineering to hold up on source selection pending review by Defense Secretary Thomas Gates Jr. On the eve of national elections, the Eisenhower Administration was reluctant to commit its successors to costly, far-reaching new military programs.

It was months before Gates's successor, Robert McNamara, got around to reviewing the TFX with his new R. and D. team, but when he did he came to some sweeping conclusions. First, the plane was the kind of weapon that coincided perfectly with his ideas about "controlled response," i.e., that our arsenal should contain a number of options to all-out nuclear war, one of which was the selective, tactical use of atomic weapons. The TFX, as he saw it, would be able to get in under enemy radar at speeds too great for foreseeable ground-to-air missiles (assuming the Russian versions were no more likely to knock down a plane flying at treetop level at better than 0.9 mach than comparable U.S. weapons). Second, turning Hank Everest's enthusiasm for the TFX to unexpected ends, McNamara made the decision that a plane of such versatility could be made to fill the requirements of the Army and Navy as well as the Air Force and, as the first fighter designed for tri-service requirements, thus become the cornerstone of his effort to cut costs.

Can a compromise fly?

This major conclusion, when transformed into policy, changed the whole course of events for the TFX. The Army, with limited and specialized combat-plane needs, managed to slip out of the TFX program (and went quietly off to work on aircraft of its own, a much simpler, lighter, and cheaper affair called the VAX). But the Navy and the Air Force were stuck with what seemed a pretty arbitrary and doctrinaire upstairs decision. Hank Everest was incensed at the Secretary's ruling. He foresaw an interminable argument on technical details among Air Force, Navy, and Defense Department experts. Moreover, still bearing scars of ancient battles with the Navy, Everest and his Air Force group feared the Navy might seize the occasion to delay the TFX to death. "The Navy's problem was different," said Everest recently. "Carriers can do the ferrying. The Navy didn't need the plane and we thought they would see the TFX as a threat. If someone else can operate without relying on this forty-knot barge called a carrier, it demolishes the carrier. Carriers did do a great job in the Pacific, but the TFX could make them less important: four hours to Europe vs. four days, from base to the Mediterranean."

The Navy was just as unhappy as Everest, but not for the reasons he ascribed. Its problem *was* different. It had long ago established the fact that it needed relatively lighter planes for carrier landings (thus would need a 55,000-pound TFX, compared to the 75,000-pound Air Force design) with stronger tail sections (to take the arresting gear). Additionally, the Navy's tactical needs were so different that a common plane could be achieved only by limiting one service or the other on capabilities. The Navy, for example, insisted that the TFX be no longer than fifty-six feet, to fit the carrier elevators. This made for a short, relatively fat fuselage. But the Air Force fuselage had to be narrow and long—its optimum length worked out to upwards of seventy feet—if it were to meet that service's basic requirements. Every increase in frontal area above forty square feet effectively increased fuel consumption. A short, fat fuselage would rob the TFX of its extreme ferry range and would shorten the time it could spend at supersonic speed at treetop level. The latter was a matter of great concern to the Air Force because its mission called for long-distance flight over missile-defended terrain. The Navy, on the other hand, would much rather have had longer loiter time over the missile-free expanses of open ocean, with only short-range supersonic boosts for interception or attack. How consequential these divergences were can be seen in the fact that the Navy's ultimate triumph in cutting the TFX fuselage down to size caused a serious reduction in the Air Force's treetop-level capability. The Air Force wanted an 800-mile radius of operation with 400 miles of that at mach 1.2; it had to settle for the same radius with only 200 miles supersonic. Nevertheless, McNamara made the bi-service concept stick. So far as he was concerned, the T in TFX stood not so much for "Tactical" as "Togetherness."

Figuring the angles

The new concept sent the contractors scurrying to revise their strategies. The preliminary strategy of a top defense contractor is to try to anticipate, say, Air Force thinking about new weapons and then get in early. ("If you don't get in at the birth," as one veteran vice-president recently declared, "you're dead.") A period of intensive "brochuresmanship" usually follows, with the contractors' representatives paying regular visits to Air Force people at Wright-Patterson and other key commands, not because it's the season to be jolly, but to be of tangible help in working out developmental problems. "You can't be effective," said a Boeing vice-president, "unless you understand what the problems are; the military aren't interested in working with you unless you have something to contribute. In the case of the TFX, we sent representatives to TAC's field operations all over the world to get firsthand information on needs. We even wrote a description of how TAC operates, which the Air Force ordered for training programs at Randolph Field. It was a manual on the whole system—maintenance, spares, even the skills required of the people who will do the maintenance job."

Obviously, in the early stages of TFX, Boeing's energies and those of the other interested contractors (Republic, Lockheed, North American, McDonnell, Douglas, Chance Vought, Northrop, Grumman, and General Dynamics) had been concentrated on keeping the Air Force happy. After the Air Force's preliminary Work Statement, each company had spent anywhere from $1 million to $3,500,000 in trying to meet or anticipate Air Force requirements. Boeing had even gone so far in trying to increase its lead as to prepare a contract proposal on a dry-run basis, a task that demanded the total energies of a hundred people for more than two months. But with the Navy forcibly injected into the picture, all strategies had to be adjusted to a whole new set of imponderables.

Since there would be tremendous, and perhaps impossible, technical difficulties in designing one plane to meet the divergent requirements of the Navy and Air Force, the airframe companies' own sense of realpolitik provoked some interesting front-office questions: Would it be better strategy to favor the Air Force in design since the Air Force would be buying fifteen hundred TFX's vs. only a couple of hundred for the Navy? Anyway, wasn't the Navy powerful enough politically to defeat McNamara and eventually win a special TFX of its own? Or would McNamara get enough support to make the TFX a symbol of his push for unification of the services, and was he likely to use it to put the military professionals in their places by making the civilian decision stick? Were the nickel-and-dime economies of the automobile business going to be imposed on the armament industry? How long would McNamara be around anyway? Washington had averaged a new Defense Secretary every eighteen months. After weighing all these factors, most of the companies must have found in McNamara's favor because most began to work for both an impartial resolution of Air Force-Navy requirements and a judicious balance of performance and cost. Republic teamed up with Chance Vought, which had a long history of producing naval aircraft. Douglas and McDonnell eventually went into partnership. General Dynamics joined forces with Grumman.

G.D.'s alliance with this "Navy company" was of tremendous importance in view of the final result; it now had a partner whose planes had made more than half of all the take-offs and landings on carriers. Moreover, the Navy knew that, with Grumman in the deal, there would be a concerted effort to meet naval requirements. As J. T. Cosby, TFX program manager at General Dynamics in Fort Worth, recollected: "Grumman made no bones about standing up for what they thought were the Navy's requirements. We learned early in the game that the Navy was a strong group, and even though the number of its planes was smaller than that of the Air Force, it knew very well how to make its feelings known."

By the same token, Boeing made a serious miscalculation. It had ignored partnership feelers put out by Grumman, deciding to go it alone. In effect, it was guessing that there would ultimately be two planes, an Air Force TFX and a Navy TFX, and so would concentrate on meeting the Air

Force requirements. And, unfortunately, the primacy Boeing gave to pleasing the Air Force shortly led it into another fateful misjudgment, this time on the choice of the engine.

Power in a paper engine

The engine competiton for the TFX—the winner would walk away with a billion-dollar contract in its hip pocket—was among three companies. Pratt & Whitney was pushing its TF-30, a Navy-sponsored power plant on which that service had already spent $30 million (it was to have been installed in the canceled Douglas Missileer, a subsonic fighter). General Motors' Allison Division offered the Rolls-Royce Spey engine, already operational on the British de Havilland transport, and redesigned by Allison to increase its performance. General Electric's initial entry was the J79, also operational as the power plant for McDonnell's Navy fighter, the F-4B, and the Air Force's F-4C. After looking over these engines, which would be a crucial element in performance and design, one of the six competing teams had chosen the Allison, the other five, including Boeing, had picked Pratt & Whitney's modified TF-30.

General Electric was left out in the cold. But even though G.E. knew that the airframe companies were already designing around the respective competitive power plants—and would be most reluctant to change—the company got to work on a new engine design, the MF295, of significantly superior performance. G.E. carefully timed the release of the news for August 1961.

The strategy was simple and daring. G.E. expected that in October the Defense Department would issue its Request for Proposal and its specifications for bids on the TFX. G.E. also banked on its ability to sell the military on including the MF295 in its list of acceptable engines. And it figured (correctly) that the time between August and October was too short for either Allison or Pratt & Whitney to top the new design. Of course the MF295 was a "paper" engine—i.e., a design fortified by a few components from other G.E. power plants. Its development would also be time-consuming, a factor of considerable importance in an aircraft already months behind schedule. But the MF295 was several hundred pounds lighter than the Allison or Pratt & Whitney engine, and was smaller both in length and in diameter. This promised relief from the crushing limitation on weight, and it also permitted the narrower fuselage so critical to the Air Force's supersonic requirements. Moreover, G.E. did a brilliant selling job—with the military, with NASA, and with the propulsion division at Wright-Patterson. The result was that in the October specifications Wright-Patterson declared the MF295 eligible for the TFX competition.

This development prompted more strategy huddles in the various airframe plants. Some temperature-taking immediately took place. Was Wright-Patterson's inclusion of the MF295 simply a localized result of inspired G.E. "brochuresmanship" or should it be taken as evidence of the services' genuine respect for the engine? The word got back that "the Air Force" was "very high" on the MF295. Boeing, which had been designing the TFX around the heavier Pratt & Whitney for two and a half years, then decided to switch to the MF295. The gamble looked eminently reasonable at the time. True, it usually takes about five years to come up with a pretty well "worked out" engine, but this clear inability to meet TFX's time schedule was counterbalanced by the probability that other difficulties with the TFX would make additional time available. The prospects for better performance were compelling. Moreover, the operational words were "Air Force" and "very high." Other contractors apparently shared Boeing's views, for North American, McDonnell, Lockheed, Douglas—indeed everyone except Republic, Chance Vought, and General Dynamics–Grumman —eventually switched to the MF295.

How to figure the computer corps

McNamara's October 1 Request for Proposal and the accompanying Work Statement signaled the official start of the great race. The finish line for TFX designs was set for December 6, nine and a half weeks away. Crammed into 250 pages of the Work Statement were the rigorous requirements: the expected performance, the logistics and support demands, and the type of environment the aircraft would have to function in. Each contractor was required to specify how he intended to make the plane, which of the three eligible engines he would use, the costs involved, the dates on which he would guarantee to reach such milestones as first flight and operational availability, how much subcontracting there would be and to whom, and so on ad infinitum, even to the names of the top people to be assigned to the job.

Simply responding to all this within the time limit would be enormously difficult, but the difficulty was compounded by the subtle requirements of contract gamesmanship. One stratagem that had worked more than once, for example, was to "buy into" a program with a proposal below cost; then renegotiate more favorable terms at contract signing time or at still later stages. Even with TFX an incentive contract (with profit scaled to accurate estimates and performance), the temptation for below-cost bidding was great: belts had been pulled pretty tight in the airframe industry—Bell had already all but starved to death—and a low bid might be the deciding factor. Yet balanced against this was the possibility that the computer corps in the Defense Department might spot a starvation bid for what it really was, a potential cost overrun. Cost overruns had become a very sore point with McNamara; he had recently discovered that final costs on major systems over a period of years had exceeded the original estimates by between 300 and 1000 percent.

It might also seem sound strategy for a contractor to try to keep as much as possible of the TFX production "in house"—substantial economies could be effected in tooling costs, and training time for labor could be minimized. Yet here, too, there was an important offsetting factor. The competition for the TFX would certainly be close, perhaps a tie; in the latter case *sub*contracting could play a decisive political role. As a Douglas executive explained it: "The only place where politics is important is if two contractors are neck and neck—then subcontracting has political advantages and can swing to the best political merchandiser. We tried to lock up a substantial part of our TFX bid with subcontracts in Missouri and Oklahoma [which the late Senator Robert Kerr intended to make a lodestone for defense industry], as well as in California." Boeing followed its usual strategy of subcontracting some 50 to 60 percent to dependable suppliers, albeit with an eye on the politically important distressed areas. G.D.-Grumman kept flexible—and perhaps increased its political leverage—by having two or three runners-up in each subcontracting category and postponing final selection until the last minute.

Commonality as philosophy

Paramount to all of these time-honored considerations, however, was the problem of commonality in this joint Air Force–Navy project. Each service was pressing for attention to its unique requirements, while Secretary McNamara insisted on maximum interchangeability. Sure, McNamara was legally in command, but the plane makers had learned the hard way that weapons seldom emerge from the chrysalis of development into full-blown production unless they have the active support of the military professionals. Nowhere was this commonality aspect of the race more carefully thought

out than in the councils of the two hungriest competitors, Boeing and
G.D.-Grumman.

General Dynamics, it so happened, was more disposed toward commonality as a philosophy than was Boeing. In building the Air Force's supersonic bomber, the B-58, G.D. had gone all out trying to please the generals. It got precious little for its pains; after bright promises that the B-58
might become the workhorse of the Strategic Air Command, the Air
Force top brass limited it to only two wings. Moreover, G.D. had spent
lots of time studying multipurpose weapons (in a vain attempt to interest
TAC, the Air Defense Command, and SAC in the B-58) and thought
the McNamara concept made a lot of sense.

"We read the Work Statement," said Frank Davis, president of G.D.'s
Fort Worth division, "as putting significant emphasis on commonality. We
went to a great deal of trouble to have a common structure, and paid some
weight penalties to do it—some performance penalties as well, on both
Navy and Air Force versions."

Better blend or better plane?

Boeing's strategy was not so much to oppose McNamara as it was to design
for the Navy and the Air Force *better* planes than their individual requirements called for. It would thus bank on the hope that the best plane
would be irresistible, regardless of commonality—making the most of its
big lead in variable-wing design over the rest of the industry. A tremendous amount of effort would be put in the Air Force version of the TFX,
for that had primacy in Boeing's view, but the separate Navy version would
also be made as attractive as possible (within the limits of Boeing's lack
of experience in designing modern Navy fighters). If all this had to be
done at the sacrifice of McNamara's dream of a single blended plane, then
so be it. Boeing was ready to gamble that the old way, pleasing the services, was still the best way, and that a bi-service TFX would ultimately be
recognized as impractical. Hadn't the Navy, even after the Work Statement was out, moved heaven and earth in vainly trying to insert a requirement that its version be able to do 0.6 mach at 35,000-foot altitudes, a
speed that would virtually have put the plane into a stall?

So with its service-oriented approach, its selection of the new G.E. engine, and its gamble on plenty of time to work out the engine "bugs,"
Boeing cut quite a different figure from its chief rival, G.D.-Grumman.

In the midst of its careful planning, Boeing began to notice that quite a lot of people were saying that its efforts were foredoomed to failure, no matter what. Indeed, these prophecies were coming so thick and fast that the company began noting them in a special scrapbook. One of its executives would report that some brass hat in the Pentagon had hinted G.D.-Grumman was going to beat Boeing out of the contract, regardless of design. Another would hear that selection of the Pratt & Whitney engine was a foregone conclusion, and this would weigh heavily against Boeing. Then there was the Texas politician who had reportedly been whispering that the Navy would hold out for a "better" design than Boeing's, and that meant one from G.D.-Grumman.

Undoubtedly the common denominator of most of these rumors was the assumption that G.D.-Grumman had more powerful political backing than Boeing, and that politics would be decisive. The Texans indeed seemed to be lined up in force. Aside from Lyndon Johnson and hard-working Congressman Wright of Fort Worth, Navy Secretary Fred Korth came from Fort Worth, and his predecessor in the job, John Connally, was the newly elected governor of Texas. Moreover, the G.D.-Grumman combination put Texas hand in hand with New York (and Teddy Kennedy was busy trying to persuade Grumman to expand into Massachusetts). But Boeing's friends from Washington state and the Midwest (Wichita) were busy too in the White House and the Pentagon.

The fact seems to be that in so far as political influence was concerned there was an immense difference between ritual and results. Congressmen habitually go through a sort of formalistic dance in behalf of their constituents, waltzing over to the White House to plead their case before Kenneth O'Donnell or Lawrence O'Brien, then doing a brisk fox-trot with one of the Pentagon's congressional liaison men or even an assistant secretary. Letters of special pleading usually follow, and when it's over all concerned can say with perfect honesty, "We gave the matter every consideration." Where these representations are more than ritualistic and do carry considerable weight within the Pentagon is in circumstances of real economic hardship. But in the case of the TFX, Congressman Wright could hardly hope to win any special consideration for General Dynamics on grounds that loss of the contract would be a severe blow to the economy of Fort Worth. McNamara's Office of Economic Adjustment, set up to gauge the impact of military procurement on sixty cities across the nation, had already informed him that if Boeing lost the TFX, Wichita would be just as hard hit as Fort Worth. The political battle appeared to be a standoff.

Proposals five feet tall

By early December 1961 the nine weeks of frantic activity came to an end for Boeing, G.D.-Grumman, and the other six remaining contractors (only Northrop of the original starting ten had dropped out). The days of computer time and wind-tunnel testing, the trade-offs in design, the compromises and intricate strategies had been synthesized into printed proposals, typically fifteen hundred pages long and five feet in height. The proposals were shipped off to Wright-Patterson and followed by the engineers who were to give the oral summations. At Wright-Patterson there was none of the good fellowship usual to industry get-togethers, for it had been growing increasingly clear that the U.S. had too many airframe companies with too little business. Competitive stances were maintained, even down to drawing straws for the order of position (the lead-off spot was bad—the audience wasn't warmed up—but being "tail-end Charlie" was even worse, for by then the military knew enough to ask questions that would curl a man's hair). The presentations were completed in three days.

Then it was the military's turn to sweat. The first job fell to the evaluation teams, each assigned to cover a particular section in all the proposals (such as avionics, costs, or logistics). Billeted together behind barbed wire and armed guards, the teams began their round-the-clock operation: a comparative rating of each element of each proposal both from the standpoint of what the contractor had said he could do and what the teams thought his performance would be. Roughly a month later they presented their findings to the TFX Source Selection Board.[1]

Boeing had done spectacularly well on performance. The company's design for its Air Force model had a ferry range of 4630 miles as against 3935 for G.D.-Grumman, the next competitor, which meant it stood alone in being able to fly a bomb from the United States to friendly bases in Japan without refueling; its lift-to-drag ratio, an indication of the wing efficiency that gave it this extreme range, was 20 vs. G.D.-Grumman's score of 16.50. In addition, it was clearly superior at treetop level—of prime importance to the Air Force—and on an 800-mile mission could fly 173 miles at mach

[1] Source Selection Boards are *ad hoc* service groups convened to recommend a winner from among the contestants for a particular weapon contract. This one was made up of Rear Admiral Frederick L. Ashworth (Navy), Brigadier General Allman T. Culbertson (Systems Command), Major Generals William W. Momyer (Tactical Air Command), T. Alan Bennett (Logistics Command), and the nonvoting chairman, Major General W. Austin Davis (Systems Command).

1.2 vs. 141 miles for the nearest competitor, G.D.-Grumman. On loiter time, Boeing's Navy version could remain on station for 4.11 hours, the next best, G.D.-Grumman, 3.66 hours. With all this, the teams raised some warning signals about giving Boeing a clear track. The engine-evaluation group reported that G.E.'s MF295, the foundation of Boeing's design, could not meet the TFX timetable, a factor of rising importance since the Tactical Air Command was determined to keep the plane strictly on schedule. Moreover, Boeing's design, while considered the best of all submitted, still fell short of the capability that both the Navy and the Air Force wanted. Nevertheless, on January 19, 1962, the Source Selection Board voted unanimously to recommend Boeing as the winner of the TFX contract.

"You can't tell what's in people's minds"

Under normal circumstances this recommendation would have gone up through channels, gathering endorsements as it went, for the military have not only a high regard for the findings of their Source Selection Boards (the members are typically officers of stature) but an ingrained disposition to believe that what comes up from below is incontrovertible. Boeing, in short, would normally have been awarded the TFX contract at this point, and ordered to rectify the design deficiencies before the specification stage.

This, indeed, was the direction in which things seemed to be heading. The Tactical Air Command declared its approval of the Boeing award, and TAC, after all, would be the prime user of the aircraft. The Logistics Command also endorsed the Source Selection Board's recommendation of Boeing. "I sat through two Pentagon briefings with a lot of people from the Navy and Air Force, Harold Brown of McNamara's staff, Air Force Under Secretary Joe Charyk, and some others from [Air Secretary] Zuckert's office," said a veteran of the TFX competition. "In neither was there any indication that there'd be a reversal of the board's recommendation. You can't tell what's in people's minds, of course, but I came away from those briefings feeling the contract would go to Boeing."

What was in people's minds, however, was the very thing that was just about to upset Boeing's applecart. In the first place there was that embarrassing business about the MF295 engine. TAC was insisting on holding the TFX to schedule. Boeing would therefore have to switch to Pratt & Whitney's TF-30. But that meant very substantial changes in design. The propulsion people at Wright-Patterson were already beginning to blush at the recollection of how they had ebulliently approved the MF295's eligibility in September, only to turn around in December and decide that it really wouldn't meet the time schedule. And the Pentagon's civilian bosses felt their own faces would be even redder if, in one breath, they declared Boeing's design had won on the basis of what it could do with the MF295, then in the next breath announced the winner would have to go through substantial redesign, and probably degradation of performance, to accommodate a different power plant (the TF-30).

Second, there was that business of commonality so dear to the civilian hearts. Over and over Air Secretary Zuckert had repeated his manifesto: "The name of the game is a single plane for *two* services." Harold Brown, Defense research chief, had carried the same message from McNamara. Brown had forced the Navy and Air Force to compromise their requirements enough so one plane was possible. Boeing's design had very low commonality—the two versions were little over 50 percent similar. Zuckert and Brown suspected that what tended to be two planes at the start would likely become two planes in fact, under the pressure of each service to get its own TFX. These two civilians found they had a powerful fellow skeptic in Lieutenant General Bernard Schriever, chief of the Air Force Systems Command and officer in charge of new program developments. After going over the Source Selection Board's findings with General Davis, Schriever weighed in with a strong recommendation that Boeing not be awarded the contract until it had produced a more complete design and a higher degree of commonality.

And finally there was the Navy's strong suspicion that if Boeing got the award then and there, the Navy might not get all that it wanted in the way of a naval TFX. The Navy had no "family" relationship with Boeing such as it had with Grumman. Therefore, it reasoned that if there was really going to be a bi-service TFX, it might be smart to have everything nailed down and all deficiencies satisfied before awarding the contract, particularly since there seemed to be no prospect of a backup plane.

Reasons for a runoff

Thus the stage was already set for a reversal when on January 24 the Air Council, plus the Navy's representative, Vice-Admiral Robert Pirie, met to consider the Source Selection Board's vote. Admiral Pirie said he'd go with Boeing if the decision had to be made that minute, but the Navy would prefer to have the substantial design problems hammered out in six to eight weeks of additional competition. Lieutenant General Dean Strother, the acting chairman, broke precedent to go behind the board's recommendation and ask Colonel Charles A. Gayle, officer in charge of the TFX evaluation teams, what *he* thought should be done. Colonel Gayle's opinion tallied with that of his boss, General Schriever, who recommended a runoff between Boeing and General Dynamics–Grumman, on grounds that this might avert the familiar trouble connected with rushing complicated weapons into development before designs had been adequately worked out. The Air Council's decision, arrived at with no loss of composure, was to reject the board's recommendation. Instead, it proposed the eight-week extended competition between Boeing and G.D.-Grumman.

For all of this, most of the experts were still betting on Boeing to win. The redesign around the new engine was not an insurmountable problem for old hands in Seattle and Wichita. The delay was only eight weeks, and it was difficult to see how G.D.-Grumman could possibly catch up to Boeing's one-year lead in general design in that time. Only those who sensed that the initial big break with procedure might well foreshadow other surprises to come had a foreboding. Just how many surprises no orthodox strategist could have foreseen. For ahead, as we shall see in the next chapter, lay not eight weeks but ten months of savage competition, important breakthroughs in design technology that brought G.D.-Grumman forward fast, and a reversal that rewrote the rules and heralded the new day in the biggest procurement business in the world.

CHAPTER X

Boeing vs. General Dynamics–Grumman:
A Crisis of Competition

(Continued)

Boeing and General Dynamics faced the special runoff like a pair of exhausted runners who had put all they had into a sprint for the finish line only to find the tape had been moved a mile farther down the track. They had been racing at top speed ever since the previous October. Both had invested a great chunk of their technical resources in the contest—Boeing had a thousand people assigned to the TFX, G.D. had made it the sole concern of virtually an entire division (Fort Worth)—and they had committed capital in equal measure. Money was pouring out of their treasuries at the rate of over $1 million a month. Now each had to shore up sagging morale and get on with another lap, one that would be just as long, just as tough, and just as mysterious as the first.

Nothing had occurred to lessen the Washington pressures. Secretary McNamara was still hell-bent on proving that a well-designed TFX could save $1 billion over the cost of giving the Air Force and Navy separate fighter planes. The Air Force Tactical Command, which had asked for the plane in the first place, was still complaining that every delay was a delay in strengthening U.S. capability in an area where it was woefully weak. The two services remained united only in the common desire to hamstring a bi-service weapon that promised more bi-service weapons to come. Rumors of political pressure flew as thick and fast as before: Boeing was alleged to be doomed before heavy Texas politicking; General Dynamics–Grumman was reported tottering to defeat as Washington Senators Magnuson and Jackson pulled the strings. But perhaps the greatest pressure was the fact that McNamara's Defense Department had simply junked the time-honored service procedure of awarding a contract to the top scorer in a competition, and then granting time for the winner to correct his deficiencies.

Instead, the Pentagon had decided to gamble that protracted competition between a pair of finalists would get it exactly what it wanted.

At the start of the second race the two finalists stacked up about like this: Boeing's design had been adjudged far superior to anybody else's—indeed, the company might already have been declared the winner had it not been led down the garden path by the Air Force and designed its plane around the wrong engine. Boeing would now have to redesign around a completely different power plant, Pratt & Whitney's modification of the TF-30. G.D.-Grumman, on the other hand, had had the good fortune to pick the P. & W. engine from the first, but even so would have to go fast and far to overcome Boeing's long technical lead.

The corporate strategies for winning the contract remained substantially the same. General Dynamics–Grumman's strategy was to come as close as it could to giving Secretary McNamara what he wanted, one plane for the two services. This meant sticking by McNamara's insistence on commonality and resisting Navy and Air Force pressure for two TFX's, separate planes designed solely to satisfy each service's requirements. Boeing continued to gamble that the defense industry's old way, pleasing the services, was still the best way, and that McNamara's dream of a bi-service TFX would ultimately be recognized as unattainable. Boeing would again go all out to satisfy the Air Force's requirements, for it had long been an Air Force-oriented company; at the same time, it would do the best it could to woo the Navy, which was mistrustful of the fact that Boeing had never made a modern Navy fighter.

But unhappily both companies were still in the dark as to how they were being judged. They knew little more than that they had until May 1 to submit entirely new proposals. How to improve the design, how to balance off one antithetical requirement against another (e.g., what weight to give to cost as opposed to performance, performance vs. logistics, logistics vs. production planning) continued to be as deliberate a mystery as ever. The Pentagon was depending on the agony of uncertainty to bring forth the best possible combination of factors. "It was like Russian roulette," recollected Roger Lewis, president of General Dynamics. "You were never sure whether the emphasis you'd put on one of a dozen elements might not be just the thing that would eventually do you in." Down the line, G.D.'s engineers saw it in the same desperate light: "Reconciling the requirements of the Navy and Air Force in a common plane was like getting equilibrium in a bag full of springs; if you pushed in here, something would pop out there." Nevertheless, when May 1 rolled around, both contractors were ready with new proposals.

The Navy opens the sea cocks

This time, as on January 19, the bi-service Source Selection Board at Wright-Patterson Air Force Base found in favor of Boeing. This time, moreover, the Air Force's top-level Air Council went along with the board. Boeing's strategy of pleasing the Air Force appeared to have been a resounding success.

Then the Navy opened up. Though it had never wanted a TFX at all, the Navy had decided earlier that—if faced with the inevitable—its best chances for a tailored naval version lay in getting an old-line Navy plane maker into the deal. G.D.'s partner, Grumman, had filled that bill. But now the G.D.-Grumman design had been officially judged inferior to Boeing's and the Navy faced the bitter prospect of having to accept what it considered a straight Air Force airplane. On top of this seeming denial of the seagoing distinctiveness of naval aviation, something else was sticking in the Navy's craw. For years its custom had been to concentrate on *design* competitions, hammering the design out with a few time-tested contractors like Grumman, or Douglas, then relying on past experience (rather than contemporary analysis) to pilot the new plane through such tricky byways as costs or production plans; the Air Force's method, inaugurated with the Atlas missile in 1956, was to hammer out *everything*—design, costs, planning, etc.—during the competition. Now, the admirals were asking themselves, what was going to happen to the Navy's procurement and development system if the Air Force's newborn Systems Command was allowed to bring off this, the biggest fighter program since World War II? So began a concerted effort, led by Vice-Admiral Robert Pirie, Deputy Chief of Naval Operations for Air, and supported by other admirals, to get the Navy a TFX of its own or at the very least a version that would not give precedence to Air Force requirements.

The Navy's initial point of attack was weight: Boeing's design was 7000 pounds heavier than the specifications called for. "This is ridiculous," said the Navy spokesmen, in voicing their protest to the Defense Department's Office of Research and Engineering. "We wanted a 40,000-pound plane but you talked us into accepting one of 55,000 pounds. Now the thing weighs 62,000 pounds. We just can't handle it on our carriers. The arresting gear won't take it and the catapulting equipment isn't powerful enough to launch that much airplane." Defense's engineers pointed out that the Navy had had no difficulty handling a 70,000-pound carrier-based bomber, the

A-5 (nee A3J), but the admirals shrugged this off with the observation that such big planes overcrowded their flight decks. "This was an emotional problem," said Dr. John McLucas, the young Deputy Director of Defense Research and Engineering. If it was, it wasn't *blind* emotion, for the Navy next attempted to confound design plans by redefining the kinds of missions it wanted the TFX to fly. This was like inviting everybody to start all over again, since it was only because Navy and Air Force missions had been painfully reconciled in months of heated discussions during 1961 that the *bi-*service TFX was even put out to contract competition. In consequence there was an altering of the design away from Air Force requirements, away from a bi-service TFX, and toward what the Navy had hankered after all along: a lower-performance, slower airplane of much less weight. Or, as a disgusted NASA designer put it, "a big black Packard."

McNamara enters the battle

All this time Secretary McNamara had stayed some distance from the battle. He had watched approvingly while Navy Secretary Fred Korth and Air Force Secretary Eugene Zuckert backed up the Air Council's orders for the special runoff between Boeing and G.D.-Grumman. Now, however, there was a split between the military and the service secretaries. Both Zuckert and Korth felt the designs of the two contestants were still unsatisfactory, while the Air Council wanted Boeing. McNamara decided that the time for direct intervention had arrived. His faith in a bi-service plane had recently been reinforced by his success in getting the Air Force to buy the Navy's spectacular new fighter, the McDonnell Phantom II, instead of reordering its veteran Republic F-105—and the initial Air Force growls had turned to murmurs of pleasure once the airmen had begun to fly the Phantoms. If the multiservice idea had worked for the Phantom, a plane already built, it should certainly work for the TFX, which was being specially designed to suit the Navy and Air Force. "But here I realized," he said, recalling the occasion, "that after eight months of work we'd come up to May and the Navy was *still* saying *neither* design met its requirements. That was a terrible setback. My first reaction was disappointment, and then disbelief, because in mid-1961 we had finally got the services to agree on a set of requirements that were basically similar."

And, being McNamara, he was concerned about something else in the bids—i.e., the estimates of costs. Both Boeing and G.D.-Grumman had submitted "hungry" bids, and Boeing in particular had bid extremely low.

These estimates, as McNamara measured them against Defense's own analyses, were full of wishful thinking.

"I asked the Secretaries of the Navy and Air Force to tell the contractors that their cost estimates were completely unreasonable," said McNamara recently. "We weren't going to accept anything like that; they were without foundation. It appeared that they were following a practice that is evident elsewhere in our society of trying to entangle a customer by a low initial bid, keeping the thought in back of the mind that it can be raised later." Why did he attach so much importance to realistic costs? Fundamentally because a significant cost overrun on a $7-billion program like the TFX not only would have to be borne by the taxpayers, but if it amounted to, say, $3 billion, this might raise the total price of the TFX to a level where it would have been wiser to put the $10 billion in a different weapon system, one that had had to be rejected on grounds of cost. "I had learned that final costs on major systems had exceeded the original estimates by between 300 and 1000 percent. Although changes accounted for some of these overruns, this is the point: if the estimates had been better, we might not have bought those particular systems. I'm not saying we wouldn't spend what it costs to get adequate defense, but we might have bought different things. I know it is difficult to estimate costs, but there's no excuse for errors of this sort—20 to 30 percent maybe, but not 300 percent."

So the recommendation of the Source Selection Board and of the Air Council for Boeing went flying back with an emphatic disapproval. Incredibly, the race went into a third lap. Instructions were sent out that both Boeing and General Dynamics–Grumman would have to continue the competition in the interests of a better design—and sounder costs.

Needless to say, McNamara's decision was received with mixed feelings by almost everyone concerned. Boeing had gained the support of the influential Air Council, but now the extra time would allow its competition to catch up. G.D.-Grumman, having risked its all on McNamara's commonality, wondered if it shouldn't hedge its bets. The Air Force was furious at this further erosion of the TFX's time lead over Soviet aircraft; the Navy was delighted with the success of its tactics. The third lap thus began in a swirl of emotions, with the contractors sternly adjured to get more commonality in their designs and at the same time to meet the Navy's specifications, weight in particular.

The Defense engineers suggested a number of ways of accomplishing the latter—e.g., thinner-gauge stainless steel, the use of titanium, reducing the amount of fuel or weapons carried, altering the missions—and by the

June 1 deadline, the groggy contractors were again ready with a whole new batch of proposals.

Then history repeated itself.

The plane or the admirals

For the third time the Source Selection Board recommended Boeing, for the second time the Air Council followed suit. Again the Navy let loose its broadsides. Boeing was admittedly leading in the competition, wrote the Chief of Naval Operations, Admiral George Anderson, but he saw "no indications" that the Navy's requirements had been met. This was too much for the civilian Secretaries. Their analysis of the two proposals indicated that the Navy's demands had reached a stage where they could be satisfied only at the sacrifice of commonality. Further concessions would undoubtedly result in two TFX's instead of the common aircraft McNamara had set his heart on. McNamara read this as a choice between one plane and several admirals, and decided on the former. Into "early retirement" went Vice-Admiral Pirie, Deputy Chief of Naval Operations for Air, and out to new jobs went a number of other Pentagon admirals. Pirie's successor, Rear Admiral William A. Schoech, and the other replacements were soon demonstrating an unsurprising amount of sweet reasonableness.

By this time, however, something akin to desperation had begun to affect all participants. The Kennedy Administration had still to come up with a new weapon system, after all the talk of stirring things up in the Pentagon. Communication between the civilian secretariat and the Source Selection Board at Wright-Patterson had broken down, to say the least, for though each was looking at the same proposals the Source Selection Board had kept recommending Boeing on one set of standards (operational characteristics) and the civilian Secretaries had kept rejecting Boeing on a different set (costs and commonality). The contractors were in a daze of fatigue and bewilderment; by then even G.D.-Grumman had begun to think of a bi-service TFX as "a philosophical concept" technologically impossible of fulfillment. McNamara considered the companies' new cost estimates to be, if anything, more optimistic than before; in fact, so unrealistic that he had little hope the "brochuresmanship" could be worked out of them within the time span of an additional race. Something clearly had to give. In the military view there had been far too much delay already, so far as security was concerned; moreover, cold-war situations such as

Viet-Nam and, potentially, Cuba cried out for a plane like the TFX. Hardware-hungry Curtis LeMay, Air Force Chief of Staff, told the Secretary: "I for one don't pay much attention to cost estimates in a competition at this time." Admiral Schoech had concurred; so had General Schriever, chief of the Air Force Systems Command, whose doubts about Boeing's costs had carried considerable weight in the Air Council's January recommendation for a runoff. McNamara decided to have one more try and one only. He insisted, however, that this final competition be held under quite a different set of rules.

Heretofore the contractors had been competing blindfolded, not knowing precisely how short of meeting specifications they were. Customarily, such measurements are withheld until after the competition is over, then the losers are told exactly where they fall short and the winner is advised what he still must do to come up to standard. Now, on McNamara's orders, both teams were to be treated as if each had actually won the competition. Air Force Secretary Zuckert and Navy Secretary Korth got off a joint letter for Colonel Charles Gayle, the TFX program officer at Wright-Patterson, telling him to loosen up. "I told Gayle," said Zuckert, recapitulating the instructions, "to give each of the contractors his impressions of the costs they used as against those he had worked up himself—so they're not in the position of competing in the dark. Put everything on the table. He would say on design, for example, we don't think the engine arrangement minimizes the danger of foreign objects, but if you just did thus and so you might solve the problem. We permitted our people this kind of talk in order to have the best plane we could get." In early July the contractors were themselves notified of the new ground rules and told that the previously secret "payoff points"—those given the most important weightings—were structural design, commonality, and reliable costs.

Ill omens and "helpful hints"

Boeing's reaction to the change of plan was to crowd on even more speed, still confident that the wider the margin of its technical superiority the more certain its ultimate victory. Yet some members of Boeing's top management could not down a sense of foreboding. Many of the disquieting rumors they had heard since the project's beginning had been subsequently borne out by events. G.D.-Grumman's choice of engine, the Pratt & Whitney TF-30, *had* won Pentagon approval over Boeing's choice, the G.E. MF295. The Navy *had* stalled for a "better" design, providing G.D.-

Grumman the time needed to perfect its own. In light of the Pentagon's reversals of the Source Selection Board and the Air Council recommendations, it had even begun to look as if there might be substance to the prediction that Boeing's intelligence had picked up from a Texas politician: G.D.-Grumman would beat Boeing out of the contract, no matter how good a TFX the latter came up with. Now, under the changed rules, G.D.-Grumman was bound to get information about the Boeing design that would help equate the two. Not that there would be an outright leakage to G.D.-Grumman at the Wright-Patterson briefings; nevertheless some hints were bound to come out in the "corridor sessions" (to use the euphemism of a retired admiral) and more would emerge by the very nature of things. "If any design contest is dragged out," explained an official of the Defense Research and Engineering staff, "the designs tend to approximate each other, through the exchange of 'helpful' ideas on what one service or the other finds deficient. There is no way of avoiding a gradual drawing together toward a common design." In fact, at this stage of the game, that would appear to be precisely what the Pentagon wanted.

G.D.-Grumman had a lot more going for it in the final race than helpful hints from the Navy; it had made a breakthrough in its designing process. In the previous nine months it had worked on a hundred-odd different TFX configurations, turning out a new one every ten days at a minimum. Complete engineering teams would work on a single design, then several designs would be brought together for comparison and the most promising sent to model shops; next the models would go to the wind tunnels, and the resultant experimental data was used to select the best of the test lot. It was roughly a three months' cycle: so much time devoted to thinking, then designing the models, building them, putting them through wind-tunnel tests, and finally evaluation. But the big bottleneck was building the models themselves—they had to be forged of stainless steel, which entailed formidable shop problems, and each required six weeks to two months to complete. With such a bottleneck, G.D.-Grumman found it almost impossible to make *gross* changes in its designs: supporting wind-tunnel data simply couldn't be got rapidly enough to substantiate the changes.

At the beginning of the final lap, however, G.D. hit on the idea of using fiberglass models. With these it was possible to go right from line drawings to fiberglass casting and come up with a finished model in only *ten days*. "That compression," as Robert Widmer, vice-president of research and engineering at General Dynamics–Fort Worth, put it, "permitted us to go back and look at the whole commonality problem again, instead of just making small changes. We could look at that great pile of designs and see whether this thing might not be headed for the monster stage." Thus when the Air Force asked G.D.-Grumman how it was going to meet requirements in the final race, Widmer told them: "We're going to start over, take another look at everything." He added, "They wanted to know how we could do it and prove the results; I told them we'd learned to build models in much faster time. They said: 'Oho! There's a guy sawing off his own legs.' But we built and tested more models in that July–September period than in the previous nine months all put together."

Zuckert's birthday present

On September 11, 1962, Boeing and G.D.-Grumman submitted their fourth and last set of technical proposals to the Source Selection Board. On October 15, Admiral Anderson reported the momentous news that the Bureau of Naval Weapons, at long last, had found a design satisfactory to the Navy; indeed, both designs were satisfactory. On November 9, Air Force Secretary Zuckert got a brightly wrapped present for his fifty-first birthday: the military's ultimate report on the competition. Both contractors were now judged capable of designing and producing the TFX, but Boeing was chosen unanimously to do so. The Source Selection Board recommended that company over G.D.-Grumman on the basis of lower quoted costs, greater weapon selectivity and carriage capability, less chance of engine damage from foreign objects, a better deceleration mechanism (thrust reversers), and superiority in all major operating characteristics. The Air Council went on record with the flat statements (1) that the winning proposal (Boeing's) provided a substantial improvement in the capabilities of the Tactical Air Command, and of the Navy as well, where G.D.-Grumman's would not provide as much, and (2) that there was a manifest and substantial advantage in Boeing's proposal over G.D.-Grumman's in limited war actions from primitive airstrips.

The report further noted that all items, costs in particular, could not be completely corrected to the satisfaction of the military and would have to rest on the contractor's say-so until further refinements were made. Time, the report added nudgingly, was of the essence: even if approval of Boeing were immediately forthcoming, there would be a slippage of roughly six months in the initial operating capability of the first tactical wing. Lined up behind Boeing was undoubtedly the most glittering array of top brass

since the Japanese surrender ceremonies aboard the battleship *Missouri*:
General LeMay, Chief of Staff of the Air Force; ten assorted generals and
admirals of the Air Council; General Walter C. Sweeney of TAC; General
Mark E. Bradley of Logistics Command; Lieutenant General Bernard
Schriever of Systems Command; Admiral Anderson, Chief of Naval Oper-
ations; Admiral William E. Ellis, Assistant Chief of Naval Operations for
Air; Rear Admiral Kleber S. Masterson, Bureau of Weapons; plus the five
general and flag officers of the Source Selection Board itself.

"That doesn't fly!"

Such a show of interservice solidarity was most impressive—especially when
viewed through the battle smoke of the preceding fourteen months; the
realization that both contractors now had the capability of building the
TFX hung like a rainbow in Secretary Zuckert's office. McNamara's hopes
for a bi-service weapon finally had substance behind them. But Zuckert
had long since learned not to approach the boss with somebody else's
unevaluated conclusions. As he remarked recently, "I had the problem of
having this guy downstairs with the bad habit of going back into the basic
documents, so after two years and many ulcers I've learned. I can't get him
just to accept the fact that four Selection Boards and umpty-ump Air
Force generals have said it's O.K. to go with a certain contractor. He'll ask
me if I've personally looked into the thing and if I say 'Yeah, I heard the
briefing,' that doesn't fly: I have to support everything I say, whether I
disagree with the conclusions or go along with them. McNamara demands
a different philosophy and approach to the source-selection problem, a
different degree of presumption you favor the experts with." And the more
Zuckert poked about behind the report's conclusions, the more he got an
uneasy feeling that this final recommendation for Boeing might be the
occasion when the civilians would have to reverse all those glittering
echelons of gold braid.

The next morning, Saturday, he and Navy Secretary Korth talked it
over and Zuckert put in a couple of hours questioning the TFX program
officer. Then Zuckert and Korth went down to see McNamara. Despite
the military's unanimous recommendation for Boeing, it was a very close
race, the Air Secretary said; in the raw score comparison, Boeing stood at
172.1, G.D.-Grumman at 175.6, only 3.5 points or less than 2 percent apart.
Boeing's prime appeal to the services was that it had designed for *maxi-*

mum specification (i.e., capability), but the company had been able to achieve this only at the expense of commonality. G.D.-Grumman's lesser appeal for the services stemmed from a design of *minimum* specification, the price it had had to pay for achieving a high degree of commonality. The chances were that Boeing's design would become even less common in the production stage, and Zuckert, recalling Bomarc and Minuteman, was also apprehensive about Boeing's costs: if they were as wrong as they seemed to be at the start, experience had taught they'd be much worse at the finish.

McNamara contented himself with a "that's very interesting," but over that weekend both he and Deputy Defense Secretary Roswell Gilpatric pored over Zuckert's material. McNamara first satisfied himself on the fundamental point that both the Navy and Air Force now considered they had designs which met their requirements, then he turned his attention to a point-by-point comparison of the competing designs. He noted the Air Force had given a significant edge to Boeing on the basis of its greater ferry range, more firepower, and the employment of thrust reversers for increased maneuverability. But he noted that the Navy, though also giving precedence to Boeing in operational features, did so to a much lesser degree. As for G.D.-Grumman, in Navy eyes its slight inferiority in weapon selectivity (the number of attachment points of bombs, missiles, etc.) and in carrying capacity was overcome by its superior supersonic performance. McNamara proceeded to an examination of the other two prime "payoff points," costs and commonality.

He soon concluded that both contractors were still unrealistic on costs, but since there just wasn't time at that stage of the game to insist that they develop more reliable figures, it came down to a matter of choosing the lesser of two unreliabilities. G.D.-Grumman had based its costs on G.D.'s extensive experience with supersonic fighter planes (the F-102 and F-106) and bombers (the B-58), and Grumman's thirty years of expertise with carrier-borne aircraft; its bid was very low, but it expected to make a small profit. Boeing's estimates stemmed from its success with *sub*sonic aircraft, like the B-47 and the 707 jet transport, large, "open" structures with much less compactness than the TFX, yet it intended to produce this relatively small, highly complex fighter at manufacturing costs per man-hour that were as much as 30 percent below those prevailing throughout the industry. To McNamara this looked as if Boeing were desperately trying to "buy into" the program and make it up later on cost overruns.

Optimism has its price

With that thought in mind he began to compare the production plans of the two contractors, for he had always held that invalid cost estimates were the result of imprecise production planning. He found that G.D.-Grumman had adopted a conservative approach in that it expected the TFX development program to demand a high level of engineering and test effort. Boeing, on the other hand, was clearly optimistic that few major problems or engineering changes would arise to challenge the validity of its extremely low engineering and cost estimates; it obviously believed that the development of the thrust reversers would give it little trouble, that the variable-sweep wing could be easily applied to the TFX configuration, that the use of well over a ton of an exotic metal, titanium, to hold the wing on would cause no important manufacturing difficulties, and that there would be only minor problems with its unique design for housing the engines. Maybe, but to McNamara the wish seemed father to the thought; it looked to him as if Boeing had seriously misjudged the difficulties to be expected in this aircraft. Then he turned to the section on commonality and Boeing's stock sank even further. There, flatly stated, was the evaluation group's opinion that Boeing was, "in effect, proposing two different airplanes from the structural point of view." Boeing's total program costs for producing the Navy and Air Force versions of a common TFX showed that it expected a saving of only $397 million in comparison with its cost of developing the two versions as separate aircraft; G.D.-Grumman reported a saving nearly twice that, $623 million.

A breakfast of billions

Bright and early the following Tuesday, November 13, McNamara, Gilpatric, Zuckert, and Air Force Under Secretary Joseph Charyk met for breakfast in Zuckert's dining room, Tuesday being the Air Force's regular day for such gatherings, and over the orange juice and scrambled eggs set themselves to weighing the relative merits of both proposals. McNamara opened with the observation that since both the Boeing and G.D.-Grumman aircraft could perform the missions required by either the Navy or the Air Force and there was no overriding margin in favor of one design as opposed to the other, the choice of a contractor could be made on other grounds than design. Gilpatric thought the commonality comparison was critical: on final evaluation G.D.-Grumman had many fewer parts in its design than Boeing. The General Dynamics total stood at 14,423, and the Fourth Evaluation Report had found that 83.8 percent of these were identical in both versions. Boeing, on the other hand, had 18,653 parts, only 60.4 percent of which were identical; so it was going to build the aircraft about halfway to completion, then "hog out" (machine away) enough of the remaining elements to suit its Navy version. Gilpatric had never heard of this being done before, he said, and neither had the tooling experts he'd talked to; he was afraid a mere 60 percent commonality would prevent Boeing from making good on the crucial $1-billion saving.

Zuckert agreed. He'd spotted the fact that Boeing intended to have two static test programs for its two versions and to him this meant the likelihood the Pentagon would eventually be confronted with two separate aircraft. Moreover, he was disturbed over the optimism of Boeing's costs; this was not a proved plane, nobody would really *know* what he was in for until it had been flown. Yet if Boeing got into difficulties and missed its estimates by 50 percent, that was a couple of billion dollars! As the talk moved on, it became clear that they were all of one mind: G.D.-Grumman should get the contract on grounds of a higher degree of commonality and the greater likelihood that it would produce the plane on schedule and within the funds earmarked for it.

The next question was, who would prepare a memorandum of record justifying the award? Plainly, this would be a ticklish job, for many Air Force noses would be out of joint over the rejection of Boeing, and if Senator Jackson, No. 2 man on the McClellan investigating subcommittee, chose to investigate the award through the committee (as he did), he'd probably get plenty of sub-rosa expertise. Zuckert, appropriately enough, volunteered for the job. Then, late that afternoon, McNamara and Gilpatric trotted over to the White House to inform the President that G.D.-Grumman had won the award, and the program would soon be under way. What did Kennedy say? Nothing. Either way, he'd be getting a headache from someone, from the unemployed citizens of Fort Worth or those of Wichita, from Washington Senators Jackson and Magnuson or Texas politicos Governor John Connally, Congressman Jim Wright, and possibly even Vice-President Johnson.

The memorandum for the record was some eight days in preparation, as Zuckert went behind the Selection Board reports to the basic findings of the evaluation teams. It received McNamara's approval on Wednesday,

November 21. Public announcement was scheduled for 11 A.M., the 24th, a Saturday, and the Secretary issued explicit instructions on just how the news was to be broken. The press was to get it first, the politicos next. Moreover, McNamara made a point of telling Navy Secretary Korth, of Fort Worth, that no Texan was to be informed prior to eleven, and that this applied most particularly to the notification of Korth's Navy predecessor, Governor Connally. But the ink was hardly dry on the memorandum of record before at least one politician showed unmistakable signs that he sensed something conclusive in the wind. Congressman Wright armed his Fort Worth office with lists of people to be notified and pecked about nervously like a mother hen all day Thursday and Friday. On Saturday at 10:59 A.M. Major General Hoisington sent the announcement down to the Pentagon's press room and at eleven sharp he and a half-dozen other officers of the Air Force's Legislative Liaison Office started ringing up the politicians. Congressman Wright heard the glad tidings at home with a face full of shaving lather and was soon bubbling over the telephone to G.D.'s Fort Worth Division. There the operator screamed, "Did we get it?" as soon as she heard who was on the line, then cut him off while she herself spread the news. The competition that had cost the military 250,000 man-hours for evaluation, and cost Boeing and G.D.-Grumman some $25 million in the ten months of runoffs, was finally all over but the shouting.[1]

New trails and new trials

Whether or not the full TFX edition—fifteen hundred planes for the Air Force, a couple of hundred for the Navy—will ultimately see the light of day is, of course, something only time will tell. We live in an era in which a single technological mutation in weaponry could take the luster off anything in our arsenal. On the other hand, the most searching "threat analysis" has uncovered nothing that might compromise the TFX. Rather, its capabilities with both atomic and conventional weapons are being counted on to work as much of a revolution in tactical warfare on the ground and at sea as has already taken place in the strategic air war. The prospect is excellent that our future Air Force will be built basically upon missiles, troop transports (like the C-141's), and F-111's, as the TFX's will be called operationally. But regardless of how much hardware may

[1] By special ruling the two contractors are to be reimbursed for their expenses incurred in the ten-month runoff period.

ultimately take to the skies, certainly the competition for the contract will
have had a lasting impact on the world of the defense contractor.

The new logic of the situation in military procurement is demanding
changes such as the TFX set in motion. In consequence, efficient management would argue for their continuance no matter who might replace
McNamara in the catbird seat. Sudden-death runoffs, such as Boeing
and G.D.-Grumman endured, could well set the pattern of future competitions insofar as highly complex weapons are concerned. On their way
into limbo are the old procedures of having the military "work out" a
design with the contractor; McNamara's Pentagon intends to rely increasingly on extended head-to-head competitions between contractors to
produce the necessary stretching of the state of the art. (This shift, in-
cidentally, will favor the Air Force's procurement system over the Navy's.)
All new weapon programs will get an increasingly rigorous going over
within the Pentagon itself to make sure they have been clearly defined
before they are put out for bidding. No matter that a hardware-hungry
industry has already been complaining of weapons being "R. and D.'d to
death," the experience with the TFX has convinced McNamara that
"we ought to buy more pencils and more brains and use them in the
requirement and design stages."

The TFX procedure also promises greater emphasis on multiservice
systems and this in turn could alter the realpolitik of procurement. Thus
it should become increasingly desirable, or even necessary, for one contractor to team up with another who has special experience with a particular
service, as G.D. did with Grumman.

Indeed, whole new corporate strategies will have to be devised if the
contractors are to profit from the lessons in the TFX: under McNamara,
corporate management is going to be put under pressures equivalent to
those that scientists and engineers live with every day in this age of
exploding technology. Incentive contracts will reward or penalize management for performance at every significant stage of weapon development.
The Pentagon is already at work on PERT (Program and Evaluation
Review Technique) systems, which will be used to keep it constantly
informed of management's ability to control costs and meet critical
deadlines; watchful eyes at Wright-Patterson will even be able to pick up
management's every lapse or failure from the computers, which supply
data to the contractors. Necessarily, the contractors will still count on the
fascination of high-performance hardware to win them votes before the
Source Selection Boards, but after the TFX, none should doubt that the
decisive vote will always be cast by McNamara—and, once the military

requirements have been met, cast for realistic costs, precise production plans, and valid timetables.

Of course, it is as yet too early for McNamara to take his bows for bringing off this remarkable venture. Some in the Bureau of Naval Weapons still maintain, "It's ridiculous to think that this long time put in on the TFX's design phase will eliminate problems; we've never built planes that didn't change: there were thirteen models of the Grumman F9F from 1946 to 1957 and six versions of the Douglas A3D." The Air Force is similarly hopeful of slipping in a consequential change or two and these could make quite a hole in the $623-million saving expected from an 84 percent common TFX. But as one of the Defense Department's young scientists observed: "Any changes that threaten the TFX's commonality will be pretty hard to sell around here." McNamara will be watching. And so inevitably will anyone who might succeed him, for the central facts on procurement any Secretary of Defense must now face are these: with fewer and fewer weapons, exhaustive review at the secretarial level is entirely practicable; with enormous costs such review is essential.

A weapon's costs and its capabilities, to adapt a favorite analogy of Defense Comptroller Charles Hitch, are like the front and rear sights of a rifle. They are not independent considerations but interdependent elements that must be properly aligned to hit the target. Even though the nation may not soon get another Defense Secretary of McNamara's caliber and force of character, by the time his successor comes along both the contractors and the military will have had lots of practice in lining up those sights.

Conclusion

In a sense the competitive struggle between Boeing and General Dynamics provides a suitable note on which to end a book about corporations in crisis. For certainly the nature of crises-to-come is nowhere more apparent than in the turbulent defense industry. There are at present only a dozen prime contractors really capable of taking on a major weapon contract and this number will undoubtedly shrink in the next decade, as the technical capabilities demanded of the contractors by complex new weapon systems tend to eliminate the smaller companies and make the bigger ones bigger and fewer. Moreover, the rise of a new managerial corps within the Pentagon, while intended to keep the contractors *out* of trouble, could become a potent source of it. When the data from a contractor's computers is immediately transmitted to the military and then posted on the latter's own PERT flow charts, management will undoubtedly find some of its decisions challenged the instant they are made. Crisis would seem to be implicit in circumstances where two sets of bosses, with different motivations but identical information, will be running one show.

Unfortunately, the defense industry is not the only one confronted by big troubles in the future. Corporate crises can be expected in many other industries and for widely varied reasons. Heightened competitive pressures are inevitable both here and abroad as the emergence of a second great contiguous marketing area, Europe's Common Market, offsets the advantages we alone once possessed. The relentless drive of technology can be counted on to make it more and more difficult for management to stay in the running—and to choose the right race. Virtual revolutions are already in the making in the printing industry (inkless reproduction), in aerospace (nucleonics), in electronics (miniaturization), in merchandising (vending machines that cater to virtually every human need save sex and shelter), where new products by new companies are challenging the supremacy of established enterprises. Profits are coming under increased pressure; the four-day week with its unconscionable increases in labor costs has now gained a foothold. Of course, if the economy were to turn downward in whole or part for very long, then many companies would be brought to book, for the shortcomings that might be concealed or ignored while operating at 70 percent of capacity precipitate a crisis at 55 percent.

Business, in short, is going to have to be a lot better than it was to stay out of trouble. Considering that it takes three to five years of blood, sweat, and tears to get a company "turned around again" after a crisis, considering the scarcity of executives competent enough to regenerate such a company (to say nothing of the bare handful willing to risk their reputations in so hazardous an undertaking), and finally considering that for some companies, as in the publishing business, one crisis creates a lack of confidence creating successive crises, the virtues of prevention must be obvious to everyone. And just as obviously, the logical way to prevent crises is by detecting them in infancy, through an understanding of their causes.

INDEX

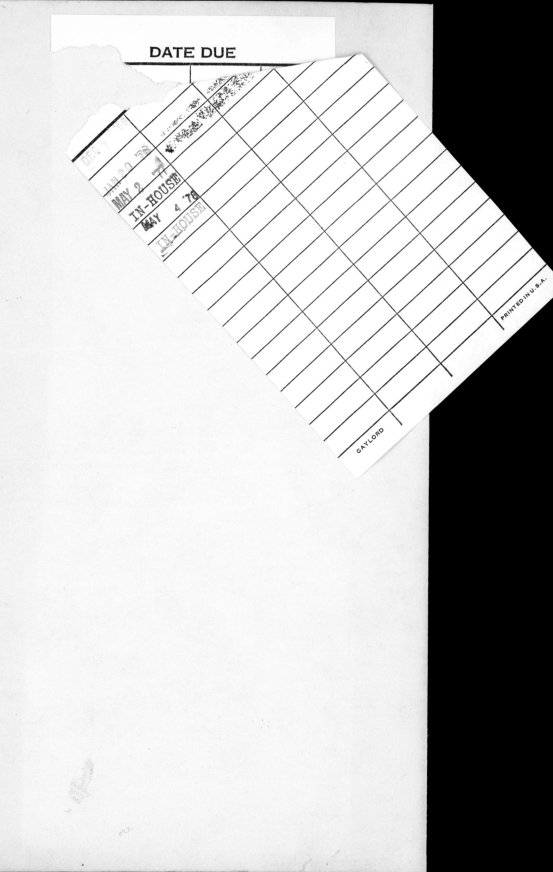

DATE DUE

DEC 7
JUN 22 '76
MAY 2 '77
IN-HOUSE
MAY 4 '78
IN-HOUSE

PRINTED IN U.S.A.

GAYLORD